I STILL
BELIEVE
IN
BUTTERFLIES

Dottie Henneberry

I STILL BELIEVE IN BUTTERFLIES

House of Prayer Ministries, Inc.
2428 Florian Court
Decatur, Illinois 62526

First Printing, August 2003

I Still Believe in Butterflies Copyright © 2003 by Dottie Henneberry

Library of Congress Catalog Card Number: 2001 135721

Published by

House of Prayer Ministries, Inc.
2428 Florian Court
Decatur, Illinois 62526
(217) 428-7077

Printed in the United States of America

ISBN 1-882825-21-7

I still believe in butterflies
For what they were, once so was I.
And like the tiny butterfly
Emerging from the past,
My life through Christ is changing
Till I fly away at last!

Dottie Henneberry
"I Still Believe in Butterflies"
Jesus Loves The Dandelion
Copyright 1980 Dottie Henneberry

"Therefore if any man be in Christ, he is a new creature; old things are passed away; behold, all things are become new."
II Corinthians 5:17

"One does not write what has already been written. One writes out of the storehouse of fresh revelation and his own personal knowledge gained through the painful experiences of growth. Ye cannot escape the growing experience without forfeiting the other. Ye shall cease writing if ye cease learning. Ye do not learn as ye write, but write as ye learn."

Frances J. Roberts
"Listen to the Silence"
COME AWAY MY BELOVED
Copyright 1973 Frances J. Roberts

Dedication and Acknowledgments

It is to my wonderful friends, Grace and Andrew "Jorgy" Jorgensen, that I dedicate this book. Jerry and I always looked forward to visiting them every fall at their mountain "haven" in North Carolina. The serenity and majestic beauty of their natural surroundings were also reflected in their lives. Their willingness to open their home and hearts to the hurting plus their eagerness to welcome pilgrims for a time of rest is surely written in God's manual of time. Grace and Jorgy came in person to be with me in my darkest hour for which I will be forever grateful.

Jorgy was called home to heaven February 26, 2003, to be with His beloved Lord forever. Grace continues their ministry on this journey of life, and I thank God that she is only a telephone call away. Thank You, sweet Jesus, for bringing these dear friends into my life!

Lovingly,
Dottie

In my acknowledgments, I want to thank my family for all of their love and devotion during a tumultuous time in my life. A very special hug goes to my eldest daughter, Viki, for her many tedious hours perfecting this manuscript.

I also wish to thank all of the doctors and nurses who watched over Jerry and me in crisis after crisis.

Lastly, I thank my Great Physician, the Lord Himself, Who guided me through the many chapters of this book. He truly is the Author and Finisher.

Contents

Foreword

I Still Believe in Butterflies by Dottie Henneberry is the saga of one woman's unflinching courage, faith and dedication through fires of affliction. It is also the story of strong family ties that provided a network of strength that nurtured each individual of this incredible family.

Life in ministry is never easy. There are unique challenges and testings. There are sacrifices to be made, discouragements and heart-rending disappointments. Because of an unshakable faith in Christ, Dottie Henneberry not only found the strength to maintain her personal integrity, but also to be an inspiration to her family. Together they continued to manifest their love for God and singleness of purpose in pouring out their lives in service for the salvation of souls.

It is truly a remarkable life story of victorious living in the face of unrelenting physical pain and seemingly insurmountable obstacles. This courageous family, inspired by Dottie's unswerving devotion, has continued to remain steadfast and vibrant in their personal lives and their varied gifts and ministries. Their vision and service have touched hundreds of lives not only in their home base of Decatur, Illinois, but out to regions beyond. They have made the world their mission field.

Dottie's personal belief in the ultimate victory of good over evil, life over death and love over strife is embodied in her choice of the title, *I Still Believe in Butterflies*. Her life is a shining example of the power of Christ to transform darkness to light and deliver the believer from captivity of the flesh to freedom in the Spirit.

To quote the old song, *"Some glad morning, when this life is over, I'll fly away!"* Every true believer can live in the light of this glorious hope. The day is coming when we will be delivered from the cocoon of this earthly experience into the freedom and glory of eternal life in His presence where there is no darkness, no pain and no sorrow and no death.

Yes, we can all believe in butterflies!

Frances J. Roberts

1

Be Instant in Season

The spirit of heaviness seemed to be hovering in the corridors of our lovely old mansion which Jerry and I had converted into the House of Prayer many years earlier. I couldn't quite put my finger on what was happening, but my spirit sensed that a spectacular spiritual storm was brewing. It was July 1, 1983, and the air was hot and humid, sending tempers and emotions soaring.

Late that evening Team I of our Christian drama team The End Time Harvesters came dragging in from an extremely discouraging tour. Everything that could go wrong, went wrong. The engine of the Truthmobile started having problems, causing the team to be late for ministry engagements and in some instances forcing them to cancel. The Truthmobile was a motor home unit that my husband Jerry had designed. The last straw was when wires started burning and the mobile unit had to be left on the side of the road until repairs could be made.

Unbeknown to my family, the girls on the team had had enough. We should have noticed the discouragement on their faces, but failed to do so. Instead, we were caught up with the approaching deadline of finishing the cover design for my family's testimony *Fortress on a Hill* which I had written.

The Fourth of July started out as a rainy day. Three of the Harvesters took off to go shopping at the mall. My oldest daughter Viki and her husband Doug decided to go to Mattoon to visit his parents, but were detained when they discovered that someone had pulled the radio out of their car and had stolen parking meter change out of my husband's vehicle. By lunch time hardly anyone was speaking. Eventually things got better when we headed to the park for the fireworks.

The next morning while working on rummage in our basement, I started reminiscing about how the Lord saved me on my 39th birthday. A beautiful psychic woman had given me a copy of Hal Lindsey's book *The Late Great Planet Earth*. The "witch" was intrigued with the book and thought I might find it interesting. Before I finished it, I was deeply convicted of my sins, renounced all of my involvement in the occult for the previous seven years and was marvelously born again, proving that God can use any means for salvation.

In one year's time, God brought all five of my children–Viki, Kim, Chris, Kirk and Cheri–to the full understanding that Jesus died for each one of them personally and that faith in Him alone was needed for the salvation of their souls. Last, but not least, came my husband Jerry, who at the age of 45 gave up his career as a district manager of the Prudential Insurance Co. of America, to serve the Lord Jesus full time. He completed three years of the Berean School of the Bible in three and one-half months. His recurring dream of a big old house to be used for the Lord's service led us to step out in faith and find it. After nine months of waiting on the Lord and living in another man's house after ours sold, we were finally able to purchase the England mansion, 401 N. College, on August 11, 1975, and convert it into the House of Prayer. God never let us down as we prayed in our groceries and mortgage payment each month.

I became a "recycler" of clothes and other treasures. Jerry said he hoped there wouldn't be rummage sales in heaven because if there were, then he knew he was in the wrong place!

I guess opposites do attract because Jerry and I were often like night and day. He was a good sport, though, and willingly distributed the goods brought in to others less fortunate. My treasures also provided many of the props our drama teams needed when ministering in churches.

A former neighbor and his new wife stopped by to visit. When they left I noticed that our son Kim and one of the Harvesters named Tim Brown were sitting in the dining room just staring into space. I wondered what was going on but did not say anything.

It was time to get supper started—a duty I always performed but now with greater intensity especially when the drama teams were home between tours. I remembered protesting when we expanded to two teams in 1982.

"But we don't have room for another team," I reasoned.

I was outnumbered by the rest of the members in my family and reluctantly gave in. Team II would stay in the United States touring while Team I prepared for several months of outreach in Australia and New Zealand.

While I was in the kitchen preparing supper, one of the Harvesters suddenly informed me she was not going to Australia. Jerry and I looked at each other in total amazement! Then another girl announced she was not going either. By then our mouths were wide opened! Visas, passports and the money for the airplane tickets had already been secured.

Viki and Kirk were devastated! Kirk informed her of the situation while Jerry and I visited with our former neighbor. Viki did all of the bookings for the teams and had spent months corresponding with Youth For Christ in Australia setting up the overseas tour. Not only would it be a terrible witness for our ministry, but it would also reflect badly on our country if we canceled the tour.

We discussed the possibility of pulling our daughter Chris from Team II and uniting her with Liz on Team I. That way we would have three males and two females. Without warning Liz remarked, "I thought you knew. I'm not going either."

We felt like the bottom of our stomachs had fallen out!

"How could this happen to us? Don't we always hear from God?" I desperately cried out.

I called my friend, Eileen Volle, who was a great prayer warrior.

"Please pray and ask God for a miracle," I urgently requested.

We both believed the girls would change their minds by morning and everything would be fine. Lo and behold, Wednesday morning came and there not only was not a miracle, two of the girls called a friend in Iowa to come and get them. At 2 p.m. a car pulled into the driveway portico and off the girls went to their homes in Iowa and Minnesota. The third girl lived in the Decatur area and she also departed.

"What do we do?" we pleaded with the Lord.

Finally the idea came to ask Kimmy Shealey if she would like to become an instant End Time Harvester and go to Australia. She was a member of our church and also sang in Kim's gospel music group called Love Notes. She had seen the skits performed many times and hopefully could learn the material quickly.

Kim was already planning to go to Australia. He and his music group had spent weeks in the recording studio on the third floor of the mansion producing a cassette tape called *Take the Time* which contained original songs composed and arranged by him. The goal was to complete the production and take duplicated copies of the tape overseas on the Australian outreach.

I called Eileen again plus a precious "saint" everyone called "Aunt Helen" and asked them to pray. Eileen called me back with the message, "The strong ones will stand." We were to continue praising the Lord, stand by and expect a miracle.

Kimmy called and was very excited. She gave me the go-ahead to start looking for new team outfits for her and Chris. Arrangements were made to have Chris leave Team II which was on tour ministering on the east coast.

Early the next morning Jerry left Decatur to drive to the Immigration Office in Chicago to get a visa and passport for Chris and Kimmy. It would take a miracle to get both of them before the scheduled departure date of August 1. The team plus Jerry and I needed to start driving that day to California. We had places to minister along the way plus several engagements in California. The team would fly out from there to New Zealand.

Jerry waited in line for hours to get the passports and visas. By the time he got to the front desk, the "closed" sign was placed right in his face. He went to the airport and picked up Chris who had flown in from the east coast. They drove home and informed us of the bad news. Jerry was determined to go back to Chicago early Monday morning.

I was scheduled to speak that day at the Decatur Women's Aglow meeting. I shared for one and one-half hours on depression and the events we had been through in the last few days. Jerry went ahead and drove to Chicago and we believed all would go well at the Immigration Office. He called that night and said he was not able to meet with anyone at the office and therefore decided to spend the night in Chicago and try again the next morning.

In the midst of all this, the pages for my first book *Fortress on a Hill* were printed and ready to be taken to the book binder in Virden. Skids loaded with the pages and covers for over 5,000 books filled our church van. As Viki made a sharp turn driving the van down Eldorado Street, papers started shifting off the skids. The van door blew open and papers went everywhere! We quickly got Kirk and Mike, my son-in-law, to help us with our near catastrophe. Mike had printed all of the pages and covers. They came to our rescue and sat on the piles of papers all the way to the book binder. With great relief we finally arrived at our destination where people were waiting to bind the books into finished products.

In record time we had published *Fortress on a Hill* which was the testimony of my family and how the House of Prayer Ministries got started. As our drama teams traveled and ministered, we received requests for information on how to start a Christian drama team. Viki encouraged Kirk to write *Harvesting The Field* which was a "how-to" Christian drama book and included three skits. The goal was to have it published before the Australian outreach. Kirk used every spare minute writing the manuscript which Viki typed and edited. She and Cheri were given complete access to Wood Printing Service where Cheri and Mike worked. Viki and Cheri typeset both manuscripts for *Harvesting the Field* and *Fortress on a Hill*. They did all of the page layouts while Mike printed both books. In three months two books were published.

Jerry called from Chicago to say he had finally gotten to see someone at the Immigration Office. All of our paperwork looked okay until the immigration officer noticed that Kimmy previously had Hodgkin's disease. No one who had cancer was allowed to enter Australia unless there was a complete medical report stating that person was 100 percent healed. Jerry wanted us to get in contact with Kimmy and have her meet him at St. Mary's Hospital at 3 p.m. so the additional paperwork could be filled out. He put the "pedal to the metal" and zoomed back to Decatur. Kimmy was waiting at the hospital for him when he arrived. He explained to her they needed to have her cancer doctor fill out the papers before she would be granted a visa. Just then Dr. G. Richard Locke came down the corridor. He was the cancer doctor who had treated her!

Kimmy ran up to him and explained the situation. The kind doctor dutifully filled out all the forms. God had triumphed!

The next day Jerry drove back to Chicago and again waited and waited in line. One of the employees stepped out to go to the restroom. Jerry approached her and explained to her our plight. She asked how she could help and we assumed everything would be taken care of.

Two days later we received an envelope from the Immigration Office. With hands trembling, we opened it only to find the Visa papers for the three girls who had left the team. Incredible! Back to the drawing board! Finally, the day before the team was to leave for California the mailman delivered the much needed packet of passports and visas. Their arrival was just in the nick of time, but then God is always on time. He watches over us to see if we really and truly believe He will come through. I thanked God for giving us the gift of faith just when we needed it most. Inwardly I hoped His source of faith would never run out.

2

Go Ye into All the World

"Ah, just one more time," I said to myself as I ran the vacuum sweeper one last time throughout the big house which boasted of 24 rooms, 10 bathrooms and a full basement. My bags were packed and we were ready to drive the Truthmobile to California with Team I of the End Time Harvesters and all of their luggage. We planned to tow Jerry's yellow Datsun nicknamed "the Yellow Lizard" behind the Truthmobile. Viki had arranged for Jerry and me to minister at several churches throughout California. The Truthmobile would be stored at the home of Kerry Abernathy, who was a former member of the End Time Harvesters and lived in Idyllwild, California. When the team came back from Australia, New Zealand and Hawaii, they would drive the Truthmobile back to Illinois.

We stayed up late the night before our departure, putting the song labels on Love Notes' *Take The Time* music cassettes and stuffing the cardboard inserts into the empty cassette boxes. Once again God's timing was perfect as we had been waiting for the printed labels and cassettes to arrive and they came that day.

With some hesitation and a lot of prayer, I said goodby to Viki and boarded the Truthmobile for our long awaited journey. I considered myself the world's worst traveler, especially when it came to camping, whereas Jerry just loved every moment out on the open road.

Our first stop was Hot Springs, Arkansas, where we met a girl named Ana who was joining Team II of the Harvesters. My dislike of camping increased greatly as we spent two nights in the camp where Ana lived. I slept very little while trying to keep flies and mosquitoes off of me. I dared any spiders to come close to me. Some of the

Harvesters persuaded me to go with them out on the lake in a paddle boat. Within minutes it started sinking. The guys immediately dove into the water and helped the boat surface. I was petrified!

We left Arkansas and continued our journey westward. Everyone was asleep when Jerry cried out, "Las Vegas ahead!" We quickly woke up to see the city's bright lights flood the area-- quite a contrast to the dark night out there.

"What a deception," I thought to myself. "That worldly light is only temporary. Only Jesus is the real Light of the world."

We finally got to the mountainous area of Idyllwild, California. We stopped at a rest area and the Harvesters quickly climbed out of the Truthmobile and ran down a steep path. They yelled back for Jerry and me to join them. Jerry cautioned me to hang onto the bushes and shrubs on my descent. I had on clunky white sandals with a heel and soon found myself picking up speed as I went down the mountain. Before long I was running faster and faster, but could not stop. Panic gripped me and I cried out, "Help, Lord!"

Suddenly, I found myself on the ground. My elbows had been my "brakes" and were buried deep in the dirt. Instantly Jerry and Kirk were by my side. Jerry was determined that I stand up on my feet. I remember him instructing me, "Whatever you do, do not look at your elbows." I later discovered that a lot of skin had been torn off and I was bleeding quite a bit.

I struggled to get to my feet but could not put any weight on my right foot. It felt like it wasn't even there! Somehow, by the grace of God, Kirk carried me up the mountain. I was placed on a make-shift bed in the back of the Truthmobile. I was covered with dirt, leaves and blood.

Finally we arrived at Kerry and Jenny Abernathy's home. Jerry helped me get to the bathroom and soon had me soaking in warm bath water. He had worked as a hospital orderly to help earn his way through college and now was tenderly cleansing my wounds. Ointment was applied to my badly scraped and bruised arms and then gauze was wrapped around them. My right foot still would not respond. It continued to swell and turned black and blue.

A prayer meeting was held that night at Abernathy's. I took

some pain medication and was able to participate. A beautiful young girl named Jeanette attended and eventually would join the End Time Harvesters. Kirk could not take his eyes off of her!

The Harvesters left early the next morning to drive to Pomona, California, where they were scheduled to minister Sunday morning. Jerry and I also left after my appointment at the local beauty shop. I was shocked to see several other people on crutches or with bandaged limbs. Apparently the area was known for its ski resorts.

We stopped at the Salvation Army Thrift Store and bought a pair of crutches for $2 so that I could get around. We then proceeded to the mall to find a pair of shoes that would fit over my badly swollen foot. I had no sooner gotten out of the car when I fell down–crutches and all. It was hard enough trying to maneuver with crutches, let alone having my arms bandaged.

We finally found a shoe store. Jerry asked for a boy's basketball shoe and literally shoved my foot inside it. The salesman winced as I grimaced in pain. Jerry asked for a pair of scissors and cut out the front top. Now I could travel in style!

We then made contact with Frances J. Roberts who lives in Ojai, California. She is the author of several books including *Come Away My Beloved*. With her permission, one of the writings in that book was included in *Fortress on a Hill*. She told me that if we were ever in California to look her up. She was delighted we took her up on her offer! She greeted us warmly at her lovely retreat home.

"Dottie and Jerry," she said, "I'm Frances and you're spending the night with me."

We were overwhelmed! "God is so good to us," I mused.

While sitting in France's kitchen and eating a delicious meal, I casually made the remark, "I wonder why we're here."

"Well, maybe God will show us and then, maybe He won't," Frances replied. She had learned to trust Him a long time ago.

We went outside and sat on her front porch just as the sun was beginning to set. All of a sudden a young man seemed to come out of nowhere and approached the front steps. His arms were bandaged in some funny wraps and he asked if he could use the phone. He seemed very nervous and kept looking all around.

Frances invited him inside. He was reluctant to enter, but I assured him it was all right and said my husband was in there and he was a minister. If anything was wrong, maybe Jerry could help him.

He informed us that he had been in a terrible fire and received burns all over his arms. The funny bandages were protecting his delicate skin. He then said he had been hiding in the ravine all day in the hot, blazing sun because the police were looking for him. He knew there was a phone at the house and he wanted to call his "wife" to come and get him.

Frances and I tiptoed out of the room while Jerry ministered to him for a long time. When we saw him later, he was a changed person! Jerry had told him about Jesus and led him in the sinner's prayer. He was bursting at the seams with joy unspeakable and full of glory! He placed another phone call and finally his girlfriend arrived. He had lied when he said she was his wife. She told us that her mother and him had been feuding. Another phone call was made and the mother arrived. With the wise counsel of the Holy Spirit, Jerry talked to them and led both the mother and the daughter to the Lord. In addition they all forgave each other. Praise the Lord!

Then came the icing on the cake. The girlfriend said the police wanted the man for just a mild traffic violation–nothing serious. Hallelujah! He was a free man in the spiritual realm as well as in the physical world. What a divine appointment God had given us!

We left the next morning in Jerry's small Datsun for a two-week ministry tour. By opening the glove compartment, I was able to rest my injured foot upon a towel, just missing the handle on the door. We traveled that way in the weeks ahead. There was no glorified comfort of air conditioning, but somehow we could always see the little cloud that followed us everywhere in the desert.

We drove to Pomona to meet up with the Harvesters at the large church where they ministered mightily. At the end of the service I broke down and cried. I guess I really lost it. Jerry and the team surrounded me and started to pray. They thought I was crying because of the ordeal with my foot and bandaged arms. I finally explained that I was crying because I was so proud of them. They had so much talent, but had given up everything to go full time for the Lord's work. I just knew many souls would be won for the Kingdom of God.

The next day we ate our last supper together before the team boarded the plane that would take them to New Zealand. Choking back the tears, I said goodby to three of my children–Kim, Chris and Kirk–and to Kimmy and Tim. Only time would tell why they were the chosen ones for this missionary outreach.

Jerry and I continued on our journey, ministering in many churches. At one place I got down on my knees to pray with someone and then could not get back up. I literally crawled across the stage to get my crutches. People must have felt sorry for me because we received the largest offering ever!

Eventually we headed to Herb and Ginny Ayers' home in Hemet, California. Ginny was one of the first person's to come to the House of Prayer when we opened its doors in 1975. The Ayers retired and left Central Illinois to settle in Hemet.

Ginny persuaded me to get an x-ray of my foot since it was not getting any better. Earlier a nurse at Kerry Abernathy's home had looked at my foot and said she was sure there was a broken bone. Her husband made the remark, "Yes, it takes a lot of faith for healing, but it takes even more faith to believe God will pay the doctor's bill." He then proceeded to give Jerry a check for $100 to cover my medical expenses.

I told the x-ray technician that out of my immediate family of seven, none of us had ever had a broken bone. After taking the x-ray he came back grinning and remarked, "You just broke your record. You have three broken toes and each one is broken in a different way."

The doctor in charge would not put a cast on my foot because the last woman he put a foot cast on, her husband carried her up the stairs and then accidently dropped her! The doctor then gave me a tetanus shot and said I might have a small reaction in a couple of days. Nothing happened until 10 days later when my entire upper arm swelled and became hot pink. It made me wonder how bad I would have gotten without the shot.

When we finally made it back to Decatur, I called my family doctor, Dr. Gordon McGhee. He recommended I see an orthopedic surgeon. Within one hour Dr. M. Stephen Huss put a cast on my right leg and foot. I decided to give him a copy of *Fortress on a Hill*. He just shouted when he saw a picture of the mansion on the front cover.

"I met my wife at a party in that house!" he exclaimed.

"It truly is a small world!" I remarked.

Later we found out it was actually the Staley mansion which was next door to us–the two blended together.

Viki kept in contact with Team I in Australia and continued booking tours for Team II in the United States. God definitely knew what He was doing when He allowed the original three girls to leave the Harvesters. Sometimes the Australian team ministered in three to four services a day. At the height of their activity, the team did 87 services in four weeks. They ministered to over 10,000 students in public schools and were allowed to give altar calls. Churches opened their doors and allowed the Harvesters to minister through Christian drama–a first for many places. It required a tremendous amount of strength, endurance and stamina on the part of the Harvesters to continuously give of themselves so others could hear the gospel message of salvation. The team also learned it was much easier traveling with five people instead of six, especially when it came time to transporting luggage.

When they arrived back in the states, the tired but exuberant Harvesters drove the Truthmobile to Dallas, Texas. Kirk was asked to speak about the Australian tour at a chapel service at Christ for the Nations Institute--the Bible college where he graduated from. What an inspiration to the future drama students at CFNI! To God be the glory, great things He has done!

3

The Two Shall Be One

December 22, 1983, was Viki's last day working as a reporter at the *Decatur Tribune*. She had been there eight years and enjoyed interviewing and writing about hundreds of people in the Central Illinois area. But the demands of booking tours for two End Time Harvester teams plus the evangelistic tours for Jerry and me was a full time job. She would now become the full time Public Relations Director for the House of Prayer Ministries, receiving a small weekly salary. She and her husband, Doug, would run the ministry and church services when we were gone. We had Sunday School, morning and evening worship services plus a Bible study on Wednesday nights.

My responsibilities included cleaning the mansion and cooking for the drama teams when they were either in training or in-between tours. In addition, I ran a clothing ministry on the side. I went to garage and church sales where I purchased clothing items and then washed and ironed them so I could resell them at two consignment shops. For 12 years I faithfully brought in 45 items a week to these shops. I clothed many, many people as well as my own family and brought in some extra money for the ministry. In addition, the rummage sales were a great source for obtaining props for the drama teams.

It didn't take long for rummage to accumulate at the House of Prayer so twice a year we had a big sale. Oftentimes the revenues from these sales either helped make a house payment or paid for a power bill. Twice a year the ministry had a booth at the local mall's bazaars. Viki and I would bake for weeks and fill our freezers with goodies to sell. Not only did the bazaars generate some income, but they also provided some great free publicity.

In my "spare" time I did latch hook to relax me. I designed and

23

completed a huge wall hanging with the End Time Harvesters' logo.

As time went on I noticed some terrible pain in my shoulders. I went back to Dr. Huss who took x-rays and said there was some deterioration of the bones. He prescribed some pain medication. The fall down the mountain a few months earlier was still giving me problems.

On February 9 in 1984 Jerry and I headed south for an evangelistic tour. Our first stop was at a church in Monroe, Georgia. Revival broke out and we were asked to stay for several nights ministering to the needs of the people. Many people came forward at the altar calls and gave their hearts to Jesus. In many instances people were healed as Jerry operated in the gift of knowledge.

As for me, I was experiencing much discomfort in my shoulders and sneezed profusely—my nose ran all the time. We stopped at one church and a man there said he "really had the anointing for praying for bad backs and if I wasn't healed after he prayed, then it was because of my unbelief." I let him pray as I reached for the tissue box. My spirit definitely was not connecting with his at all.

At another town while receiving directions from a pastor, I apologized for my runny nose and sneezing. He smiled and said softly, "Yes, it's hard on people who have allergies. Everything is budding and blooming so early this year." The wind was blowing seedlings and pollen everywhere. For the first time instead of feeling condemned, I felt like this man was someone who walked close to God. I was at peace with my situation.

We continued on with ministry in Milledgeville, Augusta, Waynesboro and other Georgian communities. On our way back to Decatur, we spent the night in Clarksville, Tennessee. We knew we were in trouble the next morning when we discovered ice and snow on our car in the motel parking lot. Some of the highway exits were closing. Vehicles were sliding off the road and landing in the ditches. By the time we reached Shelbyville, Illinois, which was about 40 miles from Decatur, deep snow was piling up everywhere. We tried following a snowplow but the driver turned around and went back because the road was so bad. We decided to keep going only to hear on the radio that all of the roads were closing. We prayed and decided to make a go for it. The sun was beginning to set and all we could see were the fence posts because the snow was so deep. Finally, we made it home.

We sneaked into the old house and stood silently in one of the doorways. It was Kirk's birthday and the Harvesters had decorated and given him a party. Suddenly someone noticed us and then it was time to really celebrate! Viki had called every prayer chain in town asking people to pray for our safety and protection. Again, the Lord had seen us through.

On March 3 one of our drama teams left to minister at Mardi Gras in New Orleans. Upon their return, they were full of stories and testimonies about what God had done. At one church service a man who recognized Kirk asked him and his "wife" to stand up. Jeanette turned red all over. "Was this prophecy or the word of knowledge in operation?" questioned the other team members.

On March 22 I was busy in the kitchen when Kirk came in and started to "butter" me up. I knew he was up to something because that was the way he always acted when he wanted something. Finally he asked, "Mom, remember when you said whichever of your sons gets engaged first, you would give him your original engagement ring?"

"Yes," I replied. "I remember. How far down the road would you like it?"

"Tonight," he said firmly.

He escorted Jeanette to the Blue Mill Restaurant for dinner and proposed to her. The next time I saw Jeanette, she was wearing my diamond ring which would be resized to fit her better. They announced their engagement at the House of Prayer's next worship service and planned to get married on September 15 at Jeanette's hometown in Idyllwild, California.

All did not flow smoothly, however, for Kirk. On April 13 while doing some back flips off of Team II leader John Reynolds, Kirk felt something go pop in his back. He was in excruciating pain. A visit to a chiropractor friend in Peoria revealed a ruptured disk. In his earlier years Kirk had been an outstanding gymnast and won first place in the floor exhibition and third place for all-around in the YMCA State Gymnastics Meet.

Now he was so contorted he could barely get around. The pain was so bad that many nights he slept on his knees, bent over a chair. It would take a long time for the disk to be repaired. My friend, Eileen Volle, brought over a traction apparatus that Kirk could hook himself into and stretch the lower part of his body, thus taking some of the pressure off of it.

The pain in my shoulders continued to get worse. The doctor put me on some other medication but it didn't seem to help. Jerry and I left for a 36-day ministry tour in the states of Arizona, Arkansas, California, New Mexico, Oklahoma and Texas. By the time we arrived at some friends' home in Albuquerque, New Mexico, I was in agony. I couldn't sit still and felt like a knife was going through my left shoulder blade. Finally my friend Nadine said, "What you really need is a good chiropractor!"

I replied, "Well, if God intends for that to happen, He'll just have to send one across my path because we have a mighty full schedule."

The following weekend we were at a prayer meeting at Kerry and Jenny Abernathy's home in Idyllwild, California. I shared my condition with a woman there and her eyes got as big as saucers. "Don't look now, Dottie, but the man who just walked in the door is a chiropractor and this is the first time he's ever come here."

Later I introduced myself to him and told him where I hurt. He interrupted me and asked if my finger went numb. When I mumbled "yes" he told me to be in his office the next morning at 10 a.m.

He took full x-rays of my neck and shoulders. Much damage had been done to the upper neck when I fell down the mountain. I would need continuous treatment but for the time being he could help relieve the pain so that I could continue traveling. He never charged a penny! God had provided!

He had heard we were coming to the prayer meeting and wanted to hear our testimony. He was so impressed that he gave his heart back to the Lord. He was delighted when I gave him an autographed copy of *Fortress on a Hill*. When Jerry and I left Idyllwild, we literally "flew down the mountain," giving God the glory.

June 25 marked my "half century." One of the Harvesters

made a huge poster with the number 50 on it. "Where had the time gone?" I asked myself.

My shoulder pain intensified so Dr. McGhee gave me cortisone shots and pain killers. Kirk was seeing a young chiropractor for his back and I decided to make an appointment. Jeff took x-rays of my left shoulder and immediately started sonic treatment. He gave me a list of exercises to do and had me wear a collar around my neck. Thus began several trips for treatments back and forth to Peoria.

Kirk still was not doing well and on June 27 he woke up with a 103° temperature and one side of his face was grossly distorted. It was also numb and paralyzed. Bell's Palsy had settled in. He decided to go ahead and fulfill a speaking engagement at Christ for the Nations in Stoneybrook, New York. His faith and trust were in the Lord that God would take care. As he walked toward the microphone across the center of the stage, he was instantly healed by God. The drooping eye and corner of his mouth were restored to normal. What a powerful testimony to God's glory and healing power!

On July 22 Jerry and I left on a 27-day evangelistic tour throughout the states of Montana, Oregon and Utah. Shortly after we got back home, two new Harvesters arrived at the House of Prayer. Dan Jones was from Oregon and Libby Almy from Montana. Twenty-nine-year-old Kim took one look at Libby and was smitten, even though she was nine years his junior. In no time they were engaged.

The ring Kim gave her was no ordinary ring. One day while hauling garbage he noticed a shiny object about ready to go into the truck's hopper. He reached down just in time and pulled out a ring. He thought it was a man's fake diamond ring and gave it to me to put in the House of Prayer's rummage sale. I was about to put $2.00 on it when I abruptly said, "Whoa, I think this might be the real thing."

Kim took it to a local jeweler who appraised it for over $500! Incredible! Kim had the diamond taken out and put into a lovely black and gold rose setting. Like his brother Kirk, Kim took Libby to the Blue Mill Restaurant and proposed to her. They set their wedding date for December 24 in Ismay, Montana. Both of my sons planned to marry within a few months time of each other.

Jerry and I left September 3 to drive to Idyllwild, California, for Kirk and Jeanette's wedding on the 15th. The ceremony was held in a little mountain church. Before long the sun seemed to disappear in the clouds and it began to get darker and darker. Just when Jerry told Kirk he could kiss the bride, there was a tremendous roar of thunder and lightening flashed everywhere. Without missing a cue, Jerry remarked, "And thank You, Father, for Your sign of approval."

"And may all your kisses have such an impact," I chimed in. Everyone roared with laughter.

Just three months later on December 20 Jerry, Kim, Kirk, Jeanette, Gene Otto and I boarded the church van to head to Montana for Kim and Libby's wedding. Gene was the Harvester who convinced Libby to join the team when it was on tour in Montana. Chris and Libby had left two weeks earlier to get everything ready for the big day.

I found the ride to Montana to be extremely uncomfortable. My shoulders, upper back and arms were in great pain and I had a terrible sore throat. While in Ismay we stayed in an old bunk house and slept on the floor. The wind howled furiously through the wall behind our heads. I was armed with a heating pad, medication and a new collar around my neck to try to ease the pain.

On Christmas Eve we drove into the parking lot of the tiny church. Libby's brother, Curtis, was riding a big tractor and scooping snow. "Isn't that nice of him?" I thought to myself. I should have known better.

Boughs of pine decorated the sanctuary. Candles were lit. It was a beautiful setting! I got a lump in my throat when Kim sang a song he composed for Libby.

During the reception there was a big commotion outside. We all raced outside to find a mammoth pile of snow in the center of the parking lot. The "get-away" car was nowhere to be found. It was buried in the snow thanks to Curtis!

On Christmas Day we started the long drive back to Decatur. The van was loaded with Christmas presents and gallons of left-over peppermint ice cream from the wedding. By the time we got to Rapid City, South Dakota, my sore throat was crying out for the ice cream, but it had all melted when the sun came out.

As we continued on our journey, it began to rain. Then the rain turned to ice the farther south we traveled. The roads became extremely slick and we just "crawled" for several hours. A little white sports car passed us at one point. A short distance later the car slipped off the road and landed in the ditch. You just couldn't stop!

That journey back on Christmas Day felt like the longest one in my life. Even though we had exchanged gifts in the van and sang carols, it just did not seem like Christmas. We finally made it home at 3 p.m. the next day. Kim and Libby arrived later that evening to set up housekeeping in Kim's old apartment in the mansion.

Sometime later I collected my thoughts on this little adventure and summed them up with the following poem.

Christmas '84

Twas the night before Christmas
As I crept like a mouse,
Toward the warmth of the fire
In the old bunkhouse.

The winds of Montana
Blustered about,
Swirling the snowflakes
With a vigorous shout.

"I'm chilled to the bone,"
I cried in dismay,
"But 'tis our son's wedding
In the town of Ismay.

I thought of my family
Who couldn't be here,
While visions of past years
Danced in the air.

The candles were flickering
In the tiny old church,
And beckoned me onward
As my feelings I nursed.

The bough on the windows
Brought scent to my nose;
Then the organ began playing
And up we arose!

A bride so lovely
Took my son's hand,
And I cried when he gave her
A gold wedding band.

At the reception that followed,
A voice called from the clatter.
We all sprang from our chairs
To see what was the matter.

The bride's brother stood laughing
And grinning so cute.
He said there'd been an avalanche
And it was a beaut!

The get-away-car
Was not to be found,
But we were mighty suspicious
Of a great white mound!

Ma Ma had her kerchief
And cried to her man,
"Oh, my dear husband,
This was not what we planned."

A pull of the tractor
      As men strained at the bit,
A grunt from the Datsun
      And she burst from the pit!

The groom and his bride
      Soon disappeared from our sight,
Wishing "Merry Christmas" to all
      And to all a good night!

I gazed at the heavens
      As the stars twinkled back.
My Father was watching
      And knew what I lacked.

So thank You, dear Father,
      For our newest addition,
And for all of these chapters
      That make up "tradition!"

4

Over Mountains and Valleys

The winter of 1985 settled in with blustery winds and freezing temperatures. It did not take long before some of the pipes in the old mansion began to freeze and burst. Each time we tried to conserve energy and save on the heat bill by closing off a room, a pipe would inevitably burst. Jerry was constantly repairing something in the old house.

The End Time Harvesters started getting more requests for their drama material after Kirk's book *Harvesting The Field* was published. The ministry decided to publish *End Time Harvesters Skit Book #1*. I was appalled by much of the so-called "Christian drama" that was out there and was determined our skits would have a strong salvation message. Kirk compiled and edited *Skit Book #1* and included four of my skits. That book proved to be so successful that in July of 1986 the House of Prayer Ministries published *End Time Harvesters Skit Book #2*. Several of my skits were also included in this book.

Our neighbor, Elmira Sparr, took care of several elderly women in her home. On Sunday afternoons I would go over and visit Lula. We found out we had something in common—we were both twins. Her sister died in her early teens from flu complications.

I told Lula about Jesus and read her some of my poems published by the House of Prayer several years earlier. She had never been taught that salvation was a free gift Jesus had purchased for everyone by dying as the sacrificial lamb on Calvary.

I shared with her that when Adam and Eve sinned in the Garden of Eden, we all inherited a sin nature and as a result deserved eternal punishment in hell fire. But, a loving God in His infinite mercy provided a plan—He would give His very best, His only begotten Son,

Jesus, in our place to be that supreme sacrifice for our sins. All who look to Him, believe on Him and His glorious resurrection plus repent of their sins will be covered by His righteousness and inherit everlasting life in His heavenly kingdom. Heaven is not attained by our good works. It is not a religion that saves us, but rather a personal relationship with Jesus Christ Who saves us. When the shadows of death envelope a believer, he is instantly with Jesus.

Lulu listened intently each time I visited her. She repented of her sins and asked Jesus to come and live in her heart. She was a changed person and those around her knew something good had happened. No longer was she grumpy; rather, she was happy and beaming because she finally had great peace. She knew Jesus and where she was going to spend eternity.

On January 14 Viki announced to everyone she was pregnant. She and Doug were excited! The baby was due at the end of August. I was in shock and had to sit down. At long last I was going to be a grandmother! I had secretly wanted to be a grandmother at the age of 39 which would have been possible if Viki had gotten married at an early age like me and had a baby. Now I would be 51 claiming that title. Viki wasn't even married by the age I had five children.

There was another rummage sale to prepare for. When we finally set up all of the tables, Jerry and I left to drive to Jacksonville for an evangelistic meeting. The speaker told Jerry he saw him with a white beard, indicating wisdom from God. He also saw Jerry winning spiritual battles by being at the altar of prayer.

The speaker then turned to me and said I had great compassion, was an edifier and a comforter. Then he spoke the following words, "I have called you. You will be coming more alive. The bondage will come off and something new is in the making."

Our friend Wayne Belcher, who had invited us to the meeting, leaned over and told me he thought I would be writing a new book.

"That will be the day," I told myself.

By mid April the tulips along our front walkway were in full bloom. Viki was also beginning to "blossom," but she didn't let her pregnancy slow her down. The House of Prayer participated in another bazaar and she and I baked most of the goodies. I also did many of the craft items. She also continued booking the tours for the drama teams.

Tension began to mount with some of the younger adults in our church. On one occasion I was bawled out for concentrating so much on the rummage and on clothing people and for not being "spiritual enough." Someone suggested that perhaps I should get a job at one of the thrift stores. And yet, a few days later I was asked to look for certain clothing items for these same people. It was a no-win situation no matter what I did.

At the May Decatur Women's Aglow meeting, the speaker asked the women to come forward for prayer. I never said a word, but the speaker began to pray over me for all the hurts that are endured by a pastor's wife. I was to rest in the Lord.

On Mother's Day I read to our church body a special poem the Lord had given me. It asks the eternal question, "What is a Mother?"

What Is a Mother?

The hand that rocks the cradle
Of a newborn that's so dear,
Singing ever so softly
For part of her is near.

The tender kiss that takes away
The pain from a battered knee.
The busy hands that forever mend
The patches mankind sees.

The loving concern of teenage years
Of worries kept inside.
Trust that bides with discipline
And love that overrides.

The tears that are shed on a wedding day
While standing meek and mild;
Yet inwardly a burst of pride
As one gives away her "child."

The contentment and the inner peace
That comes in latter time,
Knowing that this love lives on
As the road to heaven is climbed.

Our Lord must have a special place
That's higher than any other,
For those dear ones who bear the name
And are simply known as "Mother."

But wait a minute, do go on...
For by gosh, by golly,
There seems to be an added verse
To this quite splendid folly.

For though with dignity and pride
One bears the name of "Mother,"
'Tis far blessed and greater still
To be called "Grandmother!"

On June 21 Jerry and I started out on a 33-day evangelistic tour throughout several southern states. We had a wonderful time ministering in Georgia and renewing contact with several pastor friends.

We headed to Orlando, Florida, and I finally got to meet Grace and "Jorgy" Jorgensen. Jerry had met them earlier when their son Andrew met up with one of our drama teams. Our spirits bonded instantly and we stayed up for hours talking on their back porch. Frogs were croaking all around us and Disney World could be seen in the distance.

The next morning the Jorgensens took us out for dinner and made arrangements for us to receive free tickets to go see Epcot. It was a fantastic adventure witnessing all of the latest technology in laser beams and holograms. Figures appeared out of nowhere and talked as they moved about.

Jerry and I decided to try and locate a young man named Jim Johnson who had lived with us for a short while. The last we heard he was living in Palm Harbor and working as a car dealer. We made several inquiries and finally found a man who knew him and said he sometimes frequented a certain donut shop. We drove there and spotted Jim walking across the parking lot. He was absolutely stunned to see us! We talked for two hours.

He told us about his ordeal with cancer eating one of his eyes. As the doctors prepared him for surgery, some "faith healers" jumped on his bed and told him to claim and believe for his healing without surgery. He was not healed and commented he had to trust the Lord for his new plastic eyeball.

"God's ways certainly aren't man's ways," I thought to myself.

We went back to the Jorgensens and received a phone call from Viki. She had just heard from Kirk in Australia and everything was going extremely well. Because of the outstanding time of ministry by the Harvesters in 1983, the team was invited back to New Zealand and Australia. In addition, arrangements were made for them to minister for a month throughout Papua New Guinea. The overseas outreach team this time consisted of Kirk and his wife Jeanette, Chris, Neal Cline and Andrea Mueller. They were doing as many as three and four services a day. In Papua New Guinea the lines to their skits oftentimes were translated into two different languages or dialects. Team members had to be on their toes as they patiently waited for the translations and then tried to remember where they were in the skits.

Jerry and I had a great time of ministry at the Jorgensens' church. We prayed for several people who were instantly healed. Others were baptized in the Holy Spirit and spoke in tongues. Grace, Jorgy, Jerry and I stayed up til 1 a.m. thanking God and giving Him all the glory.

We left the Orlando area and continued ministering. I woke up one morning with severe burning in my bladder. I told a pastor's wife and she recommended I see a doctor. Sure enough, my white count was up and I had a bad bladder infection. A prescription was filled and we got back on the road. It was an awkward situation having God use Jerry to pray for people to get healed and then I had to go to a doctor. Again, God's ways are higher than man's ways.

On August 6 we had a baby shower for Viki. Five days later she started having contractions during church service. They were light and very sporadic. She thought it was false labor but went ahead and packed her suitcase. She knew she couldn't go to the hospital until the contractions were closer together. She decided not to attend the Women's Aglow meeting the next morning and kept timing her contractions. She called the doctor's office and was told not to come in until the contractions were 30 minutes apart and lasting about five minutes.

The next morning she started spotting and called the doctor's office. Her contractions still were not close together. Her regularly scheduled appointment was that afternoon on August 13 and unless the contractions got closer together, she should just come in for that appointment.

I insisted on driving Viki to her appointment. The nurse came out after the doctor examined her and said she needed to get to the hospital right away. She was not allowed to go home to get her suitcase. She was dilated eight centimeters!

Nervously and anxiously I drove the car to the hospital parking lot. I could hardly stay focused! Instead of letting Viki out at the front door, I inadvertently parked the car quite a distance away. She quickly got out to walk to the admittance office. When she got to the front door, hospital personnel were waiting for her with a wheelchair and quickly whisked her upstairs.

I called Jerry and told him to bring her suitcase. Doug was driving a city bus and the message was given to him to get to the hospital right away.

It took just as long for Viki to dilate the last two centimeters as she had been doing over the last couple of days. When she finally got to 10, her water was broken by a nurse and it was time to push. Everyone was taking bets in the delivery room that it would be a girl, but Viki and Doug felt all along that it would be a boy. Just a couple of quick pushes, and out came a tiny baby boy! Michael Douglas weighed 4 pounds 7 ounces and was 17 3/4 inches long. We saw him in the nursery, just kicking away. Dr. McGhee said, "He's awfully small, but he's wiry. He'll make it."

A couple of months earlier the doctor told Viki she would have a small baby that would weigh 5 pounds. Two and one-half weeks later on what should have been the due date, Michael weighed exactly 5 pounds!

He really wasn't premature because doctors consider three weeks early as being premature. He was just a low birth-weight baby. Jaundice set in and he ended up staying in the hospital while Viki was released to go home. He was placed under bright lights in his "birthday suit" to try and get his bilirubin level down. He could not drink out of a bottle and had a tube placed in his nose so he could be fed. One of the nurses called him "Peewee" and kept encouraging him to try and take a bottle–the size of a doll bottle.

On Sunday, August 18, Dr. McGhee circumcised Michael and decided he could go home, even though he only weighed 4 pounds 6 ounces. The nurses looked astonished because usually a baby has to weigh at least 5 pounds before he can be released.

"This is your first baby and your parents live in the same house as you, so they can help," the doctor remarked.

Doug's parents, Jim and Sue Scherer, came from Mattoon to see their new grandson. Grandpa Jim finally got to hold Michael. He took one look at Michael's long skinny fingers and proclaimed, "This boy will be a piano player." For several months a blue mark shaped like a music note was visible at the bridge of his nose. Michael went to his first church service that evening. Worship songs included "Song of Joy" and "I've Been Delivered."

Kirk called from Australia at the end of the month and said they were completely sold out of all our books and tapes. The crowds had been phenomenal. At one of the meetings there was literally a sea of humanity–as far as one could see there were people.

On the home front, tensions were mounting. End Time Harvesters Team I did not have a working van for the upcoming tour. In addition, some of the young adults involved at the House of Prayer blamed me for the church's slow growth. They attacked me with questions like "Did I really want to be a pastor's wife?" "Why were clothes and rummage my God?" "And what about the beer cans in the kitchen?"

I explained to them that a man with disabilities collected the cans tossed into our yard and put them in a box in the kitchen. It was his way of helping us out. When the cans accumulated, we took them to the recycling center and gave the money to missions. Jerry had heard enough and announced to the "inquisition" that it was our wedding anniversary and we were going on a date to the Dairy Queen to celebrate. We walked out, letting them try to solve their problems.

It was the age-old problem of power control. The young people wanted to show they had all the answers but disregarded the wisdom and years of experience by those who were older. Jerry and I prayed, "Lord, help us to forgive those who have hurt us."

During Jerry's next Sunday sermon, he preached on insecurity and praised my efforts of faithfulness to God's call. He spoke of Christians having "roast pastor and wife for dinner." The message seemed to get across. I was so proud of him!

Michael was gaining weight but had some physical problems. His belly button had gotten huge–the size of a golf ball. The doctor said it was an umbilical hernia that might require surgery when he was a little bit older. He had reflux and would oftentimes vomit after taking a bottle of formula. In addition, his right foot turned in and he had to wear a corrective shoe brace 24 hours a day for several months. He constantly battled ear infections and was on all kinds of antibiotics.

It was time for the annual fall bazaar. I worked like crazy baking and making crafts. Viki couldn't do as much because she had a baby to take care of and was doing all of the bookings for the teams. In addition, a drama group called Covenant Players contacted us and asked for housing while they were in the Decatur area. Jerry said yes so I was busy with meal preparations.

Before long I was tired and worn out. I just did not feel well. My shoulders and arms ached with pain and I had a sinus infection. I went to see Dr. McGhee who ordered me to take a vacation and not do any heavy manual labor. He did a blood test and the results showed I had fibrositis. He prescribed an antibiotic for the sinus infection and other medication for the inflammation in my body. To add insult to injury, the doctor's office contacted me later and said tests showed I also had a bladder infection. I had more medication to take. I went to see my chiropractor because the fibrositis was very painful. He said I would always have problems when the weather was severe or the seasons changed. Boy, did I hate growing old!

The drama team arrived home from Australia on November 26. At one point they did 70 meetings in 4 weeks and had traveled by all kinds of transportation. We talked for hours and they all took turns holding baby Michael.

It wasn't long before another meeting was called to discuss the operations of the House of Prayer. Jerry was told he must get a new building. Kim's music group "Love Notes" would go independent of our ministry. Jerry and I just sat there trying to comprehend it all.

The next day I talked to Kirk about the power struggle going on. I had witnessed it in every profession Jerry had been involved with whether it was school teaching, the insurance field and now even the ministry.

At the next board meeting I lost my position as vice president to a younger man. Even Doug voted against me and said it might not be a good idea to have a "Henneberry dynasty." Jerry was told he could not have any more salary. He only made between $100 and $150 a week and sometimes didn't even take that when the ministry was low on money.

Everything that Jerry and I had sacrificed for 10 years didn't seem to make any difference. All we once held dear was suddenly being taken over by a younger generation. I couldn't even attend the board meetings. Someone else would be making decisions they knew nothing about. My only talent seemed to be "continuous housekeeper." I cried all night. Somehow God would see us through.

On Christmas Eve we held our traditional candlelight communion service. Afterwards we gathered at Cheri and Mike's house for the family gift exchange. When everything was opened, Kim announced that he and Libby were going to have a little girl next summer. Everyone was thrilled! Number two grandchild was on the way!

As I looked back over the year with its mountains and valleys,

I thanked God for the victories He provided. He was in the "pruning business." I best summed it up with a poem I wrote before Michael was born.

The House of Prayer

It seems like only yesterday
  That the House of Prayer was born.
How well I do remember
  That August eleventh morn.

We had loaded our belongings
  And placed them in a van,
Then drove it to this parking lot
  To take our rightful stand!

The owners came in a Cadillac
  And reduced our interest loan,
Then later on this "Dollar Day"
  This place became our home!

People came from everywhere
  For in our house to stay,
Till my children came to me
  And said, "We can't go on this way."

Our church began to blossom
  As people came to see
That prayers were being answered
  By our Lord Who holds the key.

Television called our way
  And a program was set up.
For three and one-half years we ministered
  And filled the Christian's cup.

It was during this trying time
     That I sank into despair.
Depression was upon me
     As I learned of a God Who cares.

For He gave me a gift of writing
     That would lift the hearts of men
And give glory to the Father
     And the love that He transcends.

Finally it was time for Kirk
     To go away to school.
He went to Christ for the Nations
     For God's plan was really dual.

Besides a good education,
     An idea came to mind–
A drama team called End Time Harvesters
     For these closing days of time.

Then another team was formed
     And one even went "down under."
Australia and New Zealand
     Saw Satan put asunder.

In the year of eighty-two
     Love was in the air.
Viki and Doug, then Cheri and Mike
     Became a winning pair.

The nest was being shaken up
     For it was time for mom to leave.
She went with Jerry to minister
     The Christ on which they leaned.

Poems and tapes and skit books
*   Plus Fortress on a Hill,*
A "how to" book on drama
*   Were printed with great skill.*

Our family began to broaden
*   As our boys' each found the one*
They longed to spend their life with,
*   And Jeanette and Libby were won.*

Again our team is overseas
*   Saving souls from hell.*
They tell people about sweet Jesus
*   And of a heaven in which to dwell.*

Who can forget the rummage sales
*   Or the bazaars out at the mall,*
Or the crowding on the wintry days
*   For Sunday School space for all?*

Our house is running over
*   And we need a bigger place,*
But wait upon King Jesus
*   As we run this homeward race.*

And so this brings us up-to-date
*   As we ponder what lies ahead,*
For we are the conquerors for Jesus
*   And the lovely bride He'll wed.*

We'll continue to joust the enemy
*   As we always have in the past,*
And look forward to the future
*   Holding our grandchildren at last!*

5

One, Two, Three Testing

The End Time Harvesters' winter tour was scheduled to begin January 21, 1986. Team members including a new girl began arriving for intensive training shortly after the new year. Chris went back on Team I. It was getting harder and harder to find quality individuals who could handle the demands of touring and the stress of staying in different people's homes all the time. It took a certain caliber person to be able to stand up to the pressures.

There was still a stirring among the young adults that we couldn't put a finger on. Some were upset the house did not have adequate space to do everything they wanted to achieve. I prayed and asked the Lord to speak to me through His Word and opened up to Joel 2:25. *"I will restore to you the years that the locust hath eaten, the cankerworm, and the caterpillar, and the palmerworm."* I told Viki what the Lord had given me and we agreed to wait and see the fulfillment.

Jerry and I left February 24 to attend a pastor's conference sponsored by David Wilkerson in Dallas, Texas. On the first night Bob Phillips spoke on the silent judgment that was falling on preachers, but many did not even realize it.

"Today Jesus is being auctioned off and merchandised for sale. But God is greatly to be feared for He is a holy, righteous God. People want the resurrection without death and discipline. And above all, they do not want the cross–only a good-time Jesus Who makes you feel good." His comments stirred me and were the basis for a new skit I would write.

We broke for lunch and came back in the afternoon to hear David Wilkerson preach. He stopped abruptly and said he felt the Lord telling him to start ministering to the pastors and wives–much earlier than he ever did before at a conference.

For some reason Jerry and I were the first ones before him. He took both of our hands in his and said loudly, "Every demon in hell is coming against you and your ministry. Why, people are even holding meetings behind closed doors about you. But I say to you, 'I will restore to you the years that the locust has eaten, the cankerworm and the caterpillar and the palmerworm.'"

Later that evening we were riding in the same elevator with Wilkerson and I shared with him that God had given me the same verse just a few days earlier. He rejoiced, knowing he had been obedient to the Holy Spirit.

We came from the conference and started looking for a place to hold church services. On Easter Sunday we rented a building, but had to clean up everything from the drunken party the night before. The kitchen had debris everywhere and we had to get it ready for the big dinner we were going to serve after the services. I was still mopping the floor when members of the choir arrived. It would require a lot of work to hold services there every week.

Two weeks later I spoke at the Bloomington Women's Aglow meeting. I shared my testimony including my involvement in the occult. Many people came forward for prayer and said I was one of the boldest speakers.

On April 27 Jerry was scheduled to speak at Pastor Don Etnier's church, Bethel Tabernacle, located at 1110 E. Curtis in Decatur. Jerry woke up sick that morning with nausea and severe diarrhea, but he was determined to go anyway. He got through Sunday School okay, but three-fourths of the way through preaching his sermon, he turned ashen white and asked to be excused. He staggered down the aisle and motioned for me to carry on. The congregation and I ended up praying for him. When the service was over, we made a quick exit home. Jerry went straight to bed. In 24 hours he lost 13 pounds and became dehydrated.

In May Kirk suggested we publish another skit book that would contain only my skits. I had written 21 and chose *Gleaning for God* as the title. With some gentle persuasion, Frances Roberts agreed to write the foreword.

On Tuesday mornings ministers from several denominations and churches came to a prayer meeting at the House of Prayer. Jerry and Kirk were constantly praying for a new building and mentioned their request at one of the meetings. Afterwards, Pastor Don Etnier lingered around for a while and finally told Jerry and Kirk, "You have been praying and believing for a church building and I have been praying for the right pastor to take over mine. The Lord is telling me that you are the one."

Don shared that he was 75 years old and his health was not that good. He had one hip replacement and the other hip was not very good. The Sunday that Jerry preached at his church convinced Don and his wife Lura that Jerry and I were the ones to succeed them.

Jerry was hesitant because all he could see were problems with two churches uniting together. Don told Jerry to think about it while he was gone on a much-needed vacation. We decided to drive over and see the outside of the church.

It was built in the 1950's and located in a neighborhood where there were low income houses. A trailer park was behind the church. From the outside it looked small. Jerry didn't want any part of a church merger.

Don came back from his fishing trip and felt impressed to ask us again about the church. He met us at a restaurant and then took us to see the inside of the church. We were amazed to see a 150-seat sanctuary with theater seats, 10 Sunday School classrooms, a nursery, fellowship hall with a full kitchen, youth recreation room and a two-bedroom apartment behind the sanctuary.

Jerry still was not convinced this was the building God wanted for us. In desperation I sought God's Word and opened my Bible to Deuteronomy 12:11. The words that leaped out at me were, *"Then there shall be a place which the Lord your God shall choose to cause His name to dwell there; thither shall ye bring all that I command you."* I showed these verses to Jerry and my family.

Viki went to see the inside of the church and was absolutely astonished. For a long time she had been praying specifically for several features to be in the building God would give us. Everything on her prayer list was in Bethel Tabernacle!

She and Jerry decided to put out a "fleece" like Gideon in the Old Testament. If God wanted us to have Bethel Tabernacle, then three things would have to happen. First, the congregation would have to agree to change the name from Bethel Tabernacle to Harvest Christian Center. Second, the church would have to get a parking lot because church members could only park on the street. And third, the House of Prayer would have to be paid off.

In our hearts we knew the traveling ministry for the End Time Harvesters was coming to an end. It was getting harder to find competent, qualified people who could handle the rigorous demands of tours, let alone the spiritual battles that constantly arose. In addition many of the team members were getting married and wanting to start their own families. Without the income from the Harvesters, it would be hard to have enough income to pay a salary to both Kirk and Jerry, let alone meet the operating expenses of the big mansion.

On Sunday June 8 we announced to our congregation that the House of Prayer might possibly merge with Bethel Tabernacle. Everyone was ecstatic!

Our happiness and joy were short-lived, however. Kirk announced three days later that he would be leaving the House of Prayer to take the youth pastor position at a large church in town. Jerry and I were devastated! I cried all night. Instead of uniting with us at our new church, Kirk's loyalties would be elsewhere. We would be competing against each other. It was not the first time Kirk had been offered a position at another church.

Jerry was very quiet. I knew he was hurting inside. Surely it was not God's will to pit father against son. I assumed it was common courtesy not to proselyte people from other churches in their town. More and more the ministry was beginning to model the business world. Realistically, though, we simply could not afford the salary he was offered by this other church. I had to put my faith and trust in the Lord. The battle would have to be His.

Viki was elected president of the Decatur Women's Aglow chapter. She was on a committee to find women to nominate as officers and in the process felt God calling her to the role of presidency. She was elected without any opposition.

Members of the End Time Harvesters had been diligently praying for us to get a church building. When they came home a couple of days later, they were thrilled to learn about the possible merger. Tamara Reed, the team leader, recommended that we keep the mansion because God was not finished with it yet. When we took the team to see the church, Sheryl Goudy stood on the church steps and looked across the street. "I can see a big parking lot filled with cars," she envisioned.

On June 17 I noticed a little white car pull up in our back parking lot. The driver was my only brother Bob Kierlin, who was the founder and chairman of The Fastenal Company. He started the "nuts and bolts" company at the age of 28 and turned a $30,000 investment into a multi-billion dollar company with stores all over the United States and in other countries. He also founded the Hiawatha Foundation in our hometown of Winona, Minnesota. Hiawatha purchased the old defunct St. Teresa College and converted it into Cotter High School—one of the premier Catholic High Schools in America.

When I was a junior in high school, I met Jerry who was a senior at St. Mary's College in Winona. My friends and I gave the St. Teresa College girls a lot of competition concerning the boys at St. Mary's! Now my brother helped purchase the college.

I was very happy to see Bob and proud of all his accomplishments. I gave him a tour of the big house. Before he left he told me that my twin sister, Doris, was living in a home for disabled people. I was glad she was okay.

Kirk and Jeanette had a breakfast meeting at the church offering him the youth position. I kept asking God for a sign that Kirk would not leave us. I glanced out the window and saw the magnificent magnolia tree my children had given to me one Mother's Day. It had been growing quite well until an older gentleman accidently mowed it into two sections. Much to my surprise, cutting it back was exactly what the tree needed because in April it had been in full bloom.

As I looked upon it, I secretly asked my heavenly Father if I could just see one little blossom and then I would know that Kirk would be staying with us. That afternoon Doug came home from driving a city bus and casually asked, "Did you know there's a bloom on the magnolia tree way at the top?"

I went absolutely bananas! I knew in my spirit that was the confirmation I needed regarding Kirk and Jeanette. God had everything under control.

6

Beauty for Ashes

A tremendous crashing sound and intense vibration right behind our bedroom wall nearly knocked Jerry and me out of our bed.

"It's an earthquake!" I shouted.

We jumped up and raced to the window. It looked like a car was upside down in the Staley mansion's driveway next door.

"No!" Jerry cried out. "It's not next door! It's in our driveway and I'm calling the police."

I begged him not to take such action because there were some pretty wild parties next door and I didn't want any repercussions. I glanced outside again and saw two teenage boys crawl out of the car's back window. I could hear one of them say there was a phone at a grocery store four blocks away and he was going to call his mother and father and tell them there was an accident.

We hurriedly got dressed on that hot sticky night of July 13. It was actually 1:50 a.m. A few hours later would be the vote during the Sunday morning worship service at Bethel Tabernacle for that church to merge with the House of Prayer and form Harvest Christian Center. Jerry would become the pastor. It was already going to be an emotional morning and now we had an accident to contend with.

Doug and Viki quickly joined us as we headed outside. Doug said he heard screeching and saw the car headlights flash upward in their bedroom on the third floor. We were horrified to find the driveway, south porch and front yard look like a war scene. Hand carved stone pillars, huge cornerstones, stone railings and bricks were strewn everywhere. The driveway portico was heavily damaged. Upon closer examination of the smoldering car lying upside down and facing the opposite direction, we noticed the body of a young man dead in the back seat. We were in shock! It was going to be a long, long night.

I notified Kirk and Jeanette, Kim and Libby, and Mike and Cheri. Soon they arrived along with the police and firemen. Neighbors came running and said they were awakened by the loud crash.

We soon learned there had been a party and liquor was served to underage teenagers. A young man on a motorcycle had been killed earlier after leaving this party. After hearing this grizzly news, three teenagers obtained liquor and started driving around town. They came speeding down North Street and in our estimation were traveling at about 70 miles per hour. They did not realize that North Street ran straight into our driveway. They came barreling down the road and hit the big dip at the bottom of our driveway. The car became airborne and soared over 65 feet of bushes. That's when Doug saw the headlights. The car then hit the maple tree with full force, throwing the vehicle sideways and hitting the hand carved stone pillars on the south porch. The car flipped up, hitting the driveway portico and came to rest upside down. A steel beam landed on top of the car.

Viki's "reporter" instincts kicked in and she ran in to get her camera. The police arrived and told her she could not take pictures. She was furious and continued snapping anyway.

It took the firemen about an hour to remove the body of 17-year-old Todd Force out of the car. I saw tears in the eyes of the fireman who tenderly cradled him in his arms before placing the body in a yellow plastic zip bag that was placed on our front lawn.

The coroner arrived a few hours later and unzipped the bag to examine the body. He removed the boy's wallet and I heard him count out loud, "One, two, three dollars."

"Oh, my God!" I cried. "You can't even take that with you," I remarked.

An ambulance then took the body away. Around daylight the firemen came back to hose down the car. They were concerned the car could still explode and burn. A tow truck finally came to haul away the wrecked car which screeched as it was towed, scraping the driveway and leaving marks that would last for years. A bottle of hard liquor was recovered by the police.

Jerry had gone back to bed earlier saying there was nothing

else he could do and he needed his rest for the morning church service. The rest of us, including the team of Harvesters that was home in-between tours, stayed up. We eventually got ready for church.

It was already going to be an emotional morning with the vote on merging two church bodies. Now we had the additional burden of knowing a teenager had been killed in our driveway. In surveying all of the damage I wondered how God could ever work good out of the accident.

Nobody at church had heard about the accident. Finally came the church vote. Jerry was unanimously elected the pastor and the church would be renamed Harvest Christian Center. God had won a tremendous victory!

Around midnight we were awakened again by a sound coming outside of our bedroom window. It was Todd Force's mother, crying for her lost son.

For several days we had teenagers who were friends with Todd come and pay their last respects. Some left flowers on the driveway rubble. Surprisingly, the local media's coverage of the accident did not mention the tremendous damage done to our historical home and property.

One morning while talking with some of the people I noticed a man weeping at the site of the accident. It was Todd's father. He told me that Todd had spinal meningitis when he was two years old and wasn't expected to live. The doctor told him that in his teen years headaches might start up again. Todd was already experiencing them. He told his dad that two nights in a row he had the same dream that he would be killed in a car accident. As he left his parents house on the night of the accident, he turned around and told them goodbye. Todd's father commented that Todd's grandmother took him to church when he was younger. Jerry and I joined hands with this grieving father and prayed that God would comfort him.

We notified our insurance company of the accident, but no adjuster wanted the job. How do you put a dollar figure on the damage done to a historical house built in the 1800's? Someone said there was a stone quarry in Indiana that might be able to design the stone pillars, but it would probably take time and a lot of money. A friend who was a brick mason stopped by and said we'd have to go to Italy to find someone who could do the work.

A few days later Jerry and I headed to Denver, Colorado, to minister at Camp I.D.R.A.H.J.E. (I'd Rather Have Jesus). We thought we would be one of several speakers but soon learned we would be the only ones ministering three to four services a day for the next three days.

Shortly after our arrival, we were notified to call Kim immediately. We were blessed with the wonderful news that we were grandparents again! Chantelle Renee was born July 27 which was Jerry's father's birthday. Mother and baby were doing fine and went home the next day.

Before we left to drive to the camp, the Lord had given me two skits to write. The timing was perfect and we did them as the grand finale on the last night of the camp. Everyone loved "Fish Story" and "The Fad."

When we got back home we learned there were not any new recruitments for the Harvesters. God was indeed closing the door on this very successful ministry. Our time now would be spent on building up Harvest Christian Center. On September 29 the team was told their last tour would be the fall tour. It was a tough decision to make.

Two weeks later Kim and Libby announced they were moving to Flanagan, Illinois, to work at a Children's Home. Suddenly our family was splitting apart. We were still praying about Kirk's offer to be the youth pastor at a Decatur church.

With much relief and a big answer to prayer, Jerry announced on November 2 that Kirk would become the Youth Pastor at Harvest Christian Center. Rev. Don Etnier, Jerry and Chris, would be the church board members. Chris would also become the Sunday School superintendent and direct the singles group.

A week later we got the phone call that Doug's father had passed away. Doug's mom had just returned from a trip and found Jim still sitting in his chair. He had died from a brain aneurysm.

Jeanette received the tragic news on December 22 that her father was killed in a freak accident. He had delivered a table that was on his truck and somehow the truck slipped out of gear and crushed him. Kirk and Jeanette had to fly out immediately to California.

During this hectic time we were still dealing with the insurance company about the car accident. Jerry always admonished me to keep quiet and he would do the talking to the adjusters. One day, though, he was not around and so I showed an insurance adjuster where another crack or bulge had occurred by the jarring of the accident.

Finally, just before Christmas the House of Prayer received a check for $55,000 as a settlement for the damages. It was a miracle and a wonderful Christmas gift! We used the money to pay off the House of Prayer building!

Around this same time Jerry checked into the empty lot across the street from Harvest Christian Center. We could have it by paying the back taxes of $300.

The fleece that Jerry and Viki put out came to pass– changing the church name to Harvest Christian Center, paying off the House of Prayer building and getting a parking lot. God is faithful and had done His job well!

On the first anniversary of the accident I heard two women crying on our driveway. This time it was Todd Force's grandmother and aunt. I heard one of them cry out, "Oh God, if only we knew of something good that came out of all this tragedy."

I took a deep breath and told them, "Come inside, girls. Have I got a story for you!"

7

Come As a Little Child

The New Year started off with a bang! Sometime during the night of January 2, 1987, we received an emergency phone call from Kirk and Jeanette. While driving back to Decatur from the St. Louis Lambert International Airport, their car's alternator light kept coming on. They managed to coast into a gas station in Litchfield, Illinois, and were calling to see if there was any way we could meet up with them and tow their car back. I wondered how many times we had received a similar distress phone call from the Harvesters asking us to help them because their vehicle had broken down.

We met Kirk and Jeanette at a restaurant and managed to get back to Decatur around 2 a.m. I asked how everything went at her dad's funeral. Because of the holiday, they had to wait until December 26 to have it. Kirk sang Bill's favorite hymn "How Great Thou Art." Jeanette's mom was doing okay and stated that Bill truly had a divine appointment with the Lord.

Kirk said goodbye the next morning and drove to Southwestern Assemblies of God College in Waxahachie, Texas. He wanted to complete his bachelor's degree and the school would give him college credits for his ministry with the Harvesters that he could apply toward a Bachelor of Career Arts Degree.

After Kirk left, I felt an urging to write a musical. I didn't know one note from another, but years earlier had envisioned a group of people acting on stage as sailors called David's Motley Crew. I shared my ideas with several people and they all said, "Go for it."

I looked over several of the original songs that Kim and I had written over the years. I decided to write a script around them and was shocked to discover how well the songs flowed together. Two more songs were written. *Voyage* would be the musical's title and the story plot would be an allegory of the bride (the church) and her beloved bridegroom (Jesus Christ) during the last days on this earth.

The musical centered on six main characters who take a cruise on the Ship of Life and encounter a storm at sea. Steve is a songwriter married to Kathy who is having a baby in mid-life. Their 20-year-old daughter, Julie, falls in love with the handsome Captain Enright. Adding spice to the story are a spry missionary widow named Martha and a tightwad millionaire widower named Wendel. The ship's crew are the "extras" in such songs as "David's Motley Crew," "Ride O'er the Waves," "What'll We Do in Heaven?" "The Sun Is Risen" and "The Ship of Life."

Lovely ballads such as "You Are Lord," "Lost in His Loveliness," "All of My Being," "The Father's Lullaby" and "I'm Going Home" would be sung. I envisioned a soft shoe dance with the old couple singing "What Can I Say to You, Jesus?" An intensely powerful song by Julie would be "Will He Come?" depicting a Jewish wedding in the background.

"Come Away My Beloved" would be sung by the Captain to Julie as they fall in love. It would also serve as a tender wooing by the Holy Spirit for members of the audience to accept Jesus Christ as their Bridegroom and become His bride. A lovely ballet could be performed in the background with a mist engulfing the cast.

The song "Tranquility" was composed by Kim and would not have any words. It would portray a peaceful calm during the storms of life. In one week I wrote the script. Jerry read it first and loved it.

During the night of January 27, Jerry had difficulty breathing. He could breathe in easily, but had to push extra hard to exhale. He had some emphysema, but had not smoked in 12 years. He did not think he was bad enough to see a doctor and decided to go ahead and drive to Havana to visit the Belchers and share with them the musical. They absolutely loved it and truly believed God would use it for His glory.

Jerry's breathing did not get any better so he finally agreed to see Dr. McGhee who told him he was a very sick man. Jerry had waited too long to get medical attention and infection had set in. He took x-rays of his lungs and prescribed some strong medication. Jerry stayed in bed several days trying to recuperate.

Michael was 18 months old and had gotten very sick with diarrhea and vomiting. Viki, Doug and Kirk were scheduled to go to Israel on a 10-day pastors' conference, but it was touch and go with Michael's situation. On a Saturday night Dr. McGhee told Viki to meet him at his office. Michael had a virus and was given something to control the vomiting and diarrhea. Finally, he was on the road to recovery and the Scherers and Kirk headed to God's Holy Land.

Michael cried all of two minutes when they left during the early morning of February 16. He promptly dropped his shoe and the tv remote control into a bucket of water. The next day we presented Michael with his first three-wheeler bicycle. He loved it and drove all over the first floor, defying anyone who got in his way.

Jerry went back to the doctor the next day. There was some improvement, but he needed more medication.

Viki, Doug and Kirk had a wonderful time in Israel and experienced the "finger of God" several times. They would never be the same. When they walked in the door Michael screamed, "See mama! See mama!"

The next day Jerry and I left to drive to Lubbock, Texas, for his youngest sister's wedding. Candy was marrying Vasile Vezendan who had escaped out of Romania and became a free man in the United States. Candy was born when Jerry was 21 years old and in the Marine Corps.

The weather was cold and icy when we arrived. Every joint in my body yelled in pain. The wind howled and there was snow on the ground the next morning. The wedding was lovely and I enjoyed visiting with Jerry's relatives and with my sister Clarice, who we called Babe and who was married to Jerry's brother Roger.

We stopped at a rest stop in Oklahoma on the way home and met a couple from Minnesota. Jerry told them I was from Winona and remarked, "I'll bet you knew her dad Ed Kierlin." To my great surprise they not only knew him but they also knew my brother Bob. What a small world!

Jerry and I both ended up at the doctor's office when we got back home. Jerry's lungs were filling up with fluid and he needed stronger medication. I was given stronger medication for inflammation and for something to sleep at night when the pain was always the worst. How I hated growing old!

In March Kim and Libby came to visit and said they were not happy working in Flanagan. I read the script of *Voyage* to Kim and he listened intently. By the time I got to the last song, he knew it would be "The Sun Is Risen." He gave it to Libby to read and she said it was the best thing I had ever written. She asked if I could possibly write another one and they could take it on the road. I was so excited!

Viki and her officers for the Decatur Women's Aglow Chapter decided to have a style show as a fund raiser. All of the clothes had to be second hand. That would be a challenge, but I was determined to outfit several women. The style show went great! We even had a bride and the mother of the bride all dressed in rummage clothes.

My back was in terrible pain. Somehow while playing on the floor with our granddaughter, Chantelle, I pulled a muscle in my lower back. The doctor ordered a muscle relaxer and some pain pills. I was tested for a slipped disk but was told it was only strained. I had to go to the hospital for therapy treatment. Helping the Aglow ladies try on all of the clothes, only aggravated my back. In addition, I broke out with a rash due to the pain medication. Some days you just don't win at all!

The singer Mike Adkins came to Harvest Christian Center for our church's first anniversary. We went to a restaurant afterwards and I gave him a five-minute presentation of my musical *Voyage.*

"I know what you have been given is from the Lord. This musical will be done, but on God's time schedule," he commented.

He then shared about his experience in trying to get his movie *A Man Called Norman* produced. The PTL Club was scheduled to film it, but the ministry went defunct. Just when he was almost broke, Mike was notified by Dr. James Dobson that Focus on the Family wanted to produce it. God's timing was perfect and the movie was a success! I had to be patient and wait on the Lord.

A few days later Kim and Libby announced they were leaving Illinois and moving to Montana where Libby's parents owned a big ranch. They would live in Libby's hometown of Ismay which only had

18 people. She wanted to go back to college and become a teacher. Kim would tune pianos on the eastern half of Montana. I was heartbroken and had to lean on the Lord again.

During the summer months, Jerry started repairing the damage done from the car accident a year earlier. With help from Chris and Kirk, they used the old green van and a chain to move the heavy concrete cornerstone. Oftentimes when Jerry needed help, someone like Charles Volle from church would show up at just the right time.

Brick by brick, stone by stone, the work was getting done. Jerry removed the hand carved stone pedestals from the north porch and transplanted them to the south porch. Brick columns were made, concrete railings were repaired and the portico was restored. When it was all done I asked Jerry how he ever did it. He grinned widely and said, "I had a great Carpenter Who showed me how."

On September 27, 1987, I received a phone call from my brother Bob. Very calmly he told me to sit down.

"They found Doris dead in her apartment early this morning. An autopsy is scheduled but they suspect a heart attack. Her funeral will be on Monday."

I was in shock and cried all day. Mostly I was concerned about her soul. She was my fraternal twin and had big brown eyes and a round face. I had green eyes and a long face. I always considered her the prettier one of the two of us. She was mentally handicapped and had the mentality of an eight-year-old. She was held back in first grade and only went to eighth grade. I can remember "ignorant" children calling her "dumb, dumb Dorrie." I would get so angry and defend her to the core.

Now she was somewhere in eternity and I had to know where. I'd given her my poem books earlier which really upset my mother. Finally, I asked the Lord to show me if she really made it into heaven.

I started to pack but could hardly see because I was crying so hard. Kirk walked in and I told him about Doris. Suddenly I remembered something that had happened when we first moved into the mansion. We had been praying rather intensely for Doris who had been missing for 10 years. She'd had an argument with our mother and walked out the door without a coat on her back. It was the middle of

December, and Minnesota can be very cold by then.

When our dad passed away in May of 1973, there was no way we could contact Doris. We didn't even know if she was alive.

I believed in my heart she was okay, but it wasn't until the fall of 1975 that I knew God was going to answer my prayers. While interceding for her at a prayer meeting at the mansion, I heard deep within my being the words, "Doris is coming home." I looked all around to see if someone said that audibly. Again I heard the words, "Doris is coming home." The Holy Spirit was at work.

Two days later I received a letter from Babe. She stated simply, "Guess what? Doris is home." She had been living with a man in Milwaukee, Wisconsin. Earlier in life she held a job, married someone and eventually had a baby girl that was stillborn. Somehow it didn't seem fair for Doris to have such a terrible life and for me to be mightily blessed. "There but by the grace of God go I," I pondered.

While sharing with Kirk, it was as though the Lord spoke again and said, "If I cared enough to tell you about Doris coming home years ago, don't you believe I looked after her all this time too?"

That satisfied me for a while, but I needed more confirmation from God's Word. I picked up a copy of The New International Version and asked God to speak to me through it. I opened up to Deuteronomy 30:4-5 and was astonished to read, *"Even if you have been banished to the most distant land under the heavens, from there the Lord your God will gather you and bring you back. He will bring you to the land that belonged to your fathers, and you will take possession of it."* I shouted for joy!

While traveling to Winona for the funeral, I started having my doubts again and asked God for another confirmation that Doris made it into heaven. Jerry and I stopped at a rest area and a woman inside the lounge asked where we were headed.

"To Winona," I replied and then broke down crying. "I'm going to my twin sister's funeral." The lady was a Christian and just held me in her arms as she prayed for me.

When we arrived at mother's house, Babe and Roger were already there. They shared their story about encountering the pope in his popemobile. Then they turned to me and said, "You'd better sit down. We have something to tell you. They found Doris on her knees, praying." Oh, how I wanted to shout! Doris knew she was dying and was praying as a little child to Jesus.

When the funeral was over and we were back in our motel room, I reflected on the priest's remarks about Doris. He told of her simplicity, her deep frustrations about her inadequacies and her wonderful sense of humor. She would wear funny hats and entertain the elderly at nursing homes. I stared out the window, unable to go to sleep. Part of me was missing–someone I shared a bed with for nearly 19 years. Now she was gone.

Suddenly, I heard the Lord speak softly to me. "I could have taken Doris in her sleep, but you would have worried." What a beautiful and merciful God we serve!

Two weeks later I called mother to tell her that my youngest daughter, Cheri, had her first baby, Brianna, by Caesarean section because of a difficult delivery.

"Yes, I know all about that thing. I was in labor with you twins for three days and three nights. But there were few C-sections in those days," mother commented.

She went on to say that an hour after Doris was born the doctor almost went into shock and started shouting, "My God, there's another one!" I was delivered safe and sound. Now I understood Doris' condition. Her brain had taken the brunt of the horrible trauma from this difficult delivery, but I escaped without any problems.

When Jerry and I got back to Decatur after this deeply emotional time, I called Kim who was out in Montana. I told him we had just buried Doris. There was a long pause and then he gently made this observation. "Just think, mom. She's whole now. She's whole."

8

The Great Debate

The year 1988 was filled with debate about the rapture of the church. It was precipitated by a popular book stating 88 reasons why the rapture would take place that year.

In January I finally got serious with working on the musical *Voyage*. It had been a year since I had written the script, but I needed to get the music written. With a little bit of coaxing, our piano player from church agreed to write out the chords for some of the songs already on tape. LaVera Hensley came to the big mansion and accompanied me on the piano while I sang the songs. We recorded most of them on a cassette tape, but would have to wait until July to finish the remaining ones. I would see Kim then and he could help with the accompaniment.

Viki decided to stay on for another term as president of the Decatur Women's Aglow chapter. She had a dedicated group of officers who also stayed on board. The monthly meetings were now at Harvest Christian Center. I recruited some Aglow "volunteers" and had them try out some of my new skits. Everyone seemed to like them and those in the skits had a lot of fun doing them.

The middle of February brought a lot of snow and ice. Jerry dropped Chris off at work and was nearly home when he failed to come to a complete stop at the corner of Edward and North Streets. The passenger's window on our blue station wagon was still covered with ice and Jerry did not see a four-wheel drive truck going south on Edward. They collided and our blue station wagon was totaled. Both Jerry and the other driver were unhurt, but the other driver was furious. He started cursing and calling Jerry names, but calmed down and apologized when he found out that Jerry was a minister.

In a way I was secretly glad to see the wagon go because it was a stick shift. To replace it, we bought a light brown station wagon from a car salesman who used to work for Jerry years ago as an insurance agent at Prudential.

The next day after our car purchase I woke up very dizzy, but was determined to get my grocery shopping done. While backing out of a store parking lot, I misjudged the distance completely and locked our "new" wagon onto the grill work of a truck. I was so embarrassed! I couldn't move either way. Finally, two men came to my rescue. My "new" car had its first dent! Jerry was not a happy camper, but he couldn't say too much. I considered our driving escapades about even.

I continued having problems with my equilibrium and eventually found out that all the aspirin I was taking for my fibrositis was thinning my blood. I was taking as many as eight aspirin a day. As soon as I stopped taking them, my equilibrium was back to normal.

On May 10 Jerry and I left for our favorite get-away–the Smokey Mountain home of Jorgy and Grace Jorgensen in North Carolina. They decided to retire there and moved from Florida. When we arrived, the rhododendrums were in full bloom, dotting the woods and creek beds with their luscious red, pink and white flowers. They were breath-taking! "Only a glimpse of heaven," I commented to Jerry.

I shared the musical *Voyage* with Grace and she loved it. "God will use it for His glory," she remarked.

We went to a church service on Sunday morning. The pastor's wife stood before the congregation and said she was going to do something she had never done before. She felt the Lord wanted her to preach that morning instead of her husband. Her text was on false prophets and deception in the church today. Suddenly she stopped and said, "My dream is to have drama in the church, but I do not have the ability or time to write the material."

I quickly nudged Jerry and he went out to the car and brought in a set of all our skit books. When the service was over, we approached her and gave her the books.

"The Lord said we are to give these to you."

She cried and said, "Two months ago I asked God, 'Where will the writers of the scripts come from?'"

Once again I marveled at God's ability to answer prayer in His own way and in His timing. I was grateful to have been a part of this drama of life.

When we got back from North Carolina, our church's first men's softball game was scheduled. Jerry was drafted to be on the team which was sponsored by Vitagrow. Thus began our "comedy of errors." Our team had more heart than ability. We even came close to winning once!

At one of the games Doug was coerced to play because we were minus a couple of players. Someone in the outfield, who was filling in on our team, threw a ball extremely hard and it hit Doug in the mouth. Viki took him to the hospital immediately. A specialist had to be called in because of the stitches needed on the inside of his mouth. It was questionable whether he would ever be able to play the trumpet again. In time his mouth healed and he resumed playing his horn at church services.

In July Jerry and I took off to Montana to visit Kim, Libby and Chantelle. Kim and I worked day and night on several songs in *Voyage*. We used a small cassette tape recorder and finally had the finished product.

A few days after we got back from our trip I decided to play the tape at Harvest Christian Center. To my horror, there wasn't a single sound on any of it! Somehow everything had been erased! It would be back to the drawing board. I didn't know the devil could fight so hard against a musical.

With fall and winter rapidly approaching, there were several projects that needed to get done both at the mansion and at the church. Jerry and Chris painted many of the rooms in the House of Prayer, plastered several walls and worked on plumbing problems. It was a challenge keeping the "antique" bathroom equipment functioning properly in the 120-year-old mansion.

Jerry and another man started tarring the roof at Harvest Christian Center, but when it rained it still leaked. They also thought they had a leaky toilet repaired but it continued to leak. In addition, the ceiling fell in my kitchen and it had to be repaired.

Our dear friends, Charles and Eileen Volle, decided we needed to get away and therefore invited us to join them on their boat. We got out on the lake and the motor died. We drifted for hours. So much for fishing and relaxation!

On July 26 our three-year-old grandson, Michael, proudly announced to us, "The toad is going to have a tadpole to play with." I had called him "Toad" and "Toady boy" ever since he was born. Weighing only four pounds and seven ounces at birth, Michael was wrinkled and looked like an old man or a toad. We rejoiced that another grandchild was on the way and due in March of 1989.

Downtown Decatur came alive the first weekend in August as the Decatur Celebration got underway. This large street festival attracted 350,000 people from all over the Midwest. Chris stopped by the Christian stage and saw a local church group performing two of my skits, "Looking for a Christian" and "Planning Ahead." Needless to say I was delighted!

In September we had another huge rummage sale. We always needed the money for something. Inwardly I began to face the reality that one of these days the rummage sales would have to end. My body could not handle the work load. I was always worn out after the rummage sales and usually got sick

Kirk and Jeanette were anxiously awaiting the birth of their first child. On September 6 Jeanette saw her obstetrician and he sent her to the hospital. He broke her water at 2:30 p.m. but she had only dilated one centimeter. She was given labor inducement medication. After several hours she was only dilated four centimeters and the baby's heartbeat was going down. A spinal was given to Jeanette but it did not take so she was given morphine. A Caesarean section was scheduled. The next morning Jerry and I went to St. Mary's Hospital and met a beaming Kirk who said they were going to name their son Joel William. The middle name was the same as Jeanette's dad's first name and it was also Jerry's father's middle name. Joel would have the same initials as Jerry–J.W.H.

Jeanette was still very drowsy and didn't see Joel until that afternoon. He weighed seven pounds 15 ounces and was 21 inches long. His head was unusually large at 14 3/4 inches and his chest was 13 ½ inches. It had been a difficult birth and they could have lost Joel.

Jeanette told me later that even though she had suffered greatly in labor and delivery, just one look at Kirk's face when he exclaimed over and over again, "It's a boy!" erased all the pain she had endured to bring Joel into the world.

In October the Christian TV station asked Kirk and Jeanette if they would be in a commercial with Joel that would promote Christian family living. It was always thrilling to turn on the TV and see the commercial with Kirk and Jeanette gently rocking Joel in his cradle.

In November and December I continued having dizzy problems and finally went to the doctor. My blood pressure was 175 over 100! I was immediately put on blood pressure pills and given antibiotics for a sinus infection.

The end of the year came with the usual holiday shopping and church activities. Jerry even helped me set out all the candles at the church on Christmas Eve for the traditional candlelight Communion service. It's doing the little things like this together that become cherished treasures when God slowly blows out the candles of life.

The great debate of 1988 went out like a whimper. The Lord had not returned as predicted in the book *Eighty Eight Reasons Why*. It had caused quite a stir in Christian circles. Either people wanted to get their lives right with Christ or they got upset and angry because they had more living to do and wanted to stay on earth. We were all still here, but a new year was dawning on the horizon and God was directing the future scenes.

9

Ye Shall Have Trials and Tribulations

The new year had barely started when Jerry developed a bad cold that he just could not shake. Each day it seemed to sink a little lower in his chest.

The rest of the family was busy working on my latest skit book *Harvest Time*. Viki was busy editing and Cheri did the typesetting. Neal Cline, a former member of the End Time Harvesters, helped design the cover. I was already working on the next book. Ideas for skits just kept coming to me day and night and so I kept busy writing.

Kirk and Jeanette's home was broken into and several items were taken. The neighborhood was getting run down and we all knew it was just a matter of time before they would be selling their home and house hunting elsewhere.

In early February Jerry still was not feeling better. He had a bad sore throat which prevented him from doing the funeral for the daughter of a woman who attended our church. She had been killed in a terrible automobile accident. Kirk was about to have his first funeral.

Viki had her eighth month pregnancy check-up and asked the doctor how she would know when the right time would be to come in and have this baby. Michael's delivery was not like anything written in the medical books and he came early.

"Oh, it will be a long time before you have this baby. You are carrying it very high," he replied.

That night at 1 a.m. her water broke. Jerry heard noises coming from the phone next to his head. He reached over to pick it up only to hear Viki's voice telling the doctor that her water had just broken. The startled doctor told her to go to the hospital at once. I raced up the stairs and helped her pack her suitcase.

"This is a whole month early," I cried to the Lord. "Please help this baby be perfect in every way."

Doug drove Viki to the hospital in the early hours of February 8. It was cold and there was snow and ice on the ground. Viki's contractions started within an hour but she was not dilated very much. Doug left at 5:45 a.m. to drive a city bus for a few hours and then went back to the hospital. It was snowing and schools all around were closing.

The doctor examined Viki shortly after 8 a.m., but could not determine if the baby was head first or feet first. He ordered x-rays–the first ones Viki ever had in her life. An elderly man, who was the hospital volunteer pushing Viki's wheelchair, got lost trying to get her back to the labor room. Somehow they ended up in an area of new hospital construction and Viki had visions of having her baby with a bunch of "laborers" assisting delivery!

When x-rays revealed the baby was head first, Viki was given pitocin to speed up labor and delivery. A nurse told her at 11 a.m. it would probably be evening before she had that baby. Viki told Doug she couldn't take the pain much more and they prayed the baby would come sooner. By 1 p.m. she was dilated seven and the nurses were frantically calling the doctor to get there. They knew it wouldn't be long before Viki wanted to push. I was upset that I couldn't be there so Doug kept us informed with telephone calls.

The doctor finally arrived and at 1:27 p.m. out came a black haired girl weighing 6 pounds 3 ounces. Even though she weighed more than Michael, she was definitely a month early and had "peach fuzz" all over her. Doug and Viki named her Sarah Joy and believed God had a plan and purpose for her. Her liver was under-developed, causing jaundice. Her bilirubin level was high. She was placed under strong lights for several days. Viki was discharged within two days. For a second time she experienced the terrible emotions of having to leave a baby behind at the hospital. Unlike Michael, Sarah was big enough to nurse. Viki would leave home early in the morning and stay at the hospital until late evening so she could be with Sarah and feed her.

Jerry was still sick and diagnosed with a severe case of

bronchitis. He had to stay in bed and could not go up to the hospital to see his new granddaughter.

Kim and his family made an unannounced visit from Montana. It could not have come at a better time! Michael had cousin Chantelle, to play with while Viki went back and forth to the hospital.

After much intercession, Sarah finally got to come home eight days after her birth. She was still yellow with jaundice, but her bilirubin level went down and stabilized. Viki and Doug placed her near their bedroom windowsill so the sunshine would help the jaundice go away.

On Sunday after church we had all the family over for a big turkey dinner and took a family picture. All five children, their spouses and five grandchildren were together–a rare occasion as our lives got busier.

On May 8 Jerry was back at the doctor's office with a bad cold and hacking cough. It was bronchitis again and he was back on antibiotics. We did not believe it was very serious.

The Christian TV station had its annual telethon and showed clips from our "New Life" program that we aired for three and one-half years. It was amazing to see how much we had grown spiritually since the beginning of those weekly shows.

Doug received a phone call from his brother Steve informing him that their mother had fallen and broken her hip. Sue was in the hospital, down to 91 pounds and having a difficult time swallowing.

Decatur had two murders around this time and one of them occurred in the alley behind Kirk and Jeanette's house. That was one more reason for them to move somewhere else.

A reunion was planned for the End Time Harvesters. From the summer of 1981 thru the fall of 1986, 50 young men and women from the U.S. and Canada were trained in drama ministry at the House of Prayer. Many were married now and had children of their own. It was a great time of fellowship with them and their families. Although I had five children of my own, God had seen fit to give me "50" additional children who went across the country and overseas sharing the good news of Jesus.

Missionary friends of ours, Barbara and David Morris, returned from China where they had been teaching English. David shared how they gave my poem books to Christians over there. With great eagerness the Chinese read these books and remarked, "These we can understand." I was touched and praised God that the Holy Spirit helps bridge all language barriers.

Jerry and I took a quick trip to see the Jorgensens in North Carolina. For the first time Jerry had difficulty sleeping while we were there. He could not breathe very well at night with the fan on, but did better when he slept in the air conditioning.

Shortly after we returned home, we had our station wagon stolen off the back parking lot at the House of Prayer. The police said it had probably been hot wired and they would be on the lookout for it. In the meantime, we were given a white car to drive.

Two days later I was at The Castaways Store where I took clothes to be resold. An employee mentioned there was a brown station wagon on her friend's parking lot and he would like to have it removed. I didn't think too much about that until three days later when the police called and said they found our car. It was the one the lady at Castaways had been talking about! It had been hot wired and had to be towed off of the parking lot. Over 200 miles had been driven on it and the police speculated that it may have been used for a drug run. I just couldn't believe someone would steal a pastor's car!

Being a premature baby had caused Sarah's immunity system not to be very well developed. She was constantly sick with ear infections. At six months she was sent to the ear specialist. Usually doctors wait until a baby is one-year-old before tubes are put in the ears. A nurse tested Sarah's hearing and instead of having a bell shaped curve, she had a straight line. This meant she could have serious hearing problems including deafness. The doctor scheduled surgery for the next morning. Immediately we noticed a difference. Sarah was more alert and reacted to the noise around her. She could hear!

During one of Sarah's visits to Dr. McGhee, he noticed a premature closing of her fontanel. The soft spot usually remains until a child is 18 to 24 months old, allowing the brain to grow and expand. If it closes too early, then severe retardation and brain damage can occur as well as disfiguration of the face. Dr. McGhee ordered skull x-rays for the next day.

Viki came home and shared the news. I began to pray and asked the Lord for a miracle. He reminded me that Sarah meant "princess" and I believed that all princesses were beautiful.

Viki took Sarah upstairs to their living room and sat in their rocking chair, praying over Sarah. She said it was as though she heard an audible voice that said, "I am the Lord that heals you." She trusted God to do a miracle.

Finally, several days later she was notified that the x-rays revealed everything was normal. Sarah was going to be a beautiful, freckle-faced princess!

Jerry developed another bad cough which continued to get worse. He lost eight pounds and was immediately put on medication.

On September 13 Doug got the phone call that his mother had passed away. She had been diagnosed with Lou Gehrig's Disease–amyotrophic lateral sclerosis. God worked good out of her passing–Doug and Viki inherited 72 acres of farmland in Sullivan. The income from the crops would help finance the children's Christian education in the years to come.

Jerry went back to the doctor and was diagnosed with emphysema. He was given more medication and ordered to stay in bed for a few days.

On October 11, which was Jeanette's birthday, their black Labrador named Lady broke loose and wandered off. Everyone searched the neighborhood but to no avail. Jerry said he felt God would work good out of the situation. And he was right! A neighbor woman had seen Lady and brought her to Kirk and Jeanette's house. They made small talk and remarked they were going to sell their home. She mentioned that her daughter needed housing and it would be nice if she lived close to her. The daughter and husband came and bought the house contract for deed. Praise the Lord!

Kirk and Jeanette decided to move into the empty two-bedroom apartment at Harvest. That way they could save their money to buy a house. Kirk fulfilled the meaning of his name, "dweller in the church."

At the December Women's Aglow meeting several women

performed the skit "Food for Thought" which I wrote. It went over well. Later in the month church members from Harvest performed in *"Toyland"* which was a play written by Kirk. Jerry was Grandpa the narrator and had a little boy named Joshua Sutton sit on his lap, telling him the story of the Toymaker's Son coming to set the toys free from Mr. Satin's captivity.

On the afternoon of the performance, the water pipes in the downstairs kitchen at the mansion froze and burst. Water was everywhere. Jerry and Doug worked all afternoon trying to get the leaking to stop. It would be days before the water pipes in that kitchen could be used again.

The evening performance of *"Toyland"* was excellent and blessed many in the audience. It was such a success that we all agreed it should be published by the House of Prayer Ministries.

10

For Better or for Worse

During the second week of January 1990, Jerry and I drove to the Greater Washington Christian Education Conference in Beltsville, Maryland, to exhibit our skit books. Upon our arrival the muffler went bad on the car. While it was getting fixed, we walked in the cold and wind to a Chinese Restaurant to get some hot tea. We were only wearing thin rain coats and the weather did not help the sinus infection I was battling.

At the convention I was surprised to hear a lady at a booth call out my name. She was an ex-nun who overheard Jerry giving our testimony to someone and wanted to buy *Fortress on a Hill.* She then shared her testimony with me.

She entered the convent just after high school, believing this vocation would be her entrance into heaven. She became disillusioned after many years of dedication and self-denial, but never found true, lasting peace. She eventually left the strict order and found Christ as her Savior and Lord. She gave me a copy of her book entitled *Out of the Habit.* We talked for hours and thoroughly enjoyed sharing with each other.

The next day while back at our booth, I looked up to see a familiar face and heard a familiar voice from Central Illinois.

"Jerry Henneberry, what are you doing here?" It was Bruce Weaver, who had pastored a church near Decatur, but was now living in the Washington D.C. area. Immediately he invited Jerry to preach at his church on Sunday morning. Jerry accepted right away. We got lost trying to find the church and arrived late. It didn't seem to matter because the anointing of the Spirit was on Jerry and the gift of the word of knowledge operated through him. It was cold and rainy when we packed up and left for the long drive home.

When we arrived home I found an invitation to my 38th high school reunion scheduled for the last weekend in June. That meant diet time! I needed my "girlish" figure back. It was an odd number for a reunion but it was because there were only 38 girls in my 1952 graduating class at Cathedral High School. The following year the all-girls high school combined with the all-boys Cotter High School and went co-ed.

On Valentine's Day we drove our friend, Barbara Morris, to the St. Louis Airport. She was flying back to China where she taught English. By the time we got to St. Louis, the weather started getting bad and we were anxious to get back to Decatur. It was freezing rain and ice was forming everywhere.

We arrived home safe and sound. By 10:30 p.m. trees were sagging from the heavy weight of ice on their branches. Suddenly we heard a tremendous crash and our power went off. We grabbed flashlights and headed outside where we found electrical power wires hanging over the top of the kids' swing set and dangling to the bottom of the ground. Gone was our big maple tree in the front yard. It lay sprawling like a dying octopus across the driveway. All of Central Illinois was hit hard by the ice storm.

Two days later our church had a belated Valentine's spaghetti dinner for couples. Jerry was not feeling good and did not go. It was the beginning of my going alone to social functions.

The following week was the Central Illinois Sunday School Convention in Peoria. Neither Jerry nor I felt very good, but we were determined to set up and man the House of Prayer's exhibition booth. Peoria had a terrible snowstorm and the wind chill was -30°. The convention went well, but we were exhausted by the time we got home.

Rehearsals had already started at Harvest Christian Center for the short musical *"Angels, Angels"* I had written. Jerry helped me make wings for all of the angel performers. While working in the church kitchen for a "potbless," I was informed that two of the women who were in the musical had decided to leave our church. They had key roles in the musical. Kirk said "the show must go on" and he became Seraphim while I became Cherubim. It was my first time directing and acting at the same time.

Just as one crisis got over, another one developed. Only this time it was Jerry's health. His breathing became labored at night so he finally went to the doctor. He was given his first inhaler and some pills.

Easter Sunday was upon us and the production of *"Angels, Angels"* went very well. Everyone loved it!

Jerry's cough continued to get worse. The doctor ordered an arterial blood gas test and x-rays of Jerry's lungs. He had lost seven pounds and was given an antibiotic. At night, in an effort to breathe better, he would sit in a chair and sleep. Ministers who gathered for the May 3 National Day of Prayer prayed for Jerry's recovery.

It was awful watching Jerry trying to breathe. On May 7 he went back to the doctor who ordered some new medication for him. Privately, the doctor told me there was nothing more he could do for my husband.

Doug and Viki left for South Carolina to attend a conference on Jewish celebrations. The trip had been planned for months and I knew they really needed to get away. I had to babysit Michael and Sarah, but was deeply concerned about Jerry. A fellow minister stopped by to visit Jerry and begged me to take him to the hospital. I explained that we had not had any medical insurance since Jerry resigned from his job at Prudential Insurance Company to become a minister. We had lived by faith for 16 years without health insurance.

The next afternoon Chris came and took the children to the park so that I could get my hair done at New Art Beauty Studios. While talking to Betty my beauty operator, she suggested that I take Jerry to the Danville Veterans Administration Hospital. Her pastor, Rev. Wallace, had been going there for kidney treatments and was improving. We had gone to the Holy Land with Rev. Wallace several years earlier.

I came home and told Jerry about the possibility of going to Danville after Doug and Viki got back. Jerry had been a Second Lieutenant in the U.S. Marine Corps during the Korean War. We were desperate to try anything. Chris, Kirk and I planned to take him there early Monday morning.

Sunday was Mother's Day and we brought Jerry's mom to our

house for dinner. At one point Jerry whispered he was not doing well. He was gasping for air. I was so glad to see Viki and Doug walk in the door at 8 p.m.

Neither Jerry nor I could sleep well that night. I held him in my arms for hours and quoted scripture. We just counted the hours until daylight.

Kirk arrived at 6:45 a.m. and we began the race to Danville which was 90 miles away. It would be the first of many trips. By 10:30 a.m. Jerry was in an examining room at the Veterans Administration Hospital.

Between breaths, he told the young Chinese lady doctor that he had sat for seven days and nights in a chair with only one hour of sleep. He was afraid that if he coughed up sputum while lying down, he would drowned in his own fluid.

Much to our relief, he was admitted to the hospital where doctors questioned him endlessly. His arterial blood gas level was okay, but his EKG report was not as good. Mike, the young doctor in training, finally announced to us that Jerry had a full blown case of adult asthma. We couldn't believe it! We knew he had emphysema, but had no idea he also had asthma. His brother Roger had been plagued with asthma all his life, but Jerry never had a symptom.

Knowing that Jerry was in good hands, Kirk and I left the hospital around 4 p.m. We stopped for supper and Kirk asked me the ultimate question I had been dreading.

"What happens if dad should die?"

My first reaction was one of sheer denial. "Why, he wouldn't dare!" I exclaimed. Kirk proceeded to tell me that his mother-in-law never expected to be a young widow either and I needed to prepare myself.

Around midnight the next evening, Decatur experienced a terrible storm. Michael had gotten up to go to the bathroom when all of a sudden there was a huge flash of lightening. There was a loud boom followed by the sound of bricks crashing. Viki was up with Michael and thought our house was hit but instead lightening struck the two chimneys of the Staley mansion next door.

The next morning we found broken roofing tiles and chimney

bricks strewn all over our property. We relived the fatal accident in our driveway nearly four years earlier. Since the Staley mansion was also a historical home, the replacement cost for the tiles would be astronomical.

Charles and Eileen Volle made plans to drive me to Danville to see Jerry. They called and said there was no way we could get there because roads were flooded from the storm. I was extremely disappointed and decided to call the VA Hospital to check on Jerry.

I received the second blow of the day when I was informed that Jerry's condition had deteriorated and he was now in intensive care. His arterial blood gas level was very low. The medical personnel were giving him steroids to help get his breathing under control.

I called family members and friends and asked them to pray. At 6 p.m. I called the hospital back and found out Jerry was doing much better.

Not only had the storm flooded roads, but our church basement was flooded. Water was everywhere. We enlisted several volunteers to come with buckets and help mop up the mess.

Early the next morning Charles and Eileen picked me up and we headed to Danville. Debris from the storm was still scattered everywhere.

We heaved a big sigh of relief when we finally saw Jerry. He was no longer in critical condition and was being moved to a regular room.

Eileen and I went to visit the father of one of Viki's Women's Aglow officers. Kathy Blakeman's father, Walter Baumhardt, had been a patient in the VA Hospital for several years. He had been in a coma following complications from a simple operation. The night before his surgery he had accepted Jesus Christ as his Savior.

While Eileen and I were praying over Walter, a very stylish lady walked in. She was surprised to see any visitors in the room. I explained who we were and she said she was Walter's wife, Edyth. Every Wednesday she faithfully drove from Springfield to see her husband, even though he never responded. We soon became friends and left notes of encouragement for each other. I gave her my poem books and a copy of *Fortress on a Hill*. Doctors and nurses were also the recipients of my material.

The following day my youngest daughter, Cheri, drove Jerry's mother to Danville. They reported back to us that Jerry was very much improved.

My high school class reunion was coming up soon and I kept praying that somehow God would make a way for Jerry and me to be there. I even found an elegant blue dress that would be perfect for the occasion. It was marked down from $106 to $31.

Chris drove me to Danville in pouring rain. Jerry was somewhat improved, but had difficulty breathing after taking a shower. Not only was he on steroids and antibiotics, he was also using inhalers every three hours around the clock.

Viki planned to drive me two days later, but Michael was sick with tonsillitis. She stayed home with him and Chris made the trip again. Much to our dismay, Jerry had lost three more pounds.

The following day the hospital called me with the good news that Jerry was being released. I was delighted! After waiting a long time to get all of Jerry's prescriptions filled, we finally headed back to Decatur. It was great having him back home with the family again!

With great joy, I grabbed my pen and wrote on May 25 the following poem entitled "Molded by the Master."

Molded by the Master

It seems there is a moment
When God searches out mankind,
Seeking a humble servant
Through which His grace to prime.

He listens for a heart that cries
For more of God and His ways--
A desire to be molded
Under the Master's gaze.

When He finds that special one,
   He casts him into the fire
And burns away the heavy dross
   With every personal desire.

Nothing becomes more important
   Than this communion time with God.
Even the fiery flames are sweet
   When under the chastening rod.

The blazing fires intensify
   Till one can scarcely breathe,
But God is molding an image
   Through which His love will cleave.

All impurities are driven out
   As pain becomes a friend,
But the hands of God are cradling
   The tender soul He rends.

Stripped now of the world's cares,
   With faith in God supreme,
This vessel is now glowing
   For on His Lord he leans.

The trial of this suffering one
   Has turned toward God's directions.
He's endured the heat of a holocaust—
   Purged toward Christ's perfection.

Bursting from God's furnace
   With God's will for release,
There will come forth a vessel—
   The Lord's Own "Masterpiece."

One who will shine forever,
      Designed by a holy Crafter.
Oh, to be that vessel of honor
      Molded by the Master!

Two days later on a Sunday morning, Jerry surprised everyone in our church by walking in for the service. He received a standing ovation!

His recovery was short-lived. He had a bad reaction to all of the steroids he was taking. His hands began to cramp and his breathing became labored. He had been on huge doses of prednisone and instead of being weaned off it slowly, the medicine was withdrawn all at once. It was a terrible shock to his system!

To add more fuel to our fire of testing, Decatur experienced another bad storm. Lightning hit our television set, knocking it out of commission.

Jerry's breathing got worse. He literally hibernated in our bedroom where we left the air conditioner on day and night. I called Kim in Montana and explained to him the situation. He urged me to take Jerry back to Danville. Mike and Cheri also said not to wait too long this time. I called Chris and she said she would drive Jerry the next day.

It was a very rough night. Jerry struggled to breathe and sat in a chair all night. We were both scared this time.

Chris and I raced Jerry to the VA Hospital where he was admitted immediately. This time prednisone was administered directly into his veins.

No sooner had Chris and I gotten back home than Jerry called with some exciting news. Kim had just walked in the room with Chantelle. They had traveled all the way from Montana to see him. Even though he had been up for over 24 hours, Kim stayed for hours visiting with his dad. Jerry was feeling much better.

After many tests, Jerry was released from the hospital two days later. He was given a new medical program to follow that was designed specifically for him.

While Kim was around, we worked on the music for *Voyage*. We recorded the songs at Harvest Christian Center.

Pentecost Sunday was observed on June 10. Churches from several denominations gathered for a big celebration. Jerry attended and thanked everyone for their prayers. Then he shared, "Twice I was given up for dead, but God's not done with me yet."

Suddenly, everyone in the building was on his feet, clapping in thunderous applause that seemed to go on forever. It was as though the building shook as in Acts 4:19 when the early church was in one accord.

The next day at the Decatur Women's Aglow meeting someone shared about the previous evening's meeting and how God had used Jerry in a remarkable way to bring unity in the city of Decatur. To God be the glory!

Early the next morning Jerry went back to Danville for a check-up. The doctors said he was doing so well that he did not have to come back until July. They reduced his prednisone dosage in half.

On our way home I noticed a rose colored station wagon in a car dealer's parking lot. Jerry and I had been looking for a station wagon and decided to go back the next day to check it out. It was just what we needed! We traded in our old brown wagon and drove home in our new "chariot" that would carry us to my high school reunion.

Just when things were beginning to get back to normal, another storm hit three nights later. The wind blew fiercely. Around 1:30 a.m. we heard a tremendous crash and ran outside to see the enormous old ash tree fallen across the sidewalk. It was one of the biggest ash trees in the city and now it was cut off with about 60 feet of the trunk sticking up high in the air. Although on the ground, the branches reached higher than the third floor windows. When Viki and Doug looked out their bedroom windows, it looked like a jungle!

About this same time the phone rang. It was Kirk calling to say the roof had blown off the church and water was pouring in everywhere. Jerry calmly asked if there was any damage to their apartment at the church. Kirk replied, "No, we are all right and there is no damage to the sanctuary or office, but the game room, nursery and kitchen have rain pouring in."

I was stunned to hear my husband say, "Well, there's nothing you can do until morning, so turn off the lights and go back to sleep."

"Peace in the midst of the storm," I thought to myself.

During the daylight hours we noticed the ash tree hit a corner of the mansion where we had a chapel. The impact from the falling tree broke the front sidewalk. People came from everywhere looking at our "front yard jungle."

Our real emergency was at the church. It continued raining another inch. The kitchen ceiling fell during the night. The prayer room and recreation room were simply gone. Insurance adjusters came and hired a company to help with clean up. Gallons and gallons of water were sucked up by powerful vacuums. It was the first time we ever canceled a Wednesday night service. Somehow God would work good out of everything that had happened.

It was finally time for Jerry and me to depart for my high school reunion in Winona, Minnesota. We drove around the city that I called home for 19 years of my life and where I met the love of my life at a party 40 years earlier. All of my high school friends thought it was pretty cool to fraternize with the college boys. All of the girls had a crush on Jerry, but I was the one he asked for a date.

We stopped to see my mother and then went to visit my sister Colleen, who was working on our family's genealogy. We also saw my brother Bob and his wife Stefannie. As we were leaving, Bob made the remark, "I'll bet you're the youngest looking woman there." With that kind of an ego booster, I was ready for anything!

When we walked in the door, my first reaction was, "Who are all of these old people?" I could hardly believe how everyone had aged. And then it dawned on me that I was one of them!

I gave away several of my poem books to fellow classmates and they urged me to stand up when it came time for testimonials. I shared how my life had changed at the age of 39 and that Jerry and I were involved in full time ministry. I read my favorite poem "Assorted Roses." When I finished, there was utter silence. Then everyone clapped and wanted copies.

The next morning we gave a set of our skit books to the lady who had been the class president. I told Jerry we just had to give them away.

"It's up to the Lord to do the follow up," I remarked.

Later, when we got back home, I went to see Dr. McGhee because of a sinus and ear infection. I shared with him all that had happened. He simply shook his head and said, "Now I know why all these things happen to you. It's so you can share them with others and give God the glory!"

"Yes," I agreed with him and then wondered what else could possibly happen.

11

In Sickness and in Health

Our attention was now focused on getting the church repaired from the wind storm. Some news accounts reported it was actually a tornado that hit the neighborhood. Jerry wanted to be involved in all of the remodeling and rebuilding decisions. I refused to let him look at carpeting because the carpet warehouse was not air conditioned. He would just have to trust the rest of us to make the right choice.

In the meantime, the debris and tree limbs at the House of Prayer got cleaned up. The corner damaged on the house was repaired, but it would be a while before the sidewalk was fixed. There were other jobs at the mansion that needed tending to, but Jerry could not do them. He could only supervise. Since 1975 he had been the chief janitor, plumber and carpenter for the 120-year-old building, and now it was time for someone else to take over.

Jerry had a July 9 appointment at the Danville Veterans Administration Hospital to have some cysts removed from the back of his head. They were benign and we were glad to have that episode behind us. We made an appointment to have his eyes examined so that he could get a stronger lens prescription.

Jerry began to think he was on top of everything and showed up at the church to help the men who were working on the windows and fixing the rotten floor. He was right in all of the sawdust and later went back to help with installing the paneling.

On July 26 Jerry returned to Danville for a check-up and was told he was holding his own. He needed to stay on the prescribed medical course he was already doing.

The next day Kirk and Jeanette came over to see us. They

asked Joel to tell us the good news. He was going to have a sister or brother to play with! We then went to see the new house they had just bought.

August 11 was the 15th anniversary of the House of Prayer. Jerry went to the church to work on another window and breathed in all of the sawdust. He had a bad night breathing, but was determined to drive to Jacksonville the next morning to minister at a church service. It was raining and he was gasping for air. By the grace of God, we survived and made it back home. Jerry collapsed in the driveway while unloading our station wagon.

At 4 a.m. I was awakened and heard Jerry having a full blown asthma attack. I called Danville's VA Hospital, but there was no answer. I called a second time but it was too early for anyone to answer.

Jerry was not getting any better, so a couple of hours later we headed to Danville. A Pakistinian woman doctor wanted to admit Jerry for three days because he was in serious condition. Jerry insisted on coming home and finally was told he would have to take 12 pills every six hours plus antibiotics. He would also have to stay in his air conditioned bedroom. Jerry followed the doctor's orders, but his breathing continued getting worse--especially at night. He needed a miracle!

Decatur was hit with another bad storm and of all the places for lightning to hit, our television was struck again! The Persian Gulf War had just started and it was imperative that we get our tv fixed soon so we could keep up on the news overseas.

The next morning Jerry said "uncle" and knew that he had to get to the hospital fast. He could hardly breathe. I called Chris at work and she came and got us at 10 a.m. Off we raced again to Danville, praying all the way.

An Indian doctor saw Jerry and admitted him immediately. His arterial blood gas level was 74. Anything around 70 is very critical. Jerry was using inhalers every three hours, but the doctors wanted to put him on a six-hour schedule. The luxury of eight hours sleep was long gone.

Three days later Jerry was released from the hospital, but his breathing still was not good. He wanted to come home and inspect the work being done on the church. Kirk was assuming more and more of the pastoral responsibilities of the church including preaching, counseling and leading worship.

Very early Sunday morning at 1:15 a.m. Jerry had a severe asthma attack. He fell over. I called for Doug and Viki to come downstairs immediately. We all prayed and interceded for Jerry to live.

At 9 a.m. Chris and I headed back to Danville with Jerry. As soon as we arrived, Jerry was put in a wheelchair. His heart was checked and he was given a shot with adrenalin. Food was brought in, but Jerry could not eat because he was nauseous and had a terrible headache. He was given an ice bag for his head and steroids were pumped directly into his veins.

Doug drove me back to see Jerry the next day. It was nearly 100 degrees outside and very humid. We found a very sick Jerry. He had vomited for 12 hours and lost six pounds. He was on a liquid diet, but seemed to be in good spirits.

Even though Jerry was extremely sick, he did not let that stop him from preaching the truth to his roommate. The man was under such spiritual conviction that he decided to marry the woman he was living with. Soon he was inviting all of the nurses and doctors to his wedding.

When Doug and I got back home, I decided to really clean Jerry's and my bedroom. To help Jerry breathe better, I took out the carpet and put a big rug down. I even bought new curtains.

A bright spot in my day was receiving a letter from a group of Christians in Germany who wanted to distribute our skit books. It was nice having a victory instead of facing battles all the time.

Jerry was finally released, but his medicine would have to be taken every four hours instead of the six-hour interval we were hoping for. To help his breathing, he would go to the Decatur Public Library which had central air conditioning. Sometimes he and I would go to the air conditioned mall and just walk around, enjoying each other's company. It was the little things that we treasured.

Jerry seemed so much better and decided to preach the following Sunday. His sermon was "Knowing Jesus." He also insisted on helping install insulation at the church and taped five radio broadcasts at the Christian radio station in Champaign. In addition he canned several jars of home-made grape jelly.

On our 37th wedding anniversary we went to Danville for Jerry's check-up, believing for a good report. Apparently, Jerry was over-doing it and the doctor decided to increase his prednisone dosage. Also, with fall upon us and the burning of leaves, we decided to purchase an air purifier for our bedroom. Immediately Jerry began to receive good results from it.

We decided to forego participating in the annual fall bazaar at the mall, but did have another rummage sale. Even though I was wore out and had another sinus infection, Jerry and I drove to North Carolina to visit our friends the Jorgensens. It was always a lovely get-away in the Smokey Mountains. This time, however, while shopping in a store, Jerry had a bad asthma attack. He still was not fully recuperated when we started driving back to Decatur. He had a bad night of breathing at the motel we stayed at. To compound matters, he had to drive in fog the next morning. I was very concerned and just prayed since Jerry did all of the driving.

We stopped at a store in Mt. Vernon, Illinois, where I ran into Floyd Robinson, a district manager for Prudential Insurance Company. He told us he was the only manager remaining from the top 20 in all of mid-America from when he and Jerry were on that list several years earlier. All of the other men had either died or left the company. I know God arranged that "divine appointment" with Floyd to confirm my feelings about what would have happened to Jerry if he had stayed with Prudential and not surrendered his life to Jesus. I believe God would have taken Jerry earlier because of the fast-paced life and stress he constantly experienced.

It was time for Jerry to reduce the amount of prednisone he was taking. That was always hard on his system. To make matters worse, I was sick from sinus drainage.

A blessing in the midst of all this was when Michael's teacher came to our home and said Michael was a bright boy and tops in his class. That was a miracle because Viki was told shortly after his birth that he would be slow in school and not able to do things as quickly as

87

others because he was a low birth-weight baby and born early. God truly answered our prayers and had a great plan in the making for Michael.

As an alternative to Halloween, our church hosted a Hallelujah Night where participants dressed in Bible character costumes. Michael won first prize dressed as Gideon. Little Sarah was dressed as Miriam, playing a tambourine. I was Dorcus because I gave clothes away all the time. Chris came as Noah **in** the ark. She had on big rubber boots, a yellow raincoat and a cardboard box shaped like the ark. She put stuffed animals on the ark's deck. Doug won a prize for being Jonah. I powdered him white and put a fishing net with seaweed and fish over his tunic. Everyone roared with laughter!

Jerry tried as much as he could to keep active. He appeared on the Christian television station's fall telethon and taped five messages for the radio station. But with people burning leaves, he was forced to stay in his bedroom most of the time. His lungs were so sensitive that he could smell the smoke from leaves as it came down the chimney into the fireplace in our bedroom.

Chris decided to move out of her apartment on the third floor of the mansion and into the empty apartment at Harvest Christian Center. Kirk and Jeanette no longer lived there since they had bought a house. It would be convenient having someone live at the church who could turn on the heat or air conditioning and unlock the doors before service since Jerry was incapable of doing that now.

Doug and Viki decided to expand their living quarters on the third floor at the House of Prayer and took over Chris' apartment. They now had the whole third floor—bigger than most homes in the city of Decatur. They had four bedrooms, two living rooms, two bathrooms, a dining area and a kitchen.

By the time December arrived, Jerry's health was going downhill. Steroids were a part of his daily life. Although considered a miracle drug, with constant use they also caused Jerry's bones and muscles to deteriorate. More trips were made to Danville. As winter approached, there was the constant battle with the elements.

During the day of Christmas Eve, Jerry had a terrible time breathing. We decided to take him to Danville. Kirk drove and we praised God the roads had been cleared of snow. Upon arrival, Jerry was admitted to the hospital immediately and put on intravenous medication. Kirk and I stayed until mid-afternoon. We needed to get back to Decatur because our family had its traditional gift exchange that evening. Ironically, Jerry had my name that Christmas.

The next day Doug and Viki and their children went to Mattoon to celebrate Christmas with Doug's family. Kirk's family and Chris came to the mansion for a big turkey dinner I was preparing. Kim called from Montana and informed me he had talked to Jerry the night before. Chris stayed with me until evening when Doug and Viki got back from Mattoon. It was my first Christmas without Jerry.

On December 26 Cheri drove me to Danville. Jerry was so much better and off of the IV's. We stayed for a couple of hours and then headed back home.

Two days later while taking down the Christmas decorations, I received a phone call from Jerry saying he was released and could go home. Excitedly I called Kirk and we raced to Danville. Jerry was anxious to get home. The doctors put him on some new medication.

Rather than have a New Year's Eve Watch Service, our church decided not to have a get-together. It was bitter cold and many of our families had young children. In addition, Jerry had no business getting out in the cold air. We huddled on the House of Prayer's third floor and used kerosene heaters to keep warm. At midnight we looked out the windows and saw giant fireworks being shot off in downtown Decatur as part of the city's New Year's Eve Arts Celebration. As I gazed at the spectacular fireworks, I wondered what God had in store for us in 1991. I also thought about the priorities of life.

"The world doesn't know the greatest marvel of all is having the presence of Jesus and having our loved ones with us in this special moment of time," I reflected.

12

How Tender Are His Mercies

On New Year's Day 1991 I called my mother in Winona, Minnesota, to see how she was doing. She was now living in an apartment that ironically had formerly been the entrance to the hospital where my twin sister, Doris, and I were born. She was happy to be in a smaller place and said her neighbors were nice and helpful. When I hung up the phone, I immediately planned to make a beautiful wreath and flower arrangement for her new dwelling.

It was an icy first day for the year. The mansion's roofs were under heavy weight from the ice, causing some leaks in the ceilings. Jerry was unable to do any repair work because of his poor health.

By the end of January, Jerry's lungs were filling up and he could hardly breathe. We made another trip to Danville where he received some new medication and larger doses of prednisone. I was allowed to see the x-rays of his lungs and I knew they weren't good.

We came home and I decided to make an appointment with my doctor for a complete physical. I found out I had a bladder infection and mentioned I was having a lot of stomach problems after I ate certain foods.

Jerry's health problems took a turn for the worse when he started coughing up blood. We talked to Dr. Robbins in Danville and he said to allow the new medication a couple of days to work. But Jerry's situation worsened, so a flying trip was made back to Danville.

A new doctor ordered x-rays and an arterial blood gas test. I spotted Dr. Robbins in the hallway and asked him to come back and talk to Jerry. Pneumonia was suspected so Jerry was given some new antibiotics and a pain reliever and then sent home.

Jerry continued coughing up blood so on March 11 we returned to Danville. A doctor saw him immediately and said Jerry had had enough antibiotics.

"Perhaps he might have cancer," I was told.

I was very frightened at that prospect and just could not tell Jerry. My stomach churned and the fibrositis in my shoulder ached continuously.

Jerry's lungs began filling up more, causing him breathing problems. He also had the chills. The merry-go-round of sickness seemed to never end.

The House of Prayer was scheduled to exhibit skit books at a Sunday School Convention in Lincoln, Illinois, but we canceled our participation. Jerry's eyes looked like they were bleeding from the hard coughing he did. In addition he filled waste baskets with tissues containing the sputum he coughed up.

In desperation I called Chris to drive us to Danville. There was a road block and it took us 25 minutes longer to drive. Finally we arrived. What sweet words we received from the doctor. Jerry did not have cancer nor pneumonia. He had bronchitis and conjunctivitis. We left with nine prescriptions. On the way home Jerry talked about the possibility of applying early for his retirement pension from Prudential Insurance Company.

The following night Jeanette's water broke so she and Kirk hurried quickly to the hospital. Kayla Renee was born the next morning on March 23. She weighed 6 pounds and 15 ounces and was 20 ½ inches longs. A woman doctor delivered her by natural birth–so different from the Caesarian section Jeanette had with Joel.

Jerry still had pink eye and was not allowed in the hospital. Two days later Kirk pulled up in our driveway, sporting a new car and a new baby.

Forty-eight hours later, Jeanette started running a temperature and was shaking all over. An anxious Kirk drove her to the hospital's emergency room where they found out Jeanette had a severe bladder and urinary infection.

Twelve days later on May 4 we received a phone call from Mike. Cheri's water had broken at 8 a.m., but her due date was not for another six weeks. We prayed all day and night that nothing would go wrong and that the baby would be healthy and whole. Finally, at 12:12 p.m. on May 5 Mariah Danielle made her appearance into the world. She was 5 pounds and 7 ounces and had lots of coal black hair. Eventually it would turn into long golden locks that earned her the name "Goldilocks" from me. Because of the premature birth, jaundice set in just like Sarah. She was very critical for 24 hours. Finally, after 10 days Mariah was released from the hospital and went home to a very happy family.

It was time for Jerry's check-up at Danville. I saw the young intern we called Dr. Mike who had been the first one to diagnose Jerry's adult asthma. He had since left the veteran's hospital, but just happened to be there that day.

When Dr. Mike spotted Jerry, he literally jumped over people and came face-to-face with him. He hugged him and said, "Rev. Henneberry, you'll never know how much you've meant to me and how much my life has changed because of you." It was another divine appointment! I silently gave thanks to God for this "chance" meeting.

Jerry and I decided to step out in faith and drive to Montana to see Kim and his family. They were living in Miles City and had bought a house with a cabin in the back. I was battling nausea and dizziness but was determined to make the trip. Cottonwood was blowing everywhere and piling up like snow. It drifted into houses through doors and windows.

Besides the cottonwood, giant moths had made their way into the cabin behind Kim and Libby's house. Libby's mother, Joyce, helped me knock hundreds of them to the floor with brooms and then vacuum them. Because of Jerry's condition, we got to sleep in Kim's house rather than the cabin for which I was very grateful.

In the midst of difficult times, God has a way of entertaining us with the little things in life. One night I was awakened by a terrible noise coming from outside our bedroom window on the second floor. I raced to the window and looked straight into the eyes of a baby racoon sitting on top of our air conditioner, trying to come in. I woke up Jerry who was getting some much needed sleep. I threw out some pieces of chicken to the little fella.

I never should have started doing that because every night around 9 p.m. our masked bandit we nicknamed "Zorro" would faithfully come, expecting a hand-out. Zorro would walk all the way around the big house, grab the food off the air conditioner and scamper off with his reward. One night Viki videotaped Zorro staring back at us with his big bandit eyes.

Another bright spot in our lives was a letter from Moody Bible Institute which said the college was using our drama material and that it was the best available.

A missionary wrote and said she should have written us earlier about a powerful testimony concerning our drama material. She translated our skits into Spanish and witnessed hundreds and hundreds of people in Mexico and Central America coming to Jesus after seeing our skits performed. We were elated! My next skit book, *The Last Roundup*, was coming out soon.

Testing time was always around the corner. While attending a men's breakfast on a Saturday, Jerry suddenly dropped his tray. He came home sick and went straight to bed. He slept all day and ended up having the flu. Kirk had to be "instant in season" and assumed the duties of preaching the next morning's sermon.

We continued making plans to attend the North Dakota Sunday School Convention. Jerry was scheduled to teach a seminar on Christian drama and I was to teach one on writing skits.

With great reluctance on my part, we left Sept. 18 for the long drive to Minot, North Dakota. The convention ended up being a great success. On our way back home we stopped in Winona, Minnesota, and had a nice visit with my mother and sister Colleen.

Some friends made arrangements for us to spend a few days with them in a condominium in Minnesota. My friend, Pat, made a hair appointment for me at a beauty salon. The owner waited on me and told me he was a Christian. His wife wanted to divorce him. They had two children and he was heartbroken. The Lord used me to minister to him. I gave him a copy of *Fortress on a Hill*. When I went to pay my bill, he said, "There is no charge. You have given me hope again."

We were home only a few days when we took off again for a convention in Lancaster, Pennsylvania. I needed to get my hair done and found a beauty shop in the mall. This time I was not so blessed and my hairdo was a complete disaster! The poor beautician had never back-combed hair in her life and ended up rolling my hair backwards. I ended up having to set my hair all over again in the motel room.

The next morning panic set in for both Jerry and me. We had forgotten the time change in Pennsylvania! It was time to leave and I was frantically back-combing my hair. Making matters worse was the weather outside. It was pouring down rain! Jerry's breathing was affected so I ended up carrying our suitcases to the car from our second floor motel room. Somehow we made it on time to the convention and Jerry taught a seminar on drama.

We proceeded to North Carolina and stayed a few days with the Jorgensens. We had a lovely time and were able to minister at their church.

After we arrived back home, I started planning costumes for our church's Hallelujah Night, a wonderful alternative to Halloween. I persuaded Viki to be "Shirley Goodness" and I would be "Ann Mercy." Doug and Jerry wore brown robes and had black balloons attached to black paper chains around their ankles. They were Paul and Silas, singing while in prison. Needless to say, we won all the prizes!

Jerry was determined to drive his mother to his sister's house in Kalamazoo, Michigan, for Thanksgiving. Diane, who was a nurse, and Joe, who was a doctor, were always a big help when it came to medical problems. Jerry had a terrible time breathing at their house. He could not sleep at night and was up five times, gasping for air. The next morning Joe took Jerry to his office and gave him a flu shot. Jerry's immune system had deteriorated to the point where any infection could spell disaster for him.

Driving home we decided to stop in Park Forest, Illinois, where we had spent two happy, but hectic, years of our lives when Jerry worked for Prudential and commuted to Chicago. The town had changed and seemed foreign. It was raining and as usual that bothered Jerry's breathing.

On Sunday, December 1, I prepared a big turkey dinner for the family. Kirk said he had a special announcement to make and then proceeded to say baby number three was on the way--due in June.

Jerry turned 62 on December 11 and then exactly one week later was Chris' birthday. Their birthdays, Christmas and New Year's were right in a row for four consecutive weeks–always making December a very hectic month.

Chris called us at 12:30 a.m. on Sunday morning December 15. The furnace at Harvest Christian Center had quit working and she could not get it started. Jerry made two trips to the church to get the furnace going and finally decided just to stay there to make sure it didn't malfunction again. The children's big Christmas play was that morning and there would be many friends and relatives attending. The heat had to be working.

The next weekend on Friday night Jerry and I went out for supper. We stopped at church so I could put out the candles for the candlelight service. We did not stay long at the church because Jerry had a hard time breathing. I ended up driving the car home and wondered if maybe the flu was attacking Jerry.

The next evening Jerry was running a 101 degree temperature. I called Kirk to be on standby to preach the next morning in case Jerry did not make it to church. I tried to sleep in my chair in the dining room, but ended up praying all night.

Jerry ended up staying home from church the next day. At the evening candlelight service I picked out a scripture verse for him from the collection plate. Instead of taking an offering at that service, we made it a tradition for people to randomly pick a scripture verse out of the collection plate. Over and over again people would select a scripture verse that specifically applied to them for the coming year. The verse I drew out for Jerry was no exception. *"The angel of the Lord encamps around those who fear him, and he delivers them." Psalm 34:7*

A prison ministry called and asked if we could help a family for Christmas. Viki and I took some food, clothes and gifts. At the last minute I tossed in a huge brown coat in the back seat of the car. The lady was very appreciative of everything and as we turned to leave, I asked her if she could use a good winter coat. She broke down and cried, saying she really needed one. I went back to the car and got the brown coat. Now she had something to wear to church and it fit her perfectly!

That night Jerry had a terrible time trying to sleep. Kim called and after talking to him, Viki and I decided to leave at 6 a.m. to take Jerry to Danville. We thanked God Jerry had gone almost a full year without being admitted to the hospital, but it was "deja vu" with another Christmas eve spent at the VA Hospital.

Jerry was admitted immediately and given intravenous medication. His labored breathing was so hard that it was painful for me to watch him suffer. Everyone's nerves were on edge.

Viki and I headed back to Decatur around 2:30 p.m. Family members would be coming to our house in the evening to exchange gifts. It would be our second Christmas without Jerry with us.

On Christmas Day Chris picked me up at 11:30 a.m. and drove to Danville. Jerry was in a wheelchair, shaving in the bathroom, still laboring to breathe. Although he was exhausted, he visited with us as we exchanged Christmas gifts. He was in no shape to come home yet.

We got back home only to find out that Kayla, Jeanette and Joel were sick with a virus. The next day I had it. Thankfully, it only lasted 24 hours.

Chris and I headed back to Danville on December 27. Jerry was a tiny bit better and his spirit was up. Dr. Winter, chief of staff with the pulmonary division, personally took over Jerry's case and decided to start limiting the amount of prednisone Jerry was taking. This meant a slower recovery so Jerry was moved to a different room.

Chris and I decided to go back to Danville on December 30. Jerry was not much better. He coughed for three hours and his blood pressure was up. Dr. Winters decided to put him back on a higher dosage of prednisone that he could take orally.

With much hidden anxiety, Chris and I drove back to Decatur, wondering what the future held for the Henneberry family.

13

Going Through

Kim called on New Year's Day 1992 with the delightful news that my number eight grandchild would be born at the end of the month.

Two days later on Friday, Chris and I drove to Danville. Jerry was still coughing up phlegm and his blood pressure was up. We were told to come back on Monday for his evaluation check-up.

When we arrived at 11:30 a.m., Jerry was ready to leave, but we had to wait until 4 p.m. to see Dr. Winter. He and Jerry were developing a kindred spirit and could talk each other's language. Dr. Winter had undergone a kidney transplant and had to be very careful about his own condition. When Jerry finally saw the doctor, it was too late in the day for him to be discharged so we had to come back the next day. Needless to say everyone was discouraged.

By the time Chris and I got there Tuesday morning, Jerry was pacing the floor. He couldn't wait to get home! He had lost 20 pounds and was very weak. Viki fixed supper in her third floor apartment for everyone and brought all the food downstairs so Jerry would not have to climb up the stairs. Recovery would be slow this time.

Family members decided to fix up a small room downstairs on first floor that Jerry could use. His first floor office was often cold in the winter. In addition, it was filled with boxes containing the ministry's skit books. The smaller room would be easier to heat and would have the ministry's new computer. Dust and mold would be minimal so Jerry would have an easier time breathing.

Everyone went to work painting and wallpapering the walls. New carpet was installed. The "computer room" as we called it was

97

taking shape. The only problem was that every time Jerry went in there, the paint and carpet smells set off his asthma.

Jerry preached his first sermon in ages on January 19. His topic was on responsibility and trusting God. Attendance was down and several people had left our church to go elsewhere. The uncertainty of Jerry's condition was a factor. When we needed their support the most, they weren't there to encourage us. We had to trust God even more to meet the needs of the church.

On January 29 we got our eighth grandchild. Katlin Teal weighed 6 pounds and 15 ounces. Chantelle got to witness the birth of her little sister and proud papa Kim got to cut the umbilical cord.

I called my mother to tell her she was a great-grandma again. Out of the clear blue she asked if she could send me some early inheritance money. The hitch was that I could only spend it on me. I agreed and knew that God was intervening on my behalf so that my needs would be taken care of.

Jerry started receiving Social Security payments. He announced to the congregation that he would no longer be drawing a salary and decided to step down as pastor. He was turning the "reigns" over to Kirk. The congregation unanimously approved Kirk as the senior pastor.

It was a hard day for me as I had mixed emotions. I was proud of Kirk and yet I felt sad for Jerry who no longer had the strength and endurance required for being a pastor.

In early February Jerry decided to apply for his retirement pension from Prudential Insurance Company where he had worked for 18 years. To his utter amazement, he found out he would have to pass a physical. It would take a miracle, but he decided to start filling out the paperwork anyway. Everyone prayed.

Jerry had a bout with pleurisy and was in bed for several days. He insisted, though, on going to the Peoria Sunday School Convention and exhibiting our drama books. By the time we got home from that convention, he was having a hard time breathing. We made a flying trip to Danville where the doctor put him on 60 milligrams of prednisone for 10 days.

Jerry got to feeling better and was determined to keep going and not let his asthma bother him. He went to Kirk's house and helped work on cabinets and install a dishwasher. His intentions were good, but he ended up with an infection and had to take some antibiotics.

On March 19 we received the news that Lula, the little neighbor lady I had led to the Lord, had passed away. A small grave side service was held on March 23. Jerry read my poem, "Homeward Bound." I kept looking for her coffin and found out later she was in the tiny little box–she had been cremated!

On that same day I wrote the song "I'm Going Home" and sang it to Jerry. He liked it and I decided to add it to my musical *Voyage*.

Jerry made an appointment for his physical and it was scheduled for the end of April. A couple of days later the receptionist at the doctor's office called and said she had a cancellation for a 9 a.m. appointment the next morning. Would Jerry be interested in coming in then? We knew God was somehow involved and Jerry quickly said yes. He was feeling the best he had felt in a long time, his blood pressure was good and he was off the prednisone. Miraculously, he passed the physical! The only thing he wondered about was whether his asthma would prevent him from receiving his pension. He sent in all of the paperwork, mentioning the asthma. Again everyone prayed.

It was time for the annual spring ritual of taking the plastic off the windows of the mansion. Jerry insisted on helping. His kindheartedness took its toll on his health and he developed breathing problems again. By Easter Sunday he was having another asthma attack and never made it to church.

The next morning Kirk drove us to Danville. Jerry was admitted immediately to the Veterans Administration Hospital. I noticed he was put in a room which had flowers and the windows were opened. For a person having an asthma attack, these two factors were terrible!

We stayed late at the hospital and knew we needed to drive home. Jerry said he would call to keep us informed of his condition. We made plans to return on Thursday. I didn't think he was too bad off and believed he would come home soon.

I called my mother and told her the news. I thanked her for the check she sent me and we reminisced about family dinners when I was younger. She commented how she had missed Babe and me when we got married and moved so far away from home.

The next morning Cheri called the VA Hospital to check up on Jerry. He was not doing well at all. Chris and I decided not to wait until Thursday but rather drive up the next day.

To be honest, I was angry with God. Why was He permitting Jerry to suffer? I finally asked God to speak to me through scripture and give me a verse that would sustain me through this trying time. I picked up my Bible and opened it to Ezekiel 37:8-14.

"I looked, and tendons and flesh appeared on them and skin covered them, but there was no breath in them. Then he said to me, 'Prophesy to the breath; prophesy, son of man, and say to it, 'This is what the Sovereign Lord says: come from the four winds, O breath, and breathe into these slain, that they may live.' So I prophesied as he commanded me, and breath entered them; they came to life and stood up on their feet—a vast army.

"Then he said to me: 'Son of man, these bones are the whole house of Israel. They say, 'Our bones are dried up and our hope is gone; we are cut off.' Therefore prophesy and say to them: 'This is what the Sovereign Lord says: O my people, I am going to open your graves and bring you up from them; I will bring you back to the land of Israel. Then you, my people, will know that I am the Lord, when I open your graves and bring you up from them. I will put my Spirit in you and you will live, and I will settle you in your own land. Then you will know that I the Lord have spoken, and I have done it, declares the Lord.'"

"Glory!" I shouted. God had spoken to me through His Word. Jerry would live and return home. I would trust and believe God's Word no matter what happened.

Chris was late picking me up for our trip to Danville. I was outside waiting for her when I heard the phone ringing. I ran inside and it was a young intern at the VA Hospital. She didn't want to alarm me, but wanted me there as soon as possible. Jerry had taken a turn for the worse and they were hooking him up to a ventilator.

I quickly packed an over-night bag, not knowing what to

expect. Chris and I raced to Danville, praying all the way. When we got to the intensive care unit, we found a circle of doctors working on a writhing body–my husband.

He was fighting the ventilator with all his remaining strength. Dr. Winter was shouting that 60 percent of all asthmatics don't make it on a ventilator. Then the impossible happened–the power went off! Dr. Winter let out a few expletive deletes and a nurse had to manually suck the fluid from Jerry's lungs. It was a terrifying picture!

Chris helped to hold Jerry's feet as they were put in restraints. In the midst of this chaos I heard one doctor saying, "This is all in Jerry's mind. He is only doing this for attention." I had heard this same doctor tell another patient that weeks earlier. Needless to say, I did not have much faith in him.

The chaplain arrived and took Chris and me aside to prepare us for Jerry's passing away.

"No!" I cried. "He will live," I emphasized. I shared my scripture verses in Ezekiel with him, but all he could say was "I sure hope you're right."

At that instance, the Lord quickened another scripture passage to me in Philippians 4:6-7. *"Do not be anxious about anything, but in everything, by prayer and petition, with thanksgiving, present your requests to God. And the peace of God, which transcends all understanding, will guard your hearts and your minds in Christ Jesus."*

Kirk and Cheri arrived at the hospital. By then Jerry was put on oxygen and given morphine. Chris and Cheri stayed a little bit longer and then decided to go home. Kirk stayed with me during the night. I arranged some cushions on chairs and slept as comfortably as I could.

The next morning Jerry was doing better, but still fighting for his life. Kirk left at noon when Viki arrived. I was so glad to see her. I called Grace Jorgensen in North Carolina and told her my scripture verses in Ezekiel. She shouted for joy! I finally committed Jerry totally to the Lord and came home with Viki.

We made plans to return to Danville the next morning. Viki was scheduled to drive Michael and some of his classmates to St. Louis for a field trip the next morning. She explained the situation to his teacher, Bonnie White, and she understood completely. She said she would take personal charge of Michael and bring him back to our home when they got back from St. Louis. He cried and cried when Viki left him. He was concerned about grandpa and wanted to go see him. It was emotionally tough for her to leave Michael and then head to Danville, not knowing what to expect there.

When we got to Danville, we found many doctors including a heart specialist surrounding Jerry's bed. I was scared, but sat in the waiting room, hoping for some good news. Finally Dr. Winter came in and said Jerry had survived a crisis. He was in critical condition, but was improving.

At first Jerry would not look at us when we entered the intensive care unit. Eventually he became more alert and talked to us. His vital signs and arterial blood gas level were good. He was still on oxygen but off the morphine. His arms were black and blue from all of the injections. We finally said good-bye and headed back to Decatur. I called his mother and simply said, "You have your son back."

When Bonnie brought Michael back to our home, she said everyone had prayed for his grandpa. She cried when I shared with her the good news that Jerry was improving. Miracles do happen!

Chris and I returned to the VA Hospital the next day. We found Jerry very depressed. He even cried and said he never wanted to be put on a ventilator again. A nurse told us he was now on a liquid diet and using inhalers instead of getting the prednisone intravenously. We drove back to Decatur and thought our worries were over.

The next morning was Sunday and I decided to attend the morning worship service. After church Cheri picked me up and we took off for Danville. We walked off the elevator just in time to see three nurses taking Jerry up to the cardiac care unit. They thought he was having a massive heart attack.

"No!" I cried. "You will live and God will get the glory."

We were allowed to see him for a few minutes. We found out two of the nurses in the cardiac unit were Christians. One of them took one look at Jerry and proclaimed, "The peace of God is all over this man. He will live!"

Out in the hallway Cheri and I met a doctor from India. He had been called in to check Jerry for kidney failure. He said Jerry's kidneys were okay and his blood pressure was better. He pointed out that Jerry was dehydrated and had overdosed on too much medication, particularly the saline solution. It was not a massive heart attack as originally suspected.

Cheri and I decided to spend the night at the hospital. I called Mike and asked if he would come and bring my pillow and some over night items. He came as quickly as he could, but by the time he got there, our plans had changed. The power company had turned off all the power in the hospital for a seven-hour check-up. The only place that had power was the cardiac unit! It didn't take long for the hospital to cool down so we opted to go home. At least Jerry would be kept warm in the cardiac care unit. What a mighty God we serve! Again we committed Jerry into God's care and drove back to Decatur.

Viki and I arrived in Danville early the next morning. Jerry had been moved back into the intensive care unit. He had survived a terrible reaction to over-medication administered by someone by mistake.

By the next day he was sitting up in a recliner, but could only whisper. He slept on an air foam mattress. The doctor said it might be seven days before Jerry got his strength back. Praise God, he was on an uphill swing!

Viki and I drove back to see him the next day. He had been moved into a room that was two doors down from intensive care. Because he could not talk very loud, he motioned for us to come closer. He had something he wanted us to hear. When he was being hooked up to the ventilator and the power went off, he had an out-of-the-body experience.

"I was floating on the ceiling and remember looking down at all those doctors working on a body. I thought it was my cousin Lee." Jerry and Lee Henneberry had looked a lot alike when they were younger.

"I zoomed in closer and saw it was **my** body lying there. I could see you and Chris praying and rebuking the spirit of death. I was free and didn't want to come back, but I could hear you keep calling my name. In an instant I was back in the body which struggled for air and was wracked in pain."

At this point Jerry looked me in the eye and said, "If I ever start to go again, don't bring me back. I couldn't go through this again."

A short time later Jerry was moved to the Critical Care Unit so he could receive better medical attention than if he was in a regular room. By this time he weighed only 136 pounds and looked like a holocaust victim. He had bruises up and down his arms from all the machines that had been hooked up to him. A nurse told us he was a miracle because he had no chance of survival. Dr. Winter and his assistant said it would be 21 days before Jerry was well enough to be released from the hospital.

During one of our trips while enroute to the hospital, Viki and I head a familiar voice on the car radio. The Christian radio station WBGL was playing a tape Jerry had recorded a year earlier. It was like a voice from the grave! Jerry talked about the future resurrection of our bodies and going home to be with the Lord. What a mighty God we serve! His perfect timing allowed WBGL to play a tape of Jerry's at the same time we were on our way to see him. The station would never know how much it ministered to us.

I tried to keep busy while Jerry recuperated in the hospital. I baked a lot of goodies for the church bake sale that was coming up. I also worked puzzles—did anything to keep my mind off of Jerry.

We went back to see Jerry on Mother's Day. We expected him to be much better but instead the trip was a "downer." Jerry's blood pressure was back up and he was extremely weak. He could barely whisper and was having severe cramping and diarrhea. He had not been able to eat. Not only had ulcerated sores developed on the outside of his mouth where the ventilator was attached, but he had ulcers inside his mouth, throat, down his esophagus and into his stomach's lining. Because he was on so much prednisone, the sores were not healing.

We had the head nurse call Dr. Winter who put him on baby food and gave him some lozenges from his own private stock. By Thursday, Jerry was barely whispering. He wrote a note on his napkin for Dr. Winter. "Help...Reevaluate again."

Jerry was scheduled for physical therapy to help build his

strength back up. I cried as I wheeled him to his appointment. He only weighed 124 pounds–nothing but skin and bones on his six-foot frame.

Cheri went to see her dad in the hospital and decided to call Kim in Montana about his condition. He dropped everything and drove 22 hours straight with Chantelle to the VA Hospital.

Jerry was surprised and very pleased to see Kim and Chantelle. Kim helped his dad get into and out of the shower. He cried when he saw his formerly strong dad in such a pitiful state. "He has no bottom to sit on, mom. No body fat, only bones," he confided to me later.

After a few days I went back to Danville and was allowed to cut Jerry's hair. He shaved himself, but was completely exhausted by the time he got done.

Kim's wife, Libby, and their baby daughter, Katie, flew to Chicago. Kim drove there, picked them up and headed to Danville where they spent some time visiting with Jerry.

That night I received a phone call from Babe who told me to sit down. She had some bad news. Mother finally had a CAT scan and it revealed cancer of the lungs. She had been so weak that Bob and Colleen, had to hold her up to walk. Mother had smoked until she was 80, but quit cold turkey.

When I went to bed that night, I couldn't sleep. I couldn't take much more and cried out to God. "Lord, will it ever end?" Then the Lord quickened to me a poem that I had written several years earlier.

Going Through

Dear Lord, I seek deliverance
    For I cannot go on this way.
The pressures are too heavy
    As I cry to You today.

Oh, how I long to be set free
    And have everything go right,
And have my friends around me
    So I need not fear the night.

My soul lies deep in anguish.
　　　There is so much pain within.
Won't You simply take it away
　　　And let Your light shine in?

Now I see a picture—
　　　Your people pass through a sea.
Though waves surround on every side,
　　　All eyes are fixed on Thee.

The waves are piled higher.
　　　An army forms behind.
Yet Your people triumph
　　　As they march in a solid line.

Step-by-step they release their faith
　　　And are not swept clear away,
But walk on through the tempest
　　　As the Warrior leads the way!

I think You're trying to show me, Lord,
　　　That my battle belongs to You,
And release is far less important
　　　Than Your grace of "going through."

14

"And Thy Household Shall Be Saved"
Acts 16:31

On June 2 I rode in the car with Kim, Libby, Chantelle and baby Katie to Danville. Jerry beamed with pride as he held his latest grandchild. Our visit was interrupted by a telephone call from Kirk back at home. Excitedly he told us someone from Prudential Insurance Company had called about Jerry's early retirement.

"I stalled and said, 'Rev. Henneberry is not in at the moment. May I please take a message?'" Kirk responded. I thanked God for such an intelligent son!

Arrangements were made for Jerry to call "Marge" back at 1 p.m. so she could bring him up-to-date on the paper work. We wheeled Jerry down to a pay phone and prayed that the hospital noises would be drowned out and that Jerry's voice would be strong enough to be heard.

"Marge" said everything was set up and Jerry was now eligible for retirement pay as of June 1. We all shouted for joy when a grinning Jerry remarked, "I passed after all." God had given us another victory!

A day later, Viki, Michael, Sarah and I went to see "Grandpa Berry" and he was doing so much better.

Bad weather hit Decatur and torrential rains dumped tremendous amounts of water on the city. Our church was adversely affected–the ceiling above the recreation room fell in and the basement flooded. A new roof was estimated at $8,000. In addition, the ceiling in the boys' room at the mansion leaked badly. When Jerry called the next day and said he would be released on Thursday to come home, we didn't dare mention to him about the damage at Harvest Christian Center nor at the House of Prayer. We did tell him the good news that

107

the papers arrived from Prudential.

I decided to sit down and write my mother a long letter. She was failing and I did not know how much longer she would live. I poured out my heart to her and told her I loved her. I reminisced over the good times we had. I learned later that my mother had Bob read the letter to her over and over again. She was committed into God's hands.

Thursday arrived but Jerry did not get released. He was running a temperature. We were disappointed, but rejoiced he was able to sign all of the Prudential papers. He wanted to get them in the mail right away. With his weakened condition, we elected not to tell him that the Scherers' toilet on the mansion's third floor was leaking into our second floor bathroom ceiling. There were so many repairs that needed to be done, but Jerry was not in any shape to do them. The less he knew, the less he had to worry about getting them done.

Finally, on Monday, June 16, Jerry was discharged from the hospital. He had been in the hospital for two months–much of it spent recuperating in the critical care unit. He was down to 129 pounds–nothing but skin and bones. Viki drove me up there and we had to wait a long time to get 20 prescriptions filled for him. On our way home we stopped at a rest area so Jerry could use the rest room. I began to worry when it took him so long to come out of the bathroom. He was extremely weak, but finally made it back to the car.

Doug had to help Jerry climb up the many stairs of the mansion. For his homecoming, Cheri made a big sign. "Welcome home, Dad." It was a time of rejoicing! Two months of agony and near death were all behind us. God had given Jerry back to us alive and we all were extremely grateful.

Excitement was mounting in Kirk's family. Jeanette was about to deliver baby number three. The next day, on Viki's 38th birthday, Natalie Joy was born at 4:39 a.m. She weighed 8 pounds and 14 ounces and was 22 ½ inches long. She had blue eyes and black hair.

Joel was not too happy with having another sister. He wanted a baby brother. I tried to console him and commented that God had chosen him to be a big brother to two little sisters. He and cousin Michael would have to be content being the only boys in the family.

Jerry started having headaches and felt as if he was retaining fluids. He made an appointment to see the doctor in Danville. On June 25th, my 58th birthday, we headed back to the hospital. We were told the shocking news that Jerry only had one-third lung capacity. It was a bitter blow to a man who could always overcome anything by sheer willpower. The battle would no longer be his, but the Lord's.

Two days later Babe called. Mother had taken a turn for the worse. She and Roger planned to leave Arkansas early the next morning and head for Winona. All of my family prayed and interceded for mother's soul.

We also prayed for God's perfect timing for my mother's passing away. The Henneberry family reunion was scheduled for July 4 in the park in Macon, Illinois. Family members were coming from all over the country. Since Babe was married to Jerry's brother, they would need to attend Mother's funeral and the family reunion.

On Monday morning, June 29, I received a phone call from Roger. Mother had passed away at 11:30 a.m. The funeral would be in a couple of days. Ironically June 29 was Jerry's mother's 83rd birthday.

I called all of my children and told them the news. Cheri and Mike would try to go to the funeral, but had to get several things done before they could leave. Kirk and Jeanette were tied up with a brand new baby plus Kirk had responsibilities with the church. There was no way Kim and Libby could drive from Montana. Viki would have to stay home and take care of Jerry. Just Chris and I would be able to leave the next morning.

I felt sad and yet relieved that Mother did not have to suffer any more. Babe told me that Mother had requested no life support, only morphine for the pain. Whenever the morphine would wear off, her hands would start shaking. She told of seeing a magnificent light and walking toward it.

From my experience in the occult, I knew that many dying people see a light, but go down to hell. I prayed and asked God if there was any way of knowing that my Mother made it into heaven. I needed the Lord's assurance especially since Jerry would not be at my side during this emotional time.

I opened my King James Bible to Matthew 4:16. *"The people which sat in darkness saw great light; and to them which sat in the*

109

region and shadow of death, light is sprung up. " I knew this light was talking about Jesus and therefore what she saw had to be from heaven and not hell. "Yes, Lord!" I shouted.

Before the day was over I had another confirmation. A bookmark fell out from another Bible that I picked up. It stated, *"They that follow Me shall never walk in darkness."* Hope was stirring within me, but I still needed another witness.

Chris picked me up early the next morning and we made it to Winona in 6 ½ hours. We stopped at Bob and Stefannie's house and planned to stay with them.

Before long it was time to go to the funeral home for the visitation. I saw aunts, uncles and cousins I had not seen in years. At the end of the wake, the rosary was recited. Then an elderly priest stepped forward and announced, "I had the honor of taking Dorothy's hand and introducing her to the Lord Jesus Christ Who was waiting behind the scenes to receive her." Chris and I cried for joy! It was my third confirmation about where my mother was spending her eternity.

No amount of good works, nor church membership nor following various laws can earn a person's way into God's kingdom. Only by becoming like a little child, believing Jesus died on the cross to personally take away your sins and believing He rose from the dead can salvation be obtained.

The next morning we walked into the Cathedral of the Sacred Heart for the funeral Mass being performed by the bishop. The song "Amazing Grace" was being played, and I sang it especially loud. It was a sad time saying "goodby" to my mother, but now I had hope that I would I see her again in heaven.

There was a short grave side service at the cemetery. For a second I glanced down and noticed I was standing on my twin sister, Doris', grave. Just then I glanced upwards and saw a butterfly land briefly on my mother's coffin. It was symbolic of the new life in Christ my mother was experiencing.

After the big funeral dinner, Colleen called me aside and handed me several envelopes. In them were certificate of deposits worth thousands of dollars--my inheritance from Mother. I was in shock! God had granted me favor and let me know that I would be taken care of in the future. For the first time in 18 years I would be able to afford health insurance. Over and over again I praised God for being Jehovah-Jireh, my provider.

Coming home we had car trouble and had to be towed to a garage. The distributor cap needed to be replaced. As a result we arrived in Decatur several hours later than originally planned.

The Henneberry family reunion was still set for July 4 in the park in Macon. Everyone was praying Jerry would be strong enough to go and that it would not be hot and humid. It turned out to be absolutely gorgeous! Jerry sat in a lawn chair and visited for several hours with his brothers and sisters and their children. Several cousins came too. It was a wonderful day that made everyone realize how important it is to have family time together.

Jerry went back to Danville on the following Thursday for a check-up. He now weighed 137 ½ pounds. Dr. Stewart said his case was very complicated, but since he was doing well, he did not have to return until September 10. The only modification to be made was the need to double the heart medicine. Dr. Winter walked in the examining room and was shocked to see Jerry in such good condition. The chaplain also said Jerry was a living miracle.

We decided to get away for a couple of days and drove to Winona on September 25. I presented my brother with a big goose laying a golden egg with the word Fastenal on it. Bob liked it and later gave us a personal tour of Cotter High School. It had an indoor track field, indoor tennis courts and the latest technological advancements for education.

We went to the cemetery where my Dad, Mother and Doris were buried. "Death is so silent," I thought to myself.

Jerry had a very hard time breathing in the motel room we stayed at that night. Every time the heater came on, it seemed to irritate his lungs.

We made it home okay, but I noticed a few days later Jerry was fighting for air to breathe. He could not sleep and was sitting in a chair, trying to get air into his lungs.

Chris and I took him to the Danville Veterans Administration Hospital the next morning. His arterial blood gas level was down to 62 and his blood pressure was 133 over 88. Dr. Robbins admitted him right away and put him on 60 milligrams of prednisone.

The next day Jerry called me and said he was so much better. His laborious breathing was over. Big doses of prednisone always helped to stabilize his breathing, but he had to be weaned down to a minimal amount which in turn started the vicious cycle all over again.

Viki and I drove up the next day to see him. He was in excellent spirits! A nutritionist spent one-half hour informing him the need to limit his intake of salt and fast foods. The doctors were concerned about his heart and wanted him to watch his diet. Two days later Dr. Winter discharged him and told him to get out of there because there were too many diseases available for him to catch.

We decided to go visit the Jorgensens in North Carolina. Jerry always did all the driving, but now it especially gave him a feeling of independence that he desperately needed.

The closer we got to the Smokey Mountains, I began to reminisce about a poem I had written on July 24, 1989, about Grace and Jorgy's beautiful haven of retreat. I was eagerly looking forward to our "pilgrim's rest."

Pilgrim's Rest

Nestled high among the mountains
    God's sanctuary awaits–
Undaunted by the world,
    A retreat for tiring saints.

They come from all directions–
    North, south, east and west.
These birds of different feathers,
    Seeking their souls to rest.

The fearless tufted titmouse
    Greets the chickadee,
Then mingles with the mockingbird
    High in the lofty trees.

In the midst of early morning
....With joy ever expanding,
Creation pauses for a moment
....As a heron glides in for a landing!

A hummingbird fans into view
....Then quickly darts away,
While a goldfinch and a flicker
....Bask in the soft sun rays.

It is here God gathers His children
....Who come to this haven to dine.
They feed upon His loving Word
....And drink of His holy new wine.

They carry this seed ever onward,
....Seeking the lowly and meek,
Chirping the praise of God's glory
....And the "Grace" of Middle Creek!

As I thought about all of the birds, I quietly asked the Lord if I could possibly see one robin at the Jorgensens. If I did, then I would know that Jerry was going to be all right. We had hardly set down our luggage in the living room when Grace shouted, "Look out the window, Dottie. The trees are filled with robins! We've never had robins migrate here before." I wanted to believe this was a sign from God that Jerry was going to live.

We stayed downstairs, but the cold damp air affected Jerry's breathing so Grace suggested we move to an upstairs bedroom. That helped greatly! Before we knew it, it was time to head back to Decatur. As we said our goodbyes, I wondered if this would be Jerry's and my last trip together. I didn't know when I would ever see the Jorgensens again.

We stopped in Clarksville, Tennessee, so that I could shop at a mall. It was a sacrifice on Jerry's part, but he was so patient with me. He battled the cold blustery wind and would suffer for it later with a hacking cough and headache.

We made it home, but soon faced another trial in the family. Viki slipped in the church basement and used her left elbow to brace her fall. She ended up fracturing the elbow and had to put her arm in a sling for several weeks. She was concerned that she would have to wear a cast, but Dr. Kraus said if there was ever a bone a person could break and not have to be casted, it was the elbow bone. Praise the Lord!

Jerry also injured one of his elbows. He slightly bumped it and the skin came off, but he never complained.

Days later we received a phone call from Laurie who worked in an office at the VA Hospital. Excitedly, she asked if Jerry could possibly go to the University of Illinois medical building on Thursday morning. Dr. Winter wanted to present his case to the medical students. Jerry agreed, but had to be checked by a doctor before being allowed to go with Dr. Winter.

Jerry's arterial blood gas level was good, but his blood pressure was up. He was well enough to make the trip to Champaign so a van was ordered that would take Jerry, two other male patients, Dr. Winter and his wife, and me.

Dr. Winter's wife was bubbling with excitement! She told me this was the day her husband treasured the most when he could share his knowledge with the new generation of potential doctors at the university.

I sat in the audience with the medical students who were allowed to ask questions at the end of Dr. Winter's presentation. He spent about one to five minutes describing the conditions of the other two patients, but he took 35 minutes dealing with Jerry's case. He introduced Jerry as a minister and said something about Jerry even trying to make him "religious." I gave a silent "Amen" to that!

While waiting for an elevator, I told Mrs. Winter that her husband saved my husband's life. I shared about Jerry's out-of-the-body experience. Her eyes lit up and she said she would love to hear more. I asked her if she had read my book *Fortress on a Hill* which I had given to her husband. She did not know anything about it. A few days later I received a personal letter from Dr. Winter saying his wife was avidly reading the book. He planned to keep it in his own private office.

On December 11 Jerry turned 63 years old. On that same day we received word from Dr. Ronald YaDeau in the Music Department at Millikin University that a student named Rick Weber agreed to write out the music notes for the songs in our musical *Voyage*.

When Rick arrived at our house, he wondered what he was getting himself into. He had never met a family like ours! It wasn't long before we developed a kindred spirit and knew he was the man God had sent to do the job.

The church Christmas program was December 20. I read two poems I had written and gave glory and thanksgiving to Father God that Jerry was still with us. It was a very sobering moment.

Jerry and I did our Christmas shopping early. He bought me a big glider walker and I bought him a big blue recliner for our bedroom. He stayed home from church on Wednesday night and decided to assemble the entire glider. Because he put it together downstairs, he had to drag it all the way upstairs to our bedroom—one step at a time. Oh, what a lovely man I had married!

Christmas Eve was the next day and all the family members planned to gather at the mansion for the big gift exchange at 7 p.m. At exactly 6:45 p.m. the doorbell rang. Very reluctantly I went downstairs to answer the door, muttering to myself, "Who dares to interfere with our family get-together tonight?"

Lo and behold, there stood Kim and his family, grinning from ear to ear! They had traveled 22 hours straight to get there in time for the holiday gathering. It was the first time in 10 years that all of my children, their spouses and grandchildren were together for Christmas. It was also the first time in three years that Jerry was there to celebrate with us. He was the center of attention! It was a wonderful time and we took one and one-half hours to open all of the presents.

Everyone gathered together again the next day for a big turkey dinner and to have a family picture taken. A separate picture was taken of all the grandchildren. The vote was unanimous—this was the best Christmas ever! Thank You, Jesus!

15

Butterflies Are Free

Kim and Libby stayed long enough to help put in a new kitchen floor. Jerry and Libby figured out how to cut it and then the men did the work. It was finished just in time for the House of Prayer's board meeting where goals would be set for 1993.

Jerry's breathing became more labored as the days went on. He missed several Sunday services. Finally, on January 21 he called Danville, but there was no answer in the pulmonary office. We decided to wait it out and see if Jerry would get better on his own.

The next day I cooked some t-bone steaks in the broiler of my new stove. It smoked terrible and affected Jerry's breathing. He had a full blown asthma attack. He called the Veterans Hospital, only to be told by three people that they would not increase his prednisone dosage.

Three days later he was very short of air and stayed in bed a long time. He showered, but the steam bothered his breathing. He finally called Danville and spoke to Laurie. She set up an appointment for him at 11 a.m. the next day.

Chuck in pulmonary admitted Jerry to the hospital even before examining him. "Asthma is so critical in Jerry's case," he remarked.

Dr. Winter walked in the room with a pretty nurse and told Jerry to "enjoy his stay" for the next few days. He would be well taken care of!

Three days later Jerry called and said he was being released the next day. He was ready and waiting when we got there. We stopped at a restaurant for dinner and even shopped at a mall. By the time we got home, Jerry was short of air and coughing.

Viki greeted us with the wonderful news that Michael had just broken out with the chickenpox. He had been exposed numerous times before, but never got them. It was just a matter of time before Sarah would have them.

Sarah celebrated her fourth birthday in our bedroom. It was difficult for Jerry to climb the stairs to the Scherers' living quarters on third floor. She shouted with delight when she found her new bicycle hidden away in our closet.

Sarah was great "therapy" for Grandpa Berry. She would get up early in the morning and run downstairs to our bedroom to play Old Maid, Go Fish, Are You My Mother? or the Strawberry Shortcake game. Jerry would get out of his big chair and sit on the floor, playing games with Sarah. Sometimes he would read a book to her.

The Last Roundup, the new skit book which I wrote, was finally published, but needed to be bound. Jerry was determined to help punch the page holes and bind the books. It was too cold downstairs so he did it on our dining room table, resting after every few books. He got the books done just before the Peoria Sunday School convention.

Viki and Kirk left Decatur to set up the House of Prayer's exhibit booth at the convention. It had started snowing, but they were determined to get to the Peoria Civic Center and then head back before it got too late. On their way home they drove in blizzard conditions. Eight inches of snow met them when they arrived back at the House of Prayer. Viki had to turn around early the next morning and drive me to the convention so we could man our booth. Snow was piled everywhere and the roads were icy. We saw many cars off in the ditches. God had His angels watching over us when we hit some ice on the bridge. We made it safely, but noticed the adverse weather conditions affected the attendance.

Late that evening we left the convention center and drove to our motel, only to discover we did not have a reservation according to management. I called Jerry and he verified we did indeed have a reservation because he called it in. A Christian man, who also had an exhibit at the Sunday School convention, was in the motel lobby at the same time as us and offered us his room. Finally the management gave us a room where the pipes banged all night and there was no sound on

117

the television set. The next morning we turned on the tv anyway and saw where the World Trade Center in New York had just been bombed.

In March Jerry was having a hard time breathing so he was put on antibiotics. To occupy my time, I decided to design an early spring display for the church bulletin board. I made two kites, cut out the letters "I'll fly away, oh glory" and mounted them.

Jerry continued to have breathing problems. My friend, Pat Kelm, expressed her concern and we concluded Jerry needed to go to Danville, but I didn't want him out in the terrible snowy weather. Doug and Viki had just returned from the St. Louis Airport to pick up Jerry's mother and commented how treacherous the trip home was.

The next night Jerry called me into our bedroom. It was 2 a.m. and he was sitting up to breathe. He spoke to me very softly, "I may not make it this time." We held each other for a long time and finally I said, "But I still believe in miracles."

I called Laurie at the VA Hospital early the next morning and explained the situation. She said one word, "Come." Viki drove the 90 miles as quickly as she could. By the time we got Jerry to Danville, his arterial blood gas level had dropped to 67. Dr. Robbins said we should have taken Jerry there two weeks earlier. He was placed in intensive care where another man was struggling to breathe on a ventilator. I felt sorry for Jerry having to witness that scene because it brought back horrible memories from Jerry's own experience a year earlier.

Two days later on Tuesday I called Danville and was told Jerry had very little sleep and was not able to eat. His vital signs, however, were good.

The next day I planned to have Viki drive me back up to Danville, but Sarah was running a high temperature and the wind chill was -5 degrees below zero. She had tonsillitis. Just then the phone rang and it was someone from Danville calling to inform me that Jerry was being moved to another room. My heart went to the pit of my stomach! The room he was in was too noisy and he was not getting any rest. His vital signs were good and he had even walked to a chair. His arterial blood gas level was also good.

On Thursday morning, March 18, Kirk and I drove up to Danville. I raced through the hospital hall looking for Jerry's name on the door, but couldn't find it anywhere. It was as though I had been thrown against the wall. "This is the beginning of the end," I thought to myself.

We found Jerry back in the intensive care unit. Jerry had a relapse and his arterial blood gas level was dangerously low. Dr. Winter came out into the hallway and told me he was sending Jerry up to the Cardiac Care Unit. I wheeled Jerry up there. Dr. Winter left it up to us if we wanted to spend the night there or drive back home. He said he lived only four minutes away from the hospital and the nurses would be in touch with him during the night. Kirk and I opted to go home. He was optimistic that Jerry could still pull through.

Early the next morning Dr. Winter called with the words, "Come quickly. Jerry is dying." The nurses had called him three or four times during the night about Jerry's condition.

It was decided that Kirk would drive me immediately and then Viki, Chris and Cheri would leave Decatur around noon to come up.

When we arrived at the hospital, we were ushered into a small room. Dr. Winter said Jerry had gone into shock. Bacteria had now entered his bloodstream. The doctor then asked us about life support.

"No," I emphatically said.

"And no ventilator. He wants to be set free."

Kirk and I went in to see him. The nurses had tenderly bathed him and dressed him in pale blue pajamas instead of the old brown ones. Blue was his favorite color!

Jerry reached over and took my hand in his and tenderly kissed it, mouthing these words slowly and painfully between breathing oxygen, "I love you." The words that he couldn't say all those years were now coming from his heart that was rapidly deteriorating.

A dinner tray was brought in, but he couldn't eat anything. He was concerned about me and insisted I eat the dessert.

"That's my husband, always thinking of the other person," I reflected.

At one point Kirk told him we would all gladly give him one of our lungs if we could.

"But if you had one of mine, you'd be lopsided and complain," I quipped.

119

I reminisced how Jerry and I met at a party when I was 16 and he was 21 years old. He had told another man that he was going to date the prettiest girl there and I ended up being that girl. We had 39 years together.

Finally the girls arrived and Jerry rallied. He had a puzzled look on his face and beckoned me near.

"Who called?" he whispered.

"Dr. Winter," I replied.

Then he knew what we knew. With tears splashing everywhere, I held him close and said, "As much as we've prayed and believed for a miracle, the miracle is...you're going home."

Later I learned that I wrote the song "I'm Going Home" one year earlier on that same day of March 19 when my neighbor friend, Lula, died. Grief stricken, I could not sing that song right then to Jerry. My heart was aching and the words just stuck in my throat.

At one point Jerry asked what day it was. I replied it was March 19 which in the Catholic Church was St. Joseph's Day and also the day the swallows come back to Capistrano.

We asked a Christian nurse for some oil and gathered around Jerry to pray for him. At the end of our prayer, he somehow raised himself up to a sitting position and said he too wanted to pray. His only prayer was one word "strength" and then he gave us the salute of two thumbs up. Everything was okay and he was ready to go home.

Chris, Kirk and Cheri said their goodbyes and drove back to Decatur. Viki stayed with me in the room. We both prayed, sang songs and quoted scripture verses to Jerry. I actually sang one chorus over and over again, not knowing if I had the correct words. Only later did I realize how perfect it was for the present situation.

> *"I will sing praise unto the Lord.*
> *I will sing praise as long as I have my being.*
> *My meditation shall be sweet.*
> *I will rejoice in the Lord and be glad.*
>
> *Bless now the Lord, oh my soul,*
> *Praise ye the Lord.*

Bless now the Lord, oh my soul,
Praise ye the Lord."

At 4 p.m. Dr. Winter came in and said he had to leave for an out-of-state conference. He had stayed at the hospital as long as he could. His replacement was to be the very doctor who tried to tell me that Jerry's condition was psychosomatic. I asked if there was any way Dr. Robbins could be there instead. I was relieved to hear Dr. Robbins was on his way.

Jerry began to slip in and out of consciousness as Viki read the Psalms and other scripture verses to him. His eyes remained opened the whole time. I started to dose in the chair.

We had been watching the heart and blood pressure monitors all afternoon and evening. The numbers were low but there was not much fluctuation.

Around 9 p.m. two nurses came in and asked us to step out into the hall while they turned Jerry over. We were only gone a few minutes when a tall man came walking down the hall and looked at us intently. The phone where we were sitting rang and the nurse told us to come quickly.

We raced into the room and saw the numbers on Jerry's monitors go down to zero. The heart monitor had a line straight across. Jerry's eyes were still opened and he was looking upward. I held him in my arms and said, "Jerry, Jesus is here with all the angels and saints to take you to heaven. We're just jealous that we're not going with you."

I turned to the tall man, who was the chaplain, and explained. "Jerry used to say that at all the funerals he performed."

Viki gently pulled me away. "Come, mom, we have a lot to do yet. Dad is no longer here." By then the nurses were even crying.

I started out the door, but turned around for one last look at my beloved husband who was lying on his side, still looking upward.

Viki and I met with a hospital employee to make arrangements for Jerry's body to be brought to Decatur. We then started the long drive home in cold, pouring rain. We started planning a funeral that would draw others to Jesus Christ.

Such emotions engulfed me! I was a widow at 58. Life would have to go on without Jerry by my side. He would never have to worry about the weather or anything else. He was free...free as a butterfly as he flew home to the Lord Jesus Christ he had served so faithfully and loved so very, very much.

16

The Oil of Gladness for Mourning

We arrived home from Danville after midnight. Doug was still waiting up for us. We stood briefly in the Scherers' living room as I shared Jerry's homecoming. I put my hand in my coat pocket and pulled out two items. One was Jerry's wedding ring and the other item was the two dollar watch he wore. A nurse asked me to remove them. I believe it was the first time Jerry's ring was ever off his finger.

I didn't sleep much that night. I kept asking, "Why, Lord, why? Why are the good always removed from the earth so early in life?" Then I remembered that Jesus ministered on earth for only three and one-half years and died at the age of 33. And He was the Son of God!

The next morning I called Dr. McGhee and he prescribed something for me to sleep. I then called our neighbor, Elmira Sparr, and asked if she and her mother could cook two turkeys for all of the relatives and friends we would be having come in.

Viki, Chris, Kirk, Cheri and I proceeded to the funeral home to make the arrangements. A young man named Mike made it all a lot easier than I thought it would be. We decided on a beautiful oak coffin for Jerry who would be dressed in blue. Burial would be on Decatur's east side at North Fork Cemetery, not far from the honeymoon house on Melwood Avenue that Jerry bought for us. Viki and Kim used to ride their bikes in the cemetery during the summer. Our next door neighbor on Melwood used to pastor the North Fork Church adjacent to the cemetery.

Even death could not interfere with my appointment at the beauty shop. A young girl named Becky walked in while I was there.

She was one of many that we had helped during our early years of ministry. She was stunned that Jerry had died and came to the visitation with a beautiful rose in his memory.

Back home we began the preparations for a house full of people. We cleaned and set up tables for those who would be eating there after the funeral on Monday.

Kim, Libby and their girls arrived from Montana around 9:45 p.m. that evening. Kim told me he had had a dream that Jerry was going to die and that was why they drove 22 hours straight to be with us for the previous Christmas holiday. He had released Jerry then to go home to be with the Lord.

Kim needed dress clothes for the visitation and funeral. The Lord blessed! All of Jerry's clothes fit him, including his shoes.

Sunday morning at Harvest Christian Center was a memorial service in Jerry's honor. Kirk stated his dad was "perfect" and kiddingly said his dad often told him that. Kim sat with me and stood up to eulogize his father, but broke down and cried.

There was not an evening service at Harvest because the visitation was scheduled for three hours. Just before we left to go to the funeral home, I remembered I had not called my friend Frances Roberts who wrote *Come Away My Beloved*. When I told her it was Dottie, she gasped, "You have been on my mind all day. I was just going to call you." I rejoiced that my heavenly Father intertwines hearts and lives together with a kindred spirit so we can bear each other's burdens.

People stood in line for an hour to pay tribute to Jerry. He looked so handsome. He didn't have to suffer any more. Somehow God gave me the strength I needed. It was very hard on his mother, however, losing her first born who had taken such good care of her since she was widowed in 1973.

The funeral was set for 1:30 p.m. on Monday afternoon. The morning gave us all time to prepare as different family members were going to have a part in the funeral service.

When we arrived at the funeral home, Jerry's sister, Connie, presented me with a great big red rose from her son Ryan. He couldn't be there, but wanted uncle Jerry to have it. Connie said she did not know what to do with it, but I said I did.

Finally the service started. Kim and Libby recorded earlier the songs which most touched Jerry's life. Kim said he did not think he could sing them in front of everyone because he was afraid he would break down. He and Libby sang "He Touched Me," "Great Is Thy Faithfulness" and Kim's own arrangement of "Psalm 23." Doug played "Amazing Grace" on his trumpet. Every time Doug practiced the song at home, Michael cried. By the time Doug got done playing several verses, there was hardly a dry eye in the funeral home. Kirk did a wonderful job of eulogizing Jerry and praising his family members for the wonderful heritage they instilled in him.

When it was my turn to speak, I shared about the last hours of Jerry's life. I read the poem "Courage" that I had written a few years earlier. True courage is finally saying, "Lord may Thy will be done."

Next I shared my poem "Assorted Roses" that I had written on the last day of winter in 1978 while sitting on the back steps of our house, watching the last bit of snow slowly melt away. I shared with everyone that Jerry died on the last day of winter and symbolically we slowly watched his body "melt away."

Assorted Roses

As a rose I grew in the garden of life,
Till I met a Gardener so fair.
He was gathering beautiful roses
And selected them with great care.

His face was lovely to look upon;
I could hardly turn away.
Then I saw that His hands were pierced
As He held them up to pray.

What grace surrounded this beautiful Man
As ever so gently He walked.
He picked up a baby pink rosebud
As ever so sweetly He talked.

125

Next he chose an American beauty,
Its red was as crimson as blood.
I knew somewhere inside of me
This Man was someone I loved.

I waited so patiently, hid by others,
As this Gardener came closer to me.
I watched Him choose a yellow rose
While He shouted in heavenly glee!

Soon He was standing in front of me.
He seemed to pause for awhile.
I peeked my head for a better look
And believed I saw Him smile!

I quickly bowed my head in shame
For my beauty was badly faded.
My petals were all torn and tattered
As my past had been darkly shaded.

I heard a sigh and looked again
For my Gardener had shed a tear.
It fell upon my entire being
As He held me so tender and dear.

I gasped as I saw my appearance
Change into a lovely white rose.
I cried that my beautiful Gardener
Picked me as the flower He chose!

"Assorted Roses," *Lost in His Loveliness* ©1979 Dottie Henneberry

Then I took the lovely red rose from our nephew Ryan and walked over to Jerry's body in the casket. I tenderly spoke these words as I lay the flower across Jerry's chest. "Farewell, my beloved. Well done, thou good and faithful servant. Now enter into the rest that the

Lord has prepared for you. And may you smell the roses forever."

When Jerry was sick was asthma, we could not bring roses or any other flowers into the room where he was. After the funeral I had the funny thought that when I finally see Jerry in heaven his first words will be, "Woman, why did you put that silly rose on me."

Chris stood up for the grand finale of the funeral. She was going to do sign language to Ray Boltz's song "Thank You for Giving to the Lord."

The funeral home was packed with people from all walks of life including teachers, businessmen, ministers and wonderful Christian friends. An overflow room had to be opened to accommodate everyone. Those who knew Chris was going to sign the song were betting she couldn't finish it without emotionally breaking down. On the very last chorus, Chris turned and signed the song specifically to her dad in the coffin.

"Thank you for giving to the Lord. I am a life that was changed. Thank you for giving to the Lord. I am so glad you gave."

There was not a dry eye in the place. Jerry had led to the Lord many of those present or had touched their lives in a powerful way. So many people came up to my family afterwards and said they had never been to a funeral like that in all of their lives. What a testimony to God's saving grace!

As we started to leave the funeral home, Cleta Perkins, who headed up a prayer ministry in Decatur, came up to me and whispered these words of encouragement. "And you have the courage of which you spoke."

By the time we got to the cemetery, it was pouring down rain. Veterans fired a twenty-one gun salute and one of them played taps. It was a solemn, tearful moment as we said our last goodbyes, but I knew Jerry was up in heaven celebrating. The veterans presented me with a carefully folded American flag and the shells from the guns that were fired.

Family members and friends joined us back at the House of Prayer for a time of fellowship. Elmira Sparr, her mother and several women from church had been busy getting the dinner ready. It was time for the healing process to begin. Life would go on.

Later that night after everyone had left, Kim, Kirk, Doug and the Jorgensens gathered upstairs in my bedroom to help go through Jerry's clothes. Kim and Jorgy were the exact same size as Jerry. We would laugh a lot and then cry as we went through things. Michael got grandpa's pocket knife, a shell from the veterans' gun salute and grandpa's favorite blue hat.

Eventually Jerry's stationary bicycle, the dehumidifier and air purifier would come out of the bedroom. All of these reminders of the past would not be needed now.

Before closing my eyes in sleep that night, I opened Charles Spurgeon's book *Morning and Evening Daily Readings* to March 22. Words that comforted me were found in John 17:24–the evening verse. *"Father, I will that they also, whom Thou hast given Me, be with Me where I am."* The reading opened with an anguished cry about losing a loved one. *"Why does thou snatch away the excellent of the earth, in whom is all our delight?"* God's answer was that Jesus was praying in the opposite direction. *"'Father, I will that they also, whom Thou hast given Me, be with Me where I am.' Lord, Thou shalt have them. By faith we let them go."* Silently and halfheartedly, I let Jerry go.

Reality set in the next day. It was time to get the lock box out and start going through important papers. Kirk took me to the Veteran's Office and we ordered a copper tombstone that was free. The word "Reverend" would be engraved on it.

The chaplain from the Danville Veteran's Administration Hospital called and expressed his condolences to me. Dr. Winter also called and said how sorry he was that he couldn't be there for Jerry when he passed away. I thanked him and his staff for giving Jerry to us for three and one-half years. I also told him we willingly gave Jerry up because no one could bear to watch him suffer any longer. Before he hung up, Dr. Winter remarked, "God bless you."

Two days later Viki and I started tackling the desk drawers and Jerry's cabinets. Viki became my right arm. All of the strength, wisdom and confidence that Jerry had were now very apparent in Viki who was our first born.

We went through boxes of Jerry's medicine. We gave some of the new inhalers that had never been used to our family doctor. The majority of the pills were flushed down the toilet. "Jerry doesn't need these anymore," we gleefully shouted.

God's timing was perfect. I opened a drawer in my desk and found a cassette tape that was dated November 1989. I decided to play it and heard Jerry addressing the church body at Harvest Christian Center on a Sunday morning. He told the congregation he had been praying and fasting for many days. He asked God to take his life and use it for His glory so that others would come to know Jesus Christ as their Lord and Savior. I raced to my diary to find out about that day's activities and was stunned to read the two words "suffering ahead" which I had written after hearing that sermon.

In the ensuing days I emotionally held up pretty good until Easter Sunday when the congregation sang "Because He Lives" by Bill and Gloria Gaither. The last verse made me break. *"And then some day, I'll cross that river. I'll fight life's final war with pain. And then as death gives way to victory, I'll see the lights of glory and I'll know He lives."*

God gave me a beautiful poem that fused all of my feelings together as I faced the future without my constant companion by my side.

Milestone

I watched in utter amazement
    As my husband drew his last breath.
A pounding heart now silenced,
    While I in sorrow wept.

It was the saddest moment of my life
    As time stood still for me,
Yet for him, his greatest triumph
    As he sailed toward eternity.

Gone but not forgotten
    With memories so sweet,
But I must carry on alone
    For my work is incomplete.

129

Now in my dreams I search for him,
Yet can't find him anywhere.
I keep looking upward though,
And toward the heavens stare.

Some day I'll see my bridegroom
When my life on earth is done.
I'll fly in the eastern direction
Of the brilliant blazing Son!

17

Pruning Hurts, Lord

With Jerry gone, a new president needed to be elected to the House of Prayer Ministries, Inc. board of directors. Kirk was unanimously voted in. Although Kirk would be president, Viki would officially run the publishing aspect of the ministry. They would operate two ministries without their late father.

I wasn't ready for Kirk's decision to move his church office out of the House of Prayer and into Harvest Christian Center. Kirk would not be coming to the mansion as often and it made me wonder if I would need an "appointment" to see him. I realized that I had gone from the role of "pastor's wife" to "pastor's mother." I had to let go of the reigns and let a new generation take over. To be honest, it wasn't easy.

On the positive side I learned that I would be eligible for one-half of Jerry's Social Security when I reached 60 which was two years away.

I found more cassette tapes of Jerry's sermons and listened to them on Monday afternoons when I ironed clothes to take to the resale shops. I was surprised how many of the sermons dealt with death and his wanting to be home with the Lord.

On Saturday, April 24, it started storming, but I was determined to go to Jerry's burial site and see if the grave marker was up yet. When the rain let up, Doug, Viki, Michael, Sarah and I raced to the cemetery. There was no marker, but we brought a little white cross that Doug pounded into the ground. I had painted "Pa Pa Berry" on it and attached two blue roses and seven pink roses for the two grandsons and seven granddaughters. It was such an emotional time for me--I had to reason with myself that Jerry really wasn't there.

Kirk, Viki and I studied several health insurance plans for me and finally settled on one. A male nurse was supposed to interview me and take some tests. I stalled setting up an appointment because I had tremendous pain on my lower right side that went clear around my back. I could hardly walk down the steps at the mansion. Although I had been having the pain for some time, I ignored it because of all we were going through with Jerry. Now the pain intensified and always seemed to be worse at night.

One evening I received my first phone call from someone asking to speak to Jerry. I broke down and cried because that person had no idea Jerry was no longer with us. Just then I heard the scurrying of tiny feet across my dining room ceiling and into another room. "Squirrels have gotten in and they will just have to be removed," I remarked out loud. I talked a lot to myself, but justified my actions because I was now a widow and could get by with it.

I went to the doctor the next day and found out I had a bad sinus infection. He prescribed an antibiotic. While I was gone, Viki called Nelson's Pest Control to see about removing the squirrels running through the ceiling rafters and down the walls. Our black cat Midnight went nuts listening to the scurrying noise. A serviceman came out and told Viki it would be very difficult to capture the squirrels in the three-story mansion. We soon learned that our critters were actually "masked bandits."

About 3 a.m. one morning we were awakened by a terrible noise. A broken flower pot was lying on the stairway going up to second floor. The window screen was ripped. Midnight was growling fiercely. We went back to bed and when we got up in the morning there was evidence of a big fight in the house. Viki found raccoon fur in the hallway.

Later that night Viki could not sleep because of all the noise in the third floor ceiling. She got up, went out into the stairway hallway, turned the light on and looked up at the ceiling attic fan. Two masked critters stared back at her! It seems the raccoon Jerry and I had fed and named Zorro was actually a female who had babies and took up occupancy at the mansion.

Someone told Doug to put mothballs up in the cupola and that would help get rid of the raccoons. Instead, the "little darlings" took great delight batting them across the floor. Midnight went crazy listening to them! When the temperature turned 95 degrees, the smell of the mothballs about asphyxiated us. The only way we could get rid of the raccoons was by setting a trap. We borrowed one from a church member and with the lure of a chicken leg smeared with peanut butter tied inside, we caught the raccoons one-by-one. Doug drove them far outside the city limits and let them go.

I met Pat Kavanaugh, a friend from the past, at a parking lot on May 1 and poured my heart out to her. She knew what suffering was all about. She and her husband had lost their three-year-old son to cancer. Her last words to me before we departed was "Remember, Dottie, be good to yourself." I desperately needed that advice in the days ahead.

I was in severe pain on my right lower side and could not do any physical work. My good friend from church, Linda Jimison, came and helped vacuum the house. Somehow she managed to open the windows in my bedroom which had not been opened the three and one-half years Jerry was sick with asthma.

The next day I was worse and stayed in bed. Viki did not want to leave me alone so she called our neighbor Elmira Sparr to come and "babysit." I took over-the-counter medication, but nothing stopped the pain. I had a temperature and would chill and then sweat. I was also very nauseated.

On May 6 I went to see Dr. McGhee who thought I had a kidney infection. He said he could treat me at home if I promised to drink "gallons" of water and stay in bed. Viki was to be my cook and 24-hour nurse maid.

Three days later was Mother's Day. Jerry's mother and my family all gathered at the mansion for dinner. They bought fried chicken from a restaurant and I ate it for a couple of days. The pain became more intense and I had diarrhea.

On Monday Viki called Dr. McGhee who agreed to see me right away. He suspected kidney stones. I didn't think I was going to make it. I went to the hospital for x-rays and blood work. At home that night I cried to the Lord, "God, I cannot endure much more."

To my great astonishment, the report came back the next day–no kidney stones and hardly any infection in the urinalysis. My doctor called me the "mystery woman."

Although Dr. McGhee was off the next day, Viki called the office anyway. He happened to be in and said to come right away. I couldn't sit in the chair because I was in so much pain. This time he asked me what foods I had been eating. When I told him fried chicken, he announced, "It's your gallbladder and it has to come out."

It was too late to do an ultrasound. I would have to wait until Thursday to get one. Finally, my pain was going to come to an end. That night was the longest night. I couldn't sleep and the pain was intense. I put a pillow between my legs and one behind my back, but that did not seem to help. I kept the television on to try to keep my mind off of the pain.

Suddenly at 4 a.m. I was startled to see the city of Ismay, Montana, splash across the screen. That was the big town of 18 people where Kim and Libby lived. As a promotional gimmick, someone wanted to rename a city in Montana as Joe after the famous Kansas City Chiefs football star Joe Montana. Ismay was selected because it had a Post Office and the postmark would say Joe, Montana. A big celebration was planned and Joe Montana Day was proclaimed. In return, the residents of Ismay would be flown to a Kansas City Chiefs football game. Sports Illustrated did a story on the name change and published a photo of the Ismay residents. Kim and Chantelle were pictured. He told us later the magazine photographer shot pictures all day which proved to be hard on baby Katlin so Libby took her back home. Kim noted that a lot of strangers showed up and claimed to be citizens of Ismay for the day. I was so proud of my son being in Sports Illustrated that we bought all the copies we could find!

When Thursday morning finally came, I was in indescribable pain. I called my brother, Bob, to tell him my predicament, but all I got was his answering machine. I briefly stated that I was writhing in pain and the gallbladder was suspected. I mentioned that I did not have any health insurance yet.

Viki got me to the hospital for the ultrasound test and then brought me home. My neighbor Elmira stayed with me again. My friend Eileen called and gave me strict orders not to do anything, absolutely nothing, until I had my gallbladder removed.

Viki called the doctor's office and learned the doctor had just called the hospital to find out the results. It was gallstones! I was so relieved to finally find out the diagnosis and decided to admit myself to the hospital. There were no guarantees a surgeon would be there, but I could not live with the pain any longer.

God had His man waiting in the wings. Dr. Scott Sherwood was on duty and came in to see me around 4:40 p.m. Betty Rush from church had him do her gallbladder surgery and recommended him. He looked at my x-rays and scheduled surgery for the following morning.

Sharing the room with me was a little lady named Helen, who had hip surgery. We shared a lot. Around midnight the nurse came in to give me some more pain medication. I was crying softly and told her that it was exactly eight weeks to the day that I had lost my husband. Helen turned the television on and I heard a familiar voice. It was my son, Kirk, talking on the Christian tv station. I had forgotten he was to be the guest all week on a local program. He was sharing about the great loss of his father.

Finally I conked out and got some much needed sleep. When I woke up I noticed my body was lying straight out, the first time in weeks. The pain killers had done their job well.

The nurses got me prepped for surgery. I was given more medication, an electro-cardiogram was given and my legs were put in hose with an electrical current applied. I was wheeled down to surgery.

For a brief moment I knew how Jerry must have felt lying in the hospital bed. He knew he was dying, but release from suffering was just ahead. I knew when I woke up from surgery, my pain would be gone and I would be free.

After spending time in the recovery room, I was wheeled down the corridor on a stretcher. Chris was by my side. She told me Dr. Sherwood had removed one huge gallstone the size of a golf ball that had been lodged in the bile duct. That was the reason my pain was in the lower part of my body and caused my back to hurt. Amazingly, the doctor was able to remove the stone and my diseased gallbladder with laser surgery. Instead of having to be cut open, only five little marks remained by my belly button.

Cheri came to see me and fed me some sherbet. I had an IV and felt a little pain under my right rib. I was given a hypo that night and slept like a baby. I was so glad it was all over.

The next day I was given some soft foods. I got up and walked the halls. I had a few bouts of diarrhea and passed a lot of orange bile. I believe there was a lot of poison in my system.

My brother called and talked for 10 minutes. When he was 45 years old he experienced a tremendous amount of pain and admitted himself to a hospital. He ended up passing a kidney stone. When he got home, he passed another one. He then asked about my financial picture. In closing he mentioned a check was on the way. I nearly leaped out of bed shouting for joy!

Dr. Sherwood came in and said the gallbladder was very abnormal and needed to come out. The stone was 1½ inches in diameter, about the size of a large jawbreaker. I told him I wanted to give it to my daughter-in-law Libby for her classroom. He checked with the laboratory, but someone had already taken it.

I was released from the hospital on Saturday afternoon. I gave the doctor an autographed copy of my book *Fortress on a Hill*. The drain and IV were removed and I was free to go home. For the first time in months I did not have any pain climbing the stairs at the mansion. It seemed strange, though, not having Jerry meet me.

Eileen told me later about her concern regarding my gallbladder. Her mother-in-law had writhed on the floor for three days and died from gallbladder disease. I was indeed blessed to have survived!

I got stronger and the pain was gone, but I continued having cramps and diarrhea. Viki took me back to Dr. Sherwood and he suspected irritable bowel syndrome. He ordered an upper GI series of tests. While having the procedure, I mentioned to the nurse about the big gallstone I had.

"Oh, you're the one who had the whopper," she commented.

Apparently, everyone in the lab had heard about it, but no one knew who took it. Somehow it had disappeared.

Everything was okay on the upper GI tests, so the lower series were ordered. I still had no medical insurance to pay for these procedures. I was in so much pain after the lower test that I had to call Kirk to come and get me.

When I went back to Dr. McGhee, I discovered I had diverticulitis. I would have to be very careful about the foods I ate. I learned that 50 percent of the women over the age of 50 have this disease. The doctor gave me a prescription for the cramping.

My sister Babe called and said Roger had been in the intensive care unit for three days. His asthma had kicked in and his arterial blood gas level was very low. He had been on oxygen, but was getting better. Immediately I thought back to Jerry and how he had suffered with asthma.

"Oh Lord," I cried when I hung up the phone. "How I hate growing old. I long for the day when we shall all have a glorified body and rule and reign with You!"

18

Life Goes On

On June 10 a wonderful, precious "saint" went home to be with Jesus. Pearl Gilman, who was a member of Harvest Christian Center, passed away. Kirk had the funeral and women from the church helped prepare another funeral dinner.

On the day of the funeral I got up early and went downstairs to the mansion's first floor to run the carpet sweeper. All of a sudden I noticed broken glass on the library floor. Someone had picked up a big rock from the garden on the north side of our house and threw it through one of the library windows. We called the police and the officer asked if anyone was angry with us. "No, not to our knowledge," we responded. But we sure wondered why we were the victims of a random act of violence.

Doug and Viki planned a vacation to North Carolina and said they would take me to see Grace and Jorgy Jorgensen. I learned what it was like to travel with young children again!

On our way home Doug drove up Lookout Mountain in Tennessee–a place Jerry and I always liked to visit. The brakes on my station wagon got hot and by the time we got down the mountain, we were burning rubber. We coasted to a little store and let the car cool off. We found a motel nearby and got the last room before a basketball team arrived. We praised God for His provision and that we had survived.

I wasn't home very long before Chris and I flew to Montana for a mini-vacation. We actually landed in Rapid City, South Dakota, where Kim and the girls drove to pick us up. We shopped in big mall and then Kim insisted we go see Wonderland Cave. I am not a cave person, but reluctantly gave in. Soon I was walking in wet mud. Somehow I managed to slip and fall down and hit my head. Then it was time to climb back up the steps as the next tour group was ready to come down. I looked up at the winding narrow passageway and saw the faces of people looking down at me. Suddenly I hyperventilated! I thought I was going to die down there. I still don't know how I got up those horrible winding stairs.

That night we saw a double rainbow all across the sky over the little town of Ismay. I believed it was a sign of God's protection, something we would definitely need the next day when we got lost driving for hours around Libby's parents' ranch.

On Sunday we attended a community service at a little country church. The pastor was on vacation so a man named David did the preaching. Afterwards, refreshments were served and I had a chance to meet David. He said he knew me from somewhere and in the course of our conversation I found out he had used four of our skit books while in Bible school. My picture was on the back cover of some of the books. What a small world!

Back home Kirk was working on plans to extend our church parking lot located across the street. Adjacent to it was an old dilapidated house that was an eyesore to our church. We prayed that it would belong to Harvest.

One evening Chris went over to talk to the owners. Out of the clear blue they said, "By the way. We are going to move. Would your church be interested in our house?" Chris could hardly contain her excitement!

Kirk talked to someone in city government about getting a permit regarding the demolition of the house. A lady working in the office said she had been praying for a house. She drove out to see the house, liked it greatly and ended up having it moved to a lot she owned in Home Park. It was quite a spectacle watching the house go down city streets to its new site. We all marveled at how God answered everyone's prayer!

On Sept. 7 Doug and Viki discovered their Oldsmobile Cutlass Ciera had been stolen from the House of Prayer's three-car garage. A report was made to the police. Viki told a friend, who was a gang specialist for the City Police Department, about the theft and he said it was probably gang related. She questioned how that could be true because the back of her car had Christian bumper stickers.

"That kind of car makes the best one for a gang to use because it would not be suspected of illegal activity. One gang leader in Decatur drives a vehicle with a Jesus sticker on it," he pointed out. He also said a General Motors vehicle could be stolen in "two" seconds.

The next day a man from a service station on Jasper Street called to ask Doug why he left his car on the lot.

"What do you want fixed on it?" he asked.

Doug excitedly told him the car had been stolen from our garage. Curiously, Doug asked the man how he found out his name.

"I found a bank deposit ticket in the midst of all the papers strewn on the floor."

Apparently the thief or thieves had gone through the glove compartment looking for money and made a mess of the car. Among the items missing was the book used for recording mileage and automobile expenses. The car was probably used to haul stolen merchandise and by taking the record book there was no way to prove how many miles the thieves drove. The steering column was broken, the back seat was jerked out of place and the trunk lock was broken. Viki's police friend said the thieves may have wanted to use the car for a drive-by shooting but changed their mind when they couldn't open the trunk. Doug and Viki were happy to get their car back, but always had a funny feeling when they drove it somewhere. They felt violated.

On Sept. 10 and 11 the church had a rummage and bake sale to help raise money for the Building Fund. By the time everything was cleaned up Saturday evening, I was exhausted. The next day would have been my 40th wedding anniversary. I knew it would be a hard day emotionally for me so I secretly asked my heavenly Father for a special blessing on that day.

After the morning worship service, I went out to dinner with Don and Lura Etnier. When we stopped at the cashier to pay for the dinners, Lura said excitedly, "Look! Look, Dottie! Your name is on the board. You've won a free dinner!"

I praised God for this special blessing, especially since I could not remember ever signing up for the drawing.

The House of Prayer Ministries sixth skit book was about to be published. Kirk had written *Toyland* which contained five Christmas plays. The play "Toyland" could actually be done any time of the year. The front and back covers and inside pages arrived in time from the printer so that books could be collated and bound prior to the Three Rivers Sunday School Convention in Ft. Wayne, Indiana.

I traveled with four others who would be doing several skits at the convention. During the last workshop, Chris did the sign language to Ray Boltz's song "Thank You for Giving to the Lord." That was the same song Chris signed at Jerry's funeral. I sat in the back row where the workshop was being conducted and just bawled. When it was over I had to quickly regain my composure and race to our exhibit booth where people were standing in line to buy our skit books. We sold 36 skit books in 15 minutes.

On our way back to Decatur, the guys were talking about their families and how good it would be to see them again. Jeff Miller turned and asked me, "What about you, Mrs. H.? Will you be glad to be home again?"

I cried again and said, "Yes, but Jerry won't be there to greet me."

With Jerry gone, I decided to make the best of it and turned my thoughts to redecorating the old mansion. Much of the house was furnished with donated or rummage sale items. I decided to buy new drapes and curtains for the first and second floor windows. Shades and blinds were also purchased. I wanted to make the fellowship room look "homey" so I scouted around for a new living room set. I finally found something I really liked and it had matching pillows. Doug hung up burgundy swag drapes and I hung up some big wreaths I made. More pictures went up. It looked Victorian and just lovely!

I managed to get the decorating project done just in time for the Jorgensens' visit. They decided to stop by on their way home to North Carolina after visiting family members in Minnesota. I gave them a quick tour of the House of Prayer and then took them to Harvest Christian Center so they could see the church. We then went out for dinner and the Scherers met up with us. Michael and Sarah promptly

141

adopted Jorgy as a "substitute grandpa."

On Oct. 23 I drove to the North Fork Cemetery and much to my delight Jerry's marker was finally in. It was a reality check for me as I officially read his birth and death dates. I chuckled to myself how Jerry must know I would visit the site at least twice a year–during the spring and fall rummage sales that are held in that area.

The coolness of fall continued to settle in and finally the dreaded day came when we would have to turn on the furnace at the House of Prayer. Jerry had written down the instructions and posted them in the furnace room. We all held our breaths that nothing would go wrong. Praise God, everything went smoothly and we had heat in the big old house.

On Friday afternoon Nov. 19 I felt particularly depressed about the upcoming holidays, knowing how different Christmas would be without Jerry. I was resting in my big recliner and for some strange reason decided to get up and walk to the north window in the dining room. I could not believe my eyes! Under the huge pine tree, sitting among the ice and snow, was the biggest, fattest robin I had ever seen! He looked directly at me, cocked his head and then flew north.

I was speechless! We never had robins that late in November. It suddenly dawned on me what my lovely heavenly Father had arranged. I had to get up at that precise moment to look out and see a robin that had stayed behind. I had to be in the right place for our eyes to meet. I knew that I knew that Jerry was right where God wanted him and I was still greatly loved.

Christmas Eve came and all my family except Kim gathered for our traditional opening of presents. After everything was opened, Kirk presented me with a little white box. Everyone grabbed their cameras to record my reaction. Kirk warned me I might cry. Tucked inside was a porcelain baby robin! I hugged it close to me and shed a few tears.

The next day was Sunday and we had service. Kirk apologized that he did not bring anything for his monthly "show-and-tell" for the children. I stood up and said, "I know why because I brought it."

I came forward to the stage and told the congregation about Jerry's and my trip to the Jorgensens the previous fall. I shared how I had asked God to let me see one robin and then I would know Jerry would be all right. God had seen fit to send enough robins to fill all the branches of the trees, even though they never migrated there before.

I held up my tiny precious robin and concluded, "So when the 'winter' time of our life comes upon us, we too will fly off in the direction of the Son!"

19

He Carries Me

Viki and Doug surprised me by giving me a wonderful manual typewriter that I could operate. Everyone was after me to learn the computer but I always balked and remarked, "I won't be able to concentrate and will end up losing my story." I won out and retyped the musical *Voyage* for the umpteenth time. It gave me something to do during one of the coldest winters ever in Decatur. The wind chill was often 50 degrees below zero.

Doug bought a big snow blower, chained it up inside the old carriage house and then covered it up. Someone, though, managed to steal it anyway. Our guess was that someone watched Doug lock it up because a person would never know it was hidden in the garage. It would have actually taken two or three people to lift it up and load it onto a truck. It was very creepy to think we were being watched.

On January 18, 1994, the wind chill hit 60 degrees below zero and another pipe burst in the kitchen on first floor. Kirk and two men from church came to our rescue to help get it fixed. Two days later Kirk came back over and started running up the stairs. Water was leaking from the ceiling in the fellowship room. In what was Kim's old second floor apartment, we found the water rising up out of the toilet and tub and pouring out onto the floor everywhere. Someone had to empty them every two hours around the clock. I was "volunteered" and decided to sleep in my chair in the dining room so that I would be sure to get up. The temperature in my bedroom was 45 degrees and you could see your breath in the hallway. Thank God, the dining room was nice and warm.

I finally decided to call a former neighbor who was a retired plumber. He suggested we set up a heater in the basement to thaw the pipes. I checked on the heater three hours later and found the electrical cord had burned. We could have had one big fire that would have done us all in. Undoubtedly, God had His angels posted around us.

We decided to put a heater between the first and second floors. At 2:30 p.m. the ice finally melted between the walls. That night I finally got to sleep in my own bed. When we got our power bill for that month, it was $1,200–the second worst one we ever had living in the mansion. I can't imagine what the power bill would have been if we had turned the thermostat up from 65 to 70 or more degrees.

One day I received a telephone call from Kathie Blakeman, concerning her stepmom. I had visited her dad, Walter Baumhardt, many times when Jerry was a patient at the Danville Veterans Administration Hospital. Kathie told me that her dad quietly passed away the previous year on Oct. 4. He had been in a coma for eight years and the nurses found him gone early in the morning.

In the next breath, Kathie was shouting! Her stepmom, Edyth, had recently attended a revival at a church and came forward to accept Jesus Christ as her Savior and Lord. She was now going to church with Kathie. We had prayed for Edyth's salvation for a number of years and God faithfully answered our prayers.

Our annual trip to the Central Illinois Sunday School Convention in Peoria was upon us. As to be expected, snow and ice hit the area. Chris and I left Decatur around 3 p.m. on Thursday, Feb. 24, to drive to Peoria to set up our exhibit booth. As we were pulling out of the House of Prayer driveway, Kirk came running out and said to wait a minute. He felt led to make copies of his workshop notes and gave them to Chris in case the weather got so bad and he couldn't make it up to Peoria.

We made it up okay but the next day was a blizzard. Viki had originally planned to come up and Doug was going to stay home with the kids, but he got called back to work. Kirk had started out, but his car died and he was stranded as deep snow drifts began to accumulate. A friend came to his rescue and very slowly followed him home. Chris needed to teach the workshops by herself. Only four people showed up at one of the workshops held in a building a block away from the

145

Peoria Civic Center. The Youth Convention was canceled because people could not get there. Although it was a poorly attended convention, it was a new beginning for Chris. God worked Romans 8:28 in this situation. *"And we know that all things work together for good to them that love God, to them who are the called according to His purpose."*

After one of the workshops, I raced back to our booth and found a lady browsing through our skit books. She told me she worked in Dr. Winter's office at the Danville VA Hospital and recognized my name on the books. She commented that several people were praying for her boss. I marveled at God's perfect timing and divine appointment!

On March 17 Michael's third grade class came to the House of Prayer for a field trip to the historic mansion. Every student received an autographed copy of my book *Fortress on a Hill*. One of Michael's classmates made my day when he told me a person he knew got saved reading my testimony.

I dreaded March 19, the first anniversary of Jerry's departure from earth. I got my hair done that day, but it had taken longer than usual. My hairdresser quickly went out the door to plug my parking meter. In her haste, I later learned she plugged the wrong meter and I received my first parking ticket.

By the time I got home, I was discouraged. God knew I needed something to perk me up and there waiting at the front door was a floral arrangement from the Jorgensens. It was incredible to think that Jerry had been in heaven for a whole year already.

Arrangements were made for Michael to get his tonsils out on Saturday, March 26. He had been sick with tonsillitis for several years, always missing school. Finally he went to a specialist who recommended Michael not wait until the school year was over, but rather get them removed during Easter vacation. A friend of Viki's was the recovery room nurse and she said Michael had two enormous holes where the tonsils once were. The specialist later said the tonsils were some of the biggest ones he had ever seen in all of his years of practice–nearly golf ball size. He wondered how Michael ever swallowed. It took eight days before Michael could talk again.

Decatur was hit with a flash flood on April 11. Kirk had two to three inches of water in his basement. Jeanette said the water ran like a river in front of their house. Some of the ceilings at the mansion leaked. It was beginning to be more than we could handle.

We decided to cut down the 150-year-old elm tree that grew outside of the west back door. When it crashed to the ground, we were told by the tree cutter that we had made a very wise decision. The big tree was rotten inside and a big wind could have blown it onto the house, causing enormous damage.

I asked the man what it would cost to cut down the "stinko Ginko" tree that plagued us every fall. It produced thousands of orange berries that fell to the ground and if stepped on smelled like sour milk and dog excrement. People who walked on the driveway or back parking lot oftentimes would step on them. Each autumn we spent hours raking them and putting them in garbage sacks for disposal. To my amazement the man replied, "Seventy-five dollars."

"Done," I responded.

In minutes the tree was down–one of the best investments I ever made!

WFHL, the Christian TV Station on Channel 23, was getting ready to celebrate its 10th anniversary. Jerry had played a significant role helping WFHL receive a broadcasting license from the Federal Communications Commission. He volunteered a year's time to contact and interview businessmen and government officials throughout Central Illinois to garner their support for the Christian TV station and to show the need for it. Jerry also helped the station manager with the paperwork that needed to be filled out when applying for a license.

I felt inspired one night and wrote 14 stanzas on WFHL from its early history until the present. I called the poem "The Center of God's Wheel."

The Center of God's Wheel

Take my hand and walk with me
As we tour down memory lane.

Glance toward Channel 23
To see how it has gained.

That famous day of infamy
When Channel 6 was birthed,
Came from Foursquare's Dr. Helms
As a satellite was installed on earth.

The Ragsdales gave up their land
And a tower was erected.
All consecrated to God's glory
As the Holy Spirit directed.

Teffeteller became the manager
Then Houpt and Sanchez came on the scene.
Henneberry helped to raise the funds
Which till then were kind of lean.

A new show came for little kids–
"Get On Board" by name,
And then a spot called "New Life"
And TV was never the same.

More programs were being added
With Christian views to air.
WFHL took over
'Midst great faith and prayer.

It stood firm throughout the decade
Through falling stars and all,
And sought for holy repentance
While awaiting the Master's call!

A search came for a leader,
But the Lord had found His Mark.

This man of God took over
And chased away the dark.

A night of prayer was called for.
There were many needs to fill.
"Touchpoint" began to blossom
As pastors sought God's will.

And where would we be without "Coach Chris,"
Who is loved by young and old,
And Kaptain Kirk's gymnastics
Through which God's truth unfolds?

This network now is crowded
With showings day and night.
Oh, who could believe this miracle
In those early days of plight?

The years have passed so swiftly
And time is running out.
The hourglass is sifting sand
While awaiting Jesus' shout!

So gather up your treasures
And in God's work–invest.
Help support this station
And seek to give the best.

Blessings on you, Channel 23,
The big ten-O today.
May you always keep looking upward
Till we simply fly away.

To celebrate the station's 10th anniversary, a big fund-raising dinner with special guest speaker and actor Dean Jones was scheduled for May 5 at the Decatur Holiday Inn. I should have suspected something when Doug, Viki and I arrived and were given corsages to wear and then ushered up to the front table. Chris was dressed in her "Coach Chris" attire and beamed from ear-to-ear. She hosted the afternoon children's programs of Disney cartoons called "The Locker Room" and shared gospel nuggets during the commercial breaks.

When dinner was over, Mark Dreistadt asked me to come up to the podium and read my poem "The Center of God's Wheel." Everyone seemed to enjoy the trip down memory lane. As I started to walk back to my table, Mark called me back and said there was something wrong with the poem. I looked at him quizzingly and he explained, "The verse in there about your husband, Jerry, wasn't strong enough." He then reached under the podium and presented me with a plaque in Jerry's memory. He told the audience that Jerry had been in heaven for over a year now. I looked upward and said, "Jerry, this one's for you." Over 700 people wept and applauded at the same time. It was a night to remember.

One day Michael went out to get the mail and started yelling for us to come. Someone had very carefully placed a jagged piece of glass inside the mailbox. We called the police and asked what could be done to protect us and secure the mansion. The officer suggested trimming back the bushes surrounding the house so no one could hide behind them. He also recommended pounding nails into the window sills so they could not be opened. Doug did all of this, but the next day we found more glass thrown into the children's sandbox. We did not know who to suspect for this wicked course of action.

Most of the time we did not have any problems with the tenants who lived in one of the 13 apartments next door at the Staley Mansion. Once in a while, though, there were some wild parties and people would get out on the Staley roof. It would be very easy for them to step across and come over onto our roof. One big man threatened a tenant and told her if she ever reported him to the authorities, he would slit her throat. For the first time in my life I was afraid for my life. My stomach was in knots. I was the only person living on the second floor and no one occupied the first floor. Doug, Viki and their kids lived on third floor. We decided to leave the big window closed on the second floor landing throughout the summer. It would be easy for someone to come over to our roof and cut the screen and get in the house just like the raccoon did several months earlier.

We made a trip to my hometown of Winona and visited with Bob and Stefannie. Michael and Sarah were enthralled with their great uncle and aunt and their beautiful Spanish home.

"Maybe we could take turns staying with them and the Jorgensens," they remarked.

We drove to the Mall of America in Bloomington, Minnesota, and spent all day there. While looking at dresses in the Sears Store, I heard a familiar husky voice on the other side of the dress rack. I peeked around and said, "Janet Larson?" There stood Janet in person, her mouth wide opened! She was one of the 38 girls in my high school class and was at the party where I met Jerry. Another divine appointment! We had a great time catching up on news.

When we got back home, my stomach was experiencing terrible pain. I went to Dr. McGhee and he suspected an infection or possible tumor on my left ovary. He gave me some antibiotics.

That night my pain worsened. I told Cheri and she suggested I contact her gynecologist Dr. Roy Tsuda. When I called at 1 p.m. for an appointment, a miracle happened. A 3 o'clock time slot had just opened.

During the exam, Dr. Tsuda touched the lower left part of my abdomen. I almost jumped off the examining table. "Ah, yes," he said. "There is a lump or a tumor there and surgery will have to be done."

He scheduled me for a sonogram the next morning. I was feeling miserable by then so Kirk drove me. I'd had severe nausea and diarrhea during the night. When the test results came back, I learned to my astonishment there wasn't a tumor. In fact, my ovary was pretty well dried up. Instead of finding the source to my problem and obtaining a solution, it was still a mystery as to why I was in pain. I was in shock and felt depressed. I just had to trust God and believe He was in control.

Dr. Tsuda also could not believe there was not a tumor. I told him I had diverticulosis and he called me back into his office where he read out loud its symptoms from a book in his medical library. He strongly believed my diverticulosis was now diverticulitis in its acute form. He ordered some very strong antibiotics. Days of intense pain followed.

On an early August evening, Sarah rode her bike while Viki was shucking sweet corn to freeze. Sarah came in crying and one look at her left arm showed it was broken in one or two places. She had fallen off her bike and the arm just sort of hung. She knew she would be in trouble if she left her bike across the street so with her good arm she dragged it up the front yard's hill.

Viki called her doctor right away, but he wasn't home. Before she took Sarah to the hospital, she knew she needed his referral or else their insurance would not pay the medical bills. In the meantime Sarah fell asleep, probably from the shock of the accident. Finally the doctor called and said to take her to the emergency room.

The waiting room was filled with people. It was 11 p.m. before Sarah's arm was finally x-rayed. The arm was broken in two places, but because Sarah had eaten supper, she would have to wait until the next morning to have the arm set and then put in a cast.

Viki and Sarah were up early the next day and returned to the hospital where Dr. Robert Kraus set the arm and put it in a neon pink cast all the way up to Sarah's shoulder. Kindergarten would start soon for Sarah who was a lefty, so she would have to learn to write her letters and numbers right handed.

When they got home from the hospital, I thought about the ordeal and later wrote the words to the following chorus:

> *I don't know what You're doing Lord,*
> *'Cuz I can't understand*
> *All the things that are going on*
> *That'll work out good in the end!*
> *That'll work out good in the end!*

This chorus would become part of a song titled "The Ship of Life" that would be added to my musical *Voyage*.

I was still in intense pain two weeks later and called Dr. Tsuda's office. I hoped I could get a referral to see Dr. Victor Eloy who specialized in gastroenterology. He had treated my friend, Linda

Jimison, who had recently been hospitalized with diverticulitis.

My God was again working behind the scenes. Dr. Tsuda's nurse got me an appointment with Dr. Eloy at 11:30 that morning. I spent two hours in his office and he came to the conclusion that I possibly had irritable bowel syndrome, milk intolerance and either diverticulosis or diverticulitis.

Three days later I was in agony and up all night. Pain pills did nothing. Nausea was my constant companion. I decided to test the "lactate" principle and had a Peanut Buster Parfait without nuts from the local Dairy Queen. In a few hours, I was in intense pain–if it was possible for the pain to be worse. Codeine only made me hyper.

On Sunday the church elders anointed me with oil. Dr. Eloy ordered a colon test for me the next day. Linda Jimison took me and I was very grateful to her. While examining the colon, Dr. Eloy found a small tumor and promptly removed it. I almost climbed the walls! He gave me some pain medicine and sent me home to rest and wait for the biopsy report.

Viki bought baby food and made instant potatoes for me. Everything was going right through me and I was dropping weight rapidly. Finally, I called the dietician at St. Mary's Hospital and she told me what would be good to eat and not eat. I had lost 14 pounds in 8 days. Equalactin® helped me to balance the fluids in my body, but I hated the chalky, grainy taste.

Kirk took me to St. Mary's Hospital on Tuesday, August 30, at 6:15 a.m. for a panendoscopy procedure of my esophagus, stomach and upper bowel. I was extremely nauseous before I was put to sleep. A polyp was discovered and removed. Before I could be released, I had to eat some toast and drink some tea. I finally got to go home, but the terrible nausea before the test really bothered me.

I called my sister Colleen, who had been a nurse, and asked her what could have made me so nauseous for days. She mentioned post-nasal drip and I shouted, "Yes! I've gone through this so many times before, but I couldn't see the forest for the trees."

I explained to Colleen that paint and tar had always made me sick before. Doug and Kirk were tarring the roof outside my bedroom window. I even handed them the tar bucket. I breathed the fumes day

153

and night from the opened windows. How could I have been so blind?

The next day I went to Dr. McGhee. Sure enough, I had a bad sinus infection and my right ear had an infection. I felt like a hundred pound weight had lifted off me since the source of my problem was diagnosed. I tried a new antibiotic, but had a bad reaction to it so another medication was prescribed. Anytime I went out in public I took some anti-diarrheal medicine with me and made sure I knew where the restrooms were.

The biopsy on the polyp and the panendoscopy results came back and everything was fine. My new health insurance paid for half of my medical bills which I was very grateful. Slowly I began the road to recovery.

Like the famous poem "Footprints in the Sand," I knew my Lord had carried me through another valley. God wanted my full attention and to walk His way, no matter the awesome cost.

Lord of the Valley

Mountain peaks abound with pride
　　And are alluring to the eye.
Romance and great adventure
　　Await somewhere in the sky.

Lofty tops keep calling
　　And man longs to soar their heights,
Then linger in the glory
　　Of this awesome inspiring sight.

But what about the valleys
　　Where no one wants to go?
Those dark and lonely valleys
　　Of desolation and woe?

Who is willing to go on
        And stand this test of time,
Walking only with the Master
        Till all is left behind?

Who is willing to suffer
        And greet each day with pain,
Yet trusting in the Master's plan
        As He praises Jesus' name?

Who is willing to be humble
        And broken in many parts,
That Christ might be the Lover
        Who dwells within his heart?

Yes, the mountains may be attractive
        And a lovely place to stay,
But nothing really grows there
        That is worthy in any way.

But look again to the valleys
        And see great fruit abound.
It ripens in God's season,
        So luscious and profound.

Our Lord waits in the valley
        To test His saints on earth.
Soon will come the harvest
        And you'll see what your fruit is worth!

20

Seasons of Life

Suddenly summer was over and Labor Day weekend of 1994 was upon us. Viki and I met in the hallway of the second floor at 7 a.m. Monday morning. She began telling me that we simply could not afford to stay in the big mansion much longer. It was time to move on.

To her amazement, I agreed. Early that morning Viki had been reading II Chronicles chapter three in her Bible where Solomon was selected to build the temple. It was the son of David that God had selected for this task. She reasoned it was time for Kirk to start concentrating on building the church at Harvest Christian Center and not be tied down with the maintenance required at the mansion. In addition, she said we neither had the funds nor the manpower to stay on much longer.

We could continue operating a publishing ministry in a smaller house if we could find a place that had separate housing for me, housing for the Scherers and office space for the ministry. The sickness I had was taking its toil on my body and I knew I could not go on living at the mansion. It was getting harder and harder for me to keep up with the cleaning.

Chris went to Macon and brought Jerry's mom, Clara, to our home for dinner. Afterwards we took several of my grandchildren to fish at Dreamland Lake in Fairview Park. In the evening Kirk came over to talk to us. He was supposed to try and convince me of the need to sell the mansion and move on.

"How subtle my kids are," I thought to myself. Viki, Chris and Kirk had it planned all along.

It was Kirk's turn to be shocked when I interrupted him by

156

saying, "Fine, let's do it. Let's go for it!"

We joined hands and prayed. Out of the blue Kirk spoke the words about Solomon building the temple, not knowing Viki had received the same words during her morning devotional.

It would be a mammoth task getting the house ready to sell and then move out. I still was not feeling very well and could do very little physically. I sat down in my big recliner, thinking about all that had to be done. Memories from when we first moved into the mansion on August 11, 1975, flooded my soul.

We agreed John Greenleaf would be the lawyer to handle all of the legal matters. His office was just a block away. He told us he had always wanted to see the inside of the mansion and just loved it. He suggested we get Bruce Campbell of Lyle Campbell and Son Realtors to be the realtor to list the house. An appointment was set up for him to come the following Tuesday.

I decided to iron some clothes that day and listened to a couple of cassette tapes with Jerry speaking. On the first one he shared the testimony of the House of Prayer and all we had done to acquire it in 1975. He emphasized that one's time and place is ordained by God. The second tape was on obedience being better than sacrifice. Jerry emphasized that a person can take nothing with him when he leaves this world. The message ended by Jerry saying, "Remember, Solomon built the temple." I nearly dropped the iron! This was the third time we were given the same scripture verse. I firmly believed God was saying, "It is time to move on."

We called a board meeting and outlined several things that would have to be done before the house could be listed on the market. Mike said he would clean out the printing room in the basement and scrape the walls. We agreed to sell the trailer the End Time Harvesters Christian drama team used when it went out on tour. Clothes stored in the closets would be moved to the basement and eventually sold or given away. The outfits worn by the Harvesters would be sorted and gotten rid of. The craft room would need to be cleaned out. The ceiling and paneling in the girl's pink apartment needed to be repaired. The basement bathroom that was transformed into a dark room where Viki did photography for the ministry would have to be cleaned. Paint cans stored in that room would have to be sorted and pitched. Much of the furniture and household furnishings would have to be sold. We'd have to set up a huge rummage sale. I was exhausted just thinking about everything!

On September 12, which would have been my 41st wedding anniversary, Chris stopped by the mansion after conducting a Bible study at an elderly hi-rise building. She was very quiet so I knew something was bothering her. She finally said she had decided to leave WFHL Channel 23, the Christian television station. She had been Coach Chris, the host for the weekday afternoon kid's club called "The Locker Room." Her one minute commercial segments were interspersed throughout the Disney cartoons. With the arrival of the new fall show "Aladdin," she new she could no longer compete with Disney.

Aladdin would cry out to his genie for help while Coach Chris taught the children watching the shows to call on Jesus. The television station wanted to reach a larger audience and be "seeker sensitive," but Chris felt she could not compromise her beliefs.

I was very proud of her. For some time I had been appalled at the rebellion and subtle occultic practices that were coming across the Christian airways. I believed Chris would have to give an account to God on judgment day for the souls of the little ones watching the shows and being led astray.

Chris said she had no idea where God was leading her. Viki jumped up and said, "I know–the Sunday School Conventions! You'll do the drama workshops at them." Chris had a trial run teaching when she filled in for Kirk who could not make it to Peoria for the Central Illinois Sunday School Convention because of the blizzard.

I got excited and found myself saying, "I'll go with you. I have nothing to do. I could help sell the skit books. The House of Prayer Ministries will indeed go on. We'll have to get a different car. Have car, will travel."

It was getting late so Chris decided to head to her car. I was standing on the back steps watching her. She forgot her purse and came back to the house. She gave me a kiss and simply said, "I love you, mom."

158

The next day Bruce Campbell from the reality company arrived promptly at 11 a.m. We gave him a tour of the house and then sat down in the fellowship room to negotiate a selling price, but could not agree on one. After several days of wrestling with a figure, we finally agreed on $159,000. We felt that was a tremendous bargain and were hoping to get $180,000. Where else could you get a 24-room historical mansion for that price?

Bruce came back on September 21 and spent six hours with us going room-to-room, making suggestions on how we could make the house more attractive and sellable. We needed to unclutter many of the rooms and make them look big and open. The red carpeting on first floor needed to be removed so the hardwood floors could be exposed. I told Bruce it was a good thing Jerry was in his heavenly mansion because he would have balked at having to make all of those changes. But deep down inside I knew Bruce was right.

While standing in the first floor hallway near the front entrance, Bruce studied the glass doors going into our library, which was originally the parlor, and the doors going into the office, which was originally the music room.

"I think there is something under that layer of paint," he excitedly remarked.

Doug scraped the white stuff off, revealing beautiful cut glass. For 19 years I had cleaned the house and never realized the doors had beveled glass.

To spruce the place up, Viki decided to paint the outside window sills as far as she could reach. I painted chairs and did some touch up painting on the walls and the fireplaces.

The room where we had our office was filled with boxes of skit books, office equipment and supplies. It was so crowded you could not see the beautiful marble fireplace. Other distinct features in it included a plaster of paris ceiling and an oak wooden floor. The room was painted light blue and had gold trim on all the white molding. Someone told us it would cost $2,000 just to replace the ceiling. Several of us spent a weekend just trying to sort everything. Bruce recommended that we uncover the original painting above the fireplace. It depicted a naked nymph playing a flute which we did not think was very appropriate for a pastor's office. Consequently, we covered it up shortly after we moved into the mansion 19 years earlier. Slowly, we transformed the office back into its original design of a music room.

The best time to fulfill many of Bruce's suggestions was the same weekend several of us were participating in the Three Rivers Sunday School Convention in Ft. Wayne, Indiana. Viki got on the phone and called some other church people to see if they could come to the House of Prayer for a work day on Saturday, September 24. Eight people showed up. Viki distributed work lists and everyone went at it. Boxes of skit books were hauled to the church, furniture was re-arranged, the piano was moved into the original music room, windows were cleaned, the old carpet was ripped out, floors and walls were washed and a closet in a bathroom was taken apart. Even the missing antique light fixtures for one of the rooms was located. What should have taken a lot more time and required more workers, was accomplished by a small army of faithful servants. We were amazed to see the transformation when we got back from the convention.

The next night I stayed home from church and vacuumed the mansion for three hours, plus cleaned out the five fireplaces. The next day I used ammonia to clean several of the bathrooms. Suddenly I was very dizzy and could not stand up. It was very frightening! I went to the doctor and found out I had a sinus and inner ear infection. You would think I would learn to stay away from paint, chemicals and ashes which always bothered me, but no, I always managed to be around them.

Bruce Campbell and Dale Maricle came to the mansion on September 28 to measure each room in order to get an accurate measurement of the house's square footage for a real estate ad. The three floors had a total square footage of 8,200 square feet. The basement did not count but if it was added in, the house had over 10,000 square feet.

On that same day the weekly issue of the *Decatur Tribune* had a full page spread about the mansion being for sale. Viki had been a reporter for that newspaper for eight years and supplied much of the information to her former boss, Paul Osborne, the editor and publisher. Included was a picture of Jerry preaching during our early days in the mansion. It brought back lots of memories and was an emotional time for me.

The next day Kirk's children came over and little Kayla asked where Grandpa was. She was only two years old when he died, but she remembered running up the stairs and heading straight to Grandpa Berry's bedroom.

We started scanning real estate ads and looked in the multiple listing book. I figured we would sell the mansion right away and therefore needed to rush out to find somewhere to live. I even paid earnest money on a house that I thought would meet our needs, but God had other plans.

In the meantime, the mansion was getting into top form for the realtors' coffee scheduled for October 7. Area real estate salesmen were invited to see the mansion. Like many townspeople, they were curious to see the inside of the historical mansion and what condition it was in. Many were surprised at how well we had maintained and improved the building over the years. They were particularly impressed with the carved oak woodwork, oak wood floors, art glass and cut glass windows, indoor porches and the beautiful built-in china cabinet located in the original formal dining room. Someone offered us $5,000 cash for the cabinet, but we knew we had to refuse because it was part of the history of the house. Several suggested the house would make a great bed and breakfast location.

On October 25 we hosted an afternoon tea for members of the Macon County Historical Society to tour the mansion and see if any of them might be a prospective buyer. We were pleasantly surprised to learn that Leland Stanford England and his son, David, were among the first to arrive. Leland was the grandson of the England family that had remodeled most of the mansion in 1916.

Although he had never actually lived there, Leland spent every Wednesday night having dinner at the mansion with his family when he was growing up. He and his brother would race to "Granddad's library" where the big radio was and listen to "Amos and Andy." In the winter they would bed down with coverings of goose down comforters in the porch bedroom that my son Kim had as part of his apartment.

Many of the historical people gathered around Leland each

time he shared a fascinating story about the mansion. Viki asked him if he would be willing to come back so that she could videotape him going room-to-room, sharing anecdotes from his childhood. He said he would be delighted so arrangements were made for a return visit.

Before the tea was over, Viki spoke with some of the historical "experts" who expressed amazement at the bathrooms that were tiled from floor to ceiling. They marveled about the excellent condition of the tiled room that was originally the kitchen on the first floor. Viki explained to them that when we first moved in, the tile on those walls was covered with several layers of paint. Two people from the House of Prayer's congregation (one was my future son-in-law Doug) used razor blades to scrape the paint off and then polished the walls. The historical people commented that the replacement for that room's floor, wall and ceiling tile would be $10,000. To reconstruct the entire house would be around $2 million. We were beginning to think our asking price of $159,900 was a steal.

Leland England returned the following week and spent three hours going throughout the house. He had a story for each room and Viki got it all on videotape.

He shared about the buzzer his grandmother had under the carpet in the formal dining room. She used it to summon the maid to come to the dining room. Leland and his brother took great delight pressing the buzzer when grandmother wasn't around just so they could see the maid come flying down the stairs.

Grandmother was convinced one of the maids was having a gentleman caller come during the night up to the third floor where the maids' quarters were located. She would listen, but could only hear one set of footsteps. One night she decided to stay up to investigate her suspicions. Sure enough, she found a man coming up the stairs. The maid was standing on his feet as he took one step at a time! No wonder she only heard one set of footsteps!

Grandmother had a heart attack in what we called the girls' apartment. She spent the last years of her life in what became Jerry's and my bedroom. Eventually she passed away.

Realtors started calling to set up appointments for the house to be showed. Usually a homeowner leaves when a house is showed, but because of the uniqueness of the historical mansion, Viki or I helped take the realtor and prospective buyer through the house. It would take 10 minutes to turn on all the lights before someone came to see the place. Usually it would take an hour to give a tour of the mansion because we always shared the historical significance and pointed out the unique features of it. Besides, most people would get lost in the house and would not know if a door opened to a room or to a closet.

We were opposed to having an Open House primarily because of security reasons. How could we keep track of everyone in the house? As the days went on, Viki began to have second thoughts and believed an excellent way to showcase the house would be to have an open house that dovetailed with the annual Heritage and Holly Historic Candlelight Home Tour scheduled for Thanksgiving weekend. Fliers at that tour would be available inviting people to our open house which would be free.

My famous last words were, "I won't have to decorate the house this year for Christmas. Surely we'll sell the house by then." Not only did I have to decorate, I needed to start earlier in order to be ready for the November 27 Sunday afternoon open house scheduled from 1:30 to 4:30 p.m.

To keep with the historical nature of the house, I decided to decorate with a Victorian style. Francis Basil helped make wreaths and boughs. The stairway going up to second floor had greenery interwoven throughout the railing. Pink and burgundy bows accentuated the look. Candles were everywhere. My lovely white Christmas tree adorned the living room which originally was the formal dining room. We even put a Christmas tree in the corner of the large indoor sun porch where Leland England said his grandparents placed theirs.

Doug and Viki decided to go on the holiday tour of historic homes on Friday night just to see how they compared to our mansion. They noticed that every homeowner had his dining room table set with the finest china and silverware.

Chris thought it would be a good idea if we did the same. My dining room table on second floor and Doug and Viki's on third floor were set with beautiful china.

We decided to go one step further and make the breakfast room on first floor actually look like a breakfast room. It had served as Kirk's office. Beautiful bird's eye maple wood and an antique bun warmer on the radiator were features in this room. Kirk's big desk and other office equipment were removed and taken to the church. They were replaced with my old dining room table and four chairs that we found in the basement. I got busy painting them and some of the radiators in other rooms in the house. It was late at night when everything got done.

The next morning we went to church and raced home to make final preparations for the 1:30 p.m. open house. We had prayed for good weather and it was an unseasonably warm 64 degrees. It started raining and then a tornado siren sounded. We did not know if anyone would show up. Two people rang the doorbell at 1 p.m. to see the house, but Viki told them to come back later because we weren't quite ready and the open house did not start for another 30 minutes.

We made arrangements for LaVera Hensley to play Christmas carols on the piano in the music room as people toured the house. Viki and I would be stationed on the first floor to greet people and give them a guided tour of the rooms on that floor. Realtors Bruce Campbell and Dale Maracle would also be on the first floor. Chris and Kirk would be on second floor while Doug and Teresa Kapper from church would be stationed on third floor. Years ago Teresa's grandmother had been a maid in the mansion for the England family.

The weather finally cleared up and out popped the sun. Before long people were pulling up in Cadillacs and Mercedes Benz. In three hours we had 550 people tour the mansion. Most were curious and said they had always wanted to see the inside of the house. Chris said she counted over 100 people at one time on the second floor. Our realtor was overwhelmed and said he had never seen anything like it. Even the couple who arrived at 1 p.m. came back and said they liked the house.

I decided to stay home from church that night and put my feet up. The carpet I had worked so hard to keep clean was now covered with leaves and ground in mud. "But tomorrow is another day," I reasoned and house cleaning could wait. I just wanted to bask in the excitement of what had happened. Hopefully someone who went through the mansion would like it enough to buy it.

I called Lura and while sharing with her about the open house, I heard a creak on the first floor stairway. Then I heard another one. I told her to stand by because I had to investigate. All I could think was, "Which closet did someone hide in?" and then decide to come out when everyone else left. My fears were for nought because there stood our big black cat, Midnight, purring away and wondering what I was so anxious about.

I planned to leisurely take my time cleaning the house the next day when my plans were abruptly changed. Bruce Campbell called to say he would be there in one hour to show the house to a man from California who was interested in making it into a college dormitory. Needless to say, I vacuumed the house in record time!

We found a house on Decatur's west end that we really liked. Again I put earnest money down, but this still was not the one God intended for us to have. Praise God, Bruce Campbell was again able to retrieve my money. I was slowly learning not to go ahead of God's will and His timing.

On February 24 and 25 Chris and I were back at the Central Illinois Sunday School Convention in Peoria and then the following week we participated in the Ohio Christian Education Association's Ministries Conference in Akron. A week after that we were at the Eastern Iowa Christian Education Conference in Iowa City.

As Chris and I were packing up our books on March 11 to head home from Iowa, we received an emergency phone call from Viki. I was so sure it was Viki telling us that she had sold the mansion, but one look on Chris' face told me otherwise.

She very quietly told me that Charles Volle, Eileen's husband of 49 years, had a massive heart attack and died in her arms at 3 a.m. that morning. Suddenly, I felt like time stood still for me again. Instead of staying with some friends, Chris and I decided to drive straight home. Eileen would need me. When Jerry and Charles were alive, we had been a foursome. Charles always considered taking us out to dinner as his "ministry."

While driving home, Chris and I witnessed the most gorgeous sunset. "Just think, Chris, Charles has now seen the Son of God in all

His glory. I'll bet Jerry was on the welcoming committee!" I exclaimed.

As it got dark, we both saw a shooting star blaze across the sky. It reminded me of Charles who was a pilot in World War II. During Charles' burial, a small plane came out of nowhere and flew over the cemetery.

Just like me, Eileen was entering into a new season in her life. Through the dark days ahead, God would be with her. He knew from the beginning what would happen and would see her through. It reminded me of a poem that I had written years earlier about my life. Our birth and death are all recorded in God's Book of Life.

He Knows My Times Appointed

From the very beginning
God knew when I'd be born.
He gave me to my parents
On a lovely Monday morn.

He watched me in my growing years
And soon I was in my teens.
He knew how much I needed Him,
But waited behind the scenes.

He knew the man I'd marry
And brought him toward my way.
Friendship blossomed into love
On a September wedding day.

God sent me tokens of His love,
For His blessings came to five.
Our home was running over,
But was very much alive.

Then one day My Lord appeared
　　　After the darkest of my nights.
He came inside my heart to stay
　　　And began to shine His light.

His love was quite contagious
　　　And my children's lives were renewed.
Then there came that special day
　　　When my husband received Christ, too!

God knew that we'd obey Him,
　　　So we gave up all we owned.
A mansion became The House of Prayer
　　　And gospel seeds were sown.

God gave to me a special gift
　　　In the middle years of life.
I was to write of His splendor and beauty
　　　In the coming days of strife.

He knows my time's appointed,
　　　So what have I to fear?
For even when the hour is dark,
　　　I know my Lord is near.

Yes, He knows my time's appointed
　　　And all that the future brings.
So I await that moment in glory
　　　When I'll see my Lord, my King!

21

Spiritual Warfare

Spring was blossoming in all of her beauty. The birds were singing their songs of praise to their Creator and flowers were beginning to burst forth from the cold hard ground. The fall and winter seasons had passed swiftly, but still the mansion was not sold.

In desperation I prayed, asking God to speak to me through His Word. It was Saturday night, March 25. My Bible opened to Isaiah 58:12. *"Your people will rebuild the ancient ruins and will raise up the age-old foundations; you will be called Repairer of Broken Walls, Restorer of Streets with Dwellings."*

"Well," I thought to myself, "The ancient ruins and age-old foundations surely applies to a mansion that is 120 years old. The fence is slowly coming down between our house and the neighbor's next door mansion. We live on an historical street with paved red brick, a memory from the past. Now, if I only knew who 'your people were.'"

The next day was Sunday and we were having another Open House for only two hours from 1:30 to 3:30 p.m. There was hardly any publicity for this Open House and our realtor thought we might have 30 to 60 people.

Once again we were surprised to see people standing in line at 1:30. In two hours we had 250 go through our home. It was incredible! Bruce Campbell indicated we had several good prospects. One person wanted the house for a Christian bed and breakfast while one lady wanted to redo it as a museum for angels.

Three years had passed since Jerry left the old mansion and went to a much better one in heaven. I told Chris my wedding band was becoming thin and I wanted a new setting. She helped me select a mounting that had two marquise diamonds on the side plus two blue sapphires surrounding them. My diamond would be placed in the center. Because I wanted white gold, there was a waiting period of several weeks.

God's timing is perfect! I received a phone call on April 4 that my ring was ready. It was exactly 42 years earlier to the day that Jerry had given me my engagement ring. Again, I knew I was loved. When I saw the ring, I gasped! It looked like a dazzling butterfly and matched perfectly the sapphires in my watch.

The doorbell rang early on Saturday morning April 22. The Scherers had already left so I raced downstairs to see who was there, but could find no one. I went into the music room and glanced out the window where I saw a strange man standing in the front yard, staring at the house. I watched him as I hid behind the curtains and finally he left.

Around noontime I fixed myself lunch and feeling rather sleepy, I decided to take a nap in my big chair in the dining room. I vaguely remembered hearing a tremendous crash which seemed to echo through the fireplace in the dining room. I was too tired to get up. The door to the dining room was wide open.

In the afternoon I was awakened by Viki and the children running up the stairs. Viki was excited and asked if I had sold the house. All of the for-sale signs were gone! We all raced outside. Viki kept saying she smelled smoke throughout the downstairs.

To our amazement one sign was stuck in the sand box and the others were stacked up on the side of the house. Suddenly, the same stranger appeared and started asking what was the price of the house. He had some money and wanted to buy it for his friends.

A neighbor across the street saw what was going on and came over to tell us he saw that man get into the House of Prayer's van and into my station wagon. Viki, who is only 5 foot 3 inches, stood up to that man and screamed, "You get off of our property right now. If I ever see you here again I'll call the police."

The man took off running. It was then that I noticed a basement window had been broken and glass was everywhere. Viki immediately dialed 911 and the police came quickly. Apparently the man had taken a blanket out of the van and used it to cover his foot or hand to break the window. He then crawled in over a sink and proceeded to walk into every room in the basement. He left cigarette ashes and butts everywhere which was the smoke that Viki had smelled.

He placed a small table in front of another window. On the table was a box. Not knowing its contents, we had Kirk open it and found it was some of Kim's old microphones. We breathed a sigh of relief that it wasn't a bomb. The police officer said it was obvious the man was definitely planning to come back.

Apparently, the man had walked up the basement stairs and turned on the lights in many of the first floor rooms. Why he didn't come up to the second floor was a mystery except that God in His infinite mercy and grace had protected me. I believe a big angel held him off!

I shook for hours afterwards, thinking about what had happened and contemplating what I would have done if I had confronted him on the first floor or in the basement. Or worse, what if he had come up to the second floor and accosted me?

We called Bruce Campbell and told him everything that had happened. He came over right away. We discussed putting iron bars on the basement windows, but that would definitely scare away any potential buyers. Kirk found a store that stayed opened late and was able to get a window made and installed before it got dark. The next day we went through all the rooms and anointed each one with oil. We prayed and gave thanks to our loving Father God for His divine protection.

More catastrophes continued. On a Friday night just as Kirk and his family were coming up the stairs for an impromptu prayer meeting, we heard a crash coming from my bedroom. Upon inspection we found that the ceiling in my bedroom closet had fallen to the floor. Plaster was everywhere. Repairs were made and Viki about got asphyxiated painting the closet in such an enclosed area.

To add insult to injury, the raccoons were back! A different family moved in. We had to pray they wouldn't run across the ceilings whenever we showed the house to a prospective buyer.

In early May we had a big rain, causing many ceilings to leak. It was all we could do to get the buckets and towels removed before people came in to see the house.

Viki reviewed the House of Prayer's finances and realized there was only two more months of reserve. We had to sell the mansion soon or we were going to be in dire financial straights. She cried out to the Lord and opened her Bible to Romans 4:20-21. *"Yet he did not waver through unbelief regarding the promise of God, but was strengthened in his faith and gave glory to God, being fully persuaded that God had power to do what He had promised."* She held onto that promise that God was going to do something out of the ordinary and get the mansion sold.

Bruce had breakfast with the mayor and city manager on Thursday morning June 1. They had contact with a man from Bloomington who was interested in purchasing our house and the Staley mansion. They were seriously considering making our square block into an historical home base with trolley cars departing from downtown and taking people on tours to other historical homes in the city. We were ecstatic!

Later that morning Bruce brought a young man named Jim McBride to the mansion. Jim had a beautiful Japanese wife and four lovely children. They took many photographs of the inside and outside of the mansion. Jim asked lots of questions about the condition of our house and the one next door. He wanted to know what the real estate taxes were and if there were any ethnic neighbors.

On June 5 a man and his well-dressed wife arrived 10 minutes earlier than their scheduled appointment to tour the mansion. Bruce was not here yet so Viki ran over to the real estate office which was half a block away. Dale Maricle came back and helped Viki show the house. The lady loved the place, but the man was very arrogant and raced through the house. We learned he was a big financier who restored historical homes. He was the one our city leaders wanted to buy our mansion and the Staley mansion and turn them into tourist sites for the city. He was willing to spend $700,000 on both homes. He estimated he would spend $50,000 on the outside of our mansion. The only catch was that he would give us a mere $125,000 for our house.

That was considerably less than our asking price so we promptly refused his offer.

On Wednesday, June 21, Bruce called at noon and said Jim McBride would be in Japan for 10 days. He and his "partner" wanted to buy our house. A possible contract was in the making. We couldn't believe it!

On Thursday, June 29, Viki received a phone call from Sarah Weaver, a realtor with Lyle Campbell & Sons Realtors. She asked if she could show the house that afternoon or the next day. Viki opted for the next day. Hardly a day went by that she did not show the house to someone. People from California to the east coast to Florida were making appointments to see the house. There was something very appealing about purchasing a mansion for only $159,000.

On Friday afternoon Sarah came over with Dr. Wayne Kelly and his wife to show them the house. Actually, she just let Viki show them around since she knew more about its historical features and where the rooms were located. Viki was surprised to learn the Kellys had been the first ones to come see the house during the open house on Thanksgiving weekend. Viki had told them they were too early and needed to come back later.

Wayne loved the old house when he went through it then, but because they had just purchased a house on William Street, he said it wasn't economically feasible for him to consider owning two houses. When they noticed there was still a for sale sign, they decided to come take a second look. Dr. Kelly was a neurologist and the rent on his medical office had just been raised. The mansion would be quite unique for his medical practice.

They went outside and Viki showed them the carriage house. When they got to the north side of the house, Dr. Kelly commented there was something missing from the north porch. Viki took a deep breath and started to explain that the hand carved stone pillars were removed to the south porch because there had been an accident several years earlier. She did not like telling the story about the teenage getting killed in the driveway when she showed the house. She was afraid it would frighten people away from buying it.

Before Viki could proceed any further, Dr. Kelly stopped he

and said, "I already know all about the accident. My receptionist is married to the driver of that car. He has changed his life around since then."

That remark sent chills up Viki's spine. She knew beyond a shadow of a doubt that Dr. Kelly was the buyer. He said the house would be perfect for his medical office and for his family to live in. In addition, the Imaging Center, was just across the street and he could send his patients there for MRI's.

Viki discovered that Dr. Kelly was a Messianic Jew. She knew from scripture that the Jews were God's chosen people. Could Dr. Kelly possibly be the answer to the scripture verse the Lord gave me in Isaiah?

Then an amazing thing happened. Both Dr. Kelly and Jim McBride offered the same proposal of $145,000. Incredible! It was the same amount! McBride wanted a 30-day closing, would not need a zoning change and would give a larger amount of earnest money. He had contacted the health and fire departments to see what would be required to convert the House of Prayer into a bed and breakfast facility.

Bruce noted that if one of the buyers actually produced more earnest money then that would help matters. He said he would convey what had transpired to Sarah Weaver and ask her if the Kellys could produce more earnest money. If they agreed, then he and Sarah would meet at 6:30 a.m. the next morning and write a new contract. The Kellys could sign it at 7:30 a.m. and then Bruce and Sarah would bring the contract to us at 8:30 a.m.

Just as planned, the Kellys went to Lyle Campbell & Sons Realty early the next morning to sign a contract to purchase the mansion. Bruce and Sarah then came over and Viki signed four copies of the four page contract. Dr. Kelly had put more earnest money down. The closing date would be on or before September 1 with the sale contingent on financing and getting the zoning changed for medical offices. The Kellys were also interested in buying some of the furniture in the mansion.

Afterwards we marveled at our Lord and His sense of humor. On Labor Day we made the decision to sell the house, and did we ever "labor" getting the house ready to put on the market, while on the Fourth of July we received our "independence" when the Kellys signed the contract to purchase the mansion. God truly is amazing!

On July 19 the Historical and Architectural Sites Commission approved Dr. Kelly's petition for an Historic Neighborhood Use Zoning Permit. Their recommendation would now go to the City Plan Commission which would decide on August 3 about the zoning petition. If it passed the City Plan Commission, then the Decatur City Council would vote on August 21 either in favor of or against the zoning change.

Since it seemed pretty certain that we would get the mansion sold, we needed to decide on a house to buy. Time was running out! We made a list of seven homes to see including one on Florian Court that was much cheaper than what we had been looking at. The multiple listing book stated that it had over 2,600 square feet and was listed at $77,500. We hadn't even bothered to look at houses in that price range because none had the space we needed.

It ended up that the house on Florian Court was the last one to see. We pulled into the driveway and argued whether to go in. The house looked small from the outside and only had a single car driveway.

We knocked on the door and Viki was surprised to be greeted by Debbie Simon. Her children had attended Northwest Christian Campus. As we walked through the house, we discovered the Simons had added on about 1,000 square feet, but were not finished with all of the remodeling. The den was completed and an upstairs bedroom had been added, but nothing had been done to the bathroom. It did not have any electrical wiring or plumbing—only insulation. The north wall in the bedroom also had insulation from floor to ceiling, but was covered up with floor length drapes.

What was so wonderful about this tri-level house was that this bedroom and bathroom were upstairs and separate from the rest of the house. Most of the houses we had looked at had an apartment or living quarters for a parent or in-law in the basement or above a garage. I'm very sensitive to mold and dust and knew we could not buy a house where I had to live in the basement. Simons' house provided the best accommodations!

There were three other bedrooms, a full bathroom and a half bathroom that would be perfect for Doug, Viki, Michael and Sarah. The living room was nice size and could accommodate a piano and other furniture. Off to the side there was a dining room area. The kitchen was big and had a long counter top that would be perfect for Viki to set food on. There was even a dishwasher–a luxury item not found in the old mansion. Sliding glass doors from the kitchen opened up to an outside patio–perfect for cooking on the grill. Michael and Sarah got very excited when they saw the woods and a creek behind the house.

In addition to adding a master bedroom and den, the Simons added a family recreational room downstairs complete with a fireplace. I quickly began envisioning my own kitchen, dining room and living room in that spacious area. It even had doors to a small walk-out patio.

A large utility room was on the other side of the rec room. To Viki's delight there was a room which formerly served as a family room that would be perfect for an office for the House of Prayer Ministries. There were even built-in shelves in the room.

Simons' asking price was $77,500. Earlier that morning Doug went to a church to give blood. Another man was also giving blood and Doug overheard him tell someone that he and his wife offered $63,000 for a house on Florian Court–the same one we were interested in. With that figure to go by, we decided to offer $70,000. The Simons countered with $73,000 and we in turn offered $71,500 plus asked for the refrigerator and patio furniture. They accepted!

"We have a house!" Bruce exclaimed.

All of the months of waiting and looking at houses let us know God's timing was perfect. Simons' house had only been on the market for three weeks and it met our needs perfectly. Nothing else came close to it for both price and size. We estimated it would cost $15,000 or more to do the remodeling for my living area and to put in a double-wide driveway.

On August 3 we attended the zoning meeting with the City Plan Commission. After much discussion including Jim McBride's protests and that of another historical home owner, the city official in charge of zoning finally said that Dr. Kelly's petition met the intent for an Historic Neighborhood Use zoning and recommended it be approved and sent to the City Council. A roll call vote was taken and the measure passed unanimously–6 to 0 in favor of Dr. Kelly. We were ecstatic!

In addition to dealing with the mansion, we also spent time going over to the house on Florian Court. We had the property surveyed to see if a double wide driveway could be put in. All of the carpet in the Scherers' bedrooms and living room would need to be replaced. The bathrooms and kitchen would need a sub-floor before linoleum could be laid. We had a lot of work to do. We talked to a Christian friend and he agreed to work on the house for $5.00 a hour. Praise God for His provision!

Monday, August 21, was the final hurdle on whether Dr. Kelly would actually be able to purchase the mansion. The City Council would vote that night on an ordinance granting a Special Use Permit for Dr. Kelly allowing him to purchase the historic England mansion. If the council refused to allow the permit, then the sale of the mansion would not go through and we could not purchase the house on Florian Court.

With much prayer we arrived at the City Council chambers. We knew it was a spiritual battle and prayed for God's divine intervention. Finally the vote was taken and it was unanimous–7 to 0 in favor of Dr. Kelly. We felt like shouting!

The next day on August 22 we met at First National Bank to close on the sale of the House of Prayer. When the papers were all signed, Bruce commented that his father, Lyle, and my husband, Jerry, were probably in heaven shouting for joy for a job well done. Over and over again we praised God that He had "hand-picked" Bruce to be our realtor, personal confidant and friend during this trying time of our lives. He was the "father image" we needed while Jerry was gone.

It had been nearly a year since the decision was made to sell the House of Prayer. As we told so many people, there are seasons in our lives and the "season" for us to live in the big mansion was coming to an end. However, it was not the end for the House of Prayer Ministries; rather, it was a new beginning.

We contracted with a man from our church to rip out the old carpet and install new carpet throughout the Florian Court residence. He was under a very tight schedule because we hired a professional moving company to move the big furniture pieces and boxes out of the House of Prayer to Florian Court on Friday, August 25. Before new flooring could be laid in the bathrooms, sub floors had to be put in. All of the carpet laying had to be done before the movers came.

Besides helping with the moving, Viki was busy getting Michael and Sarah ready for school. Their first day was August 24. What a blessing that Northwest Christian Campus was less than a mile away! On nice days the kids could ride their bikes.

The next night Bruce blessed us with a catered supper. The food hit the spot after a hard, hot day of moving. Kirk and his family joined us for a "picnic" style meal on the floor of the old fellowship room. I hoped my grandchildren would remember this great big mansion and some day realize the sacrifices their grandparents made while doing the Lord's work

The following evening the Scherers spent their first night in their new home on Florian Court. I elected to stay at the mansion with our cat, Midnight, to "guard" the house.

Two days later Chris and I made several trips back and forth to the new house before attending the funeral of a friend of mine. We had helped her out in the early days of the House of Prayer. It was a small funeral, but very emotional for me because it was in the same funeral home where Jerry's had been.

I went back to the House of Prayer to clean it one last time. A repairman was already there working on the old furnace and boiler. Slowly and sadly, I said good-bye to the various rooms and shut the doors. All I could think about was how different it was from when we first arrived 20 years earlier. The big old house rang out with laughter then, but now it was so quiet.

Jerry and I only had $15,000 to use as a down payment on the place. We had no congregation and no income. But by God's grace, we experienced miracle after miracle of His provision. We had nothing to our names but each other and a mighty God Who loved us.

My beloved husband was now gone and our children had their

177

own lives to live. I was left alone to say one final good-bye. With tears spilling down my face and hardly able to see, I got into my station wagon filled with the last load of treasures. I tried to sing, but the notes got stuck in my throat. Within two blocks of my new address, I saw a boy on a bicycle by the side of the road. It was Michael waiting for Grandma to "come home!"

22

Changes, Changes, Changes

I knew I was in God's perfect will, but how I hated change! The older I get, the more I resent change. To my dismay, I found out I was pretty set in my ways, but had to bend in order to survive.

Jerry and I had been a team for 39 years. We both did things quickly and then basked in the pleasure of our accomplishments. With Jerry gone, I had to rely on others to help get things done. Kirk, however, was busy pastoring the church and working two part-time jobs. Doug was a perfectionist and therefore tackled projects rather meticulously. I was very frustrated and felt like a fish out of water.

I liked everything beautiful and in order. I wanted rooms with lovely floral arrangements and beautiful pictures. The Scherers, on the other hand, could care less about having everything fancy. They were conservative when it came to interior decorating and did not consider that a top priority.

Since the remodeling work on my living quarters would not be completed for another month or so, I slept on Sarah's bottom bunk bed which did not lend itself to very much privacy.

Viki was busy working part-time at Northwest Christian Campus, doing church activities and running the House of Prayer Ministries. I decided to unpack some of their belongings and arrange their furniture. I had to do something to keep occupied! As usual, I overdid it and suffered with fibrositis. It felt like a knife was cutting my shoulder blade so I made an appointment to see the chiropractor.

I had several treatments and applied icy hot at bed time to help the pain. One night when it was very hot and humid, Sarah's bedspread from the top bunk fell down, hung across my bed and cut off my air supply.

"That does it!" I cried out.

I felt like I was suffocating in an enclosed coffin. I ran out to the living room and slept on a recliner chair for the next few weeks until my bedroom was completed.

I had to relinquish the reins for much of the decision making regarding the ministry and let Viki take over. She did a good job filling her father's shoes, but it was hard for me to let go.

September 9 would have been Charles and Eileen Volle's 50th wedding anniversary and September 12 would have been my 42nd wedding anniversary. We "girls" decided to make a tradition of celebrating our anniversaries together by going out to eat.

I wanted to do something special for Eileen and found a copper music box that was shaped like an airport hangar. When the key was wound up, the hangar opened and a tiny airplane came out and flew in a circle, playing "Laura's Song" from Dr. Zchivago. I also purchased a gorgeous gold heart pin and placed it in the plane's cockpit. Eileen just cried when she opened the gift.

I met some of our neighbors and was pleased to learn that Tim Littrell and his family lived across the street. He and Kim were classmates in high school. Tim said if I ever needed help with anything to let him know. I took him up on his offer several times!

Living next door on the east side of our house were Ken and Mabel Howlett. I was pleased to learn that Mabel had a special love for cats and enjoyed having our cat Midnight come over and visit. She was also fond of Michael and Sarah. We became great friends.

Next door on the other side of us were Mark and Jodi Ferriell and their three boys. Mark knew Jerry when he was in the insurance field and was amazed when Jerry went into the ministry.

Chris and I had a Sunday School Conference to attend in Michigan on Sept. 21. On our way back home, we stopped in Park Forest, Illinois, where we lived for two years while Jerry worked in Prudential's Home Office in Chicago. I was stunned to see the famous shopping mall I frequented every Friday night closed up like a ghost town. The dilapidated buildings were in ill repair. The once packed parking lot was deserted and weeds sprang up all over it. Once again I was reminded how quickly the things of this world go back to the dust of the earth. Everything is vanity!

On a happier note, my bedroom was almost ready for me to move into. I cleaned out the debris and Chris painted the trim. White carpet was installed and my beautiful new four-piece bedroom suite with etched gold roses was set up. I purchased a burgundy bedspread and pillows that matched the wallpaper. The television set was put on top of the chest of drawers and the desk fit perfectly under the new picture window facing the woods. I finally had a place to call my own!

Chris started sanding the cabinets for my kitchen. David Morris helped us hang them and then Chris and Viki painted them a light powder blue. David added the finishing touch by fastening the gold knobs. The kitchen floor linoleum resembled a blue and white marble pattern. Finally my downstairs living area was beginning to take shape.

On the fireplace mantel I put pictures of my children and grandchildren. Underneath it I put a family picture that was taken the last Christmas before Jerry died. On each side of the picture I put silhouettes of Jerry and me that we had made when we visited the Atlantic City Boardwalk shortly after we were married. Above the picture and silhouettes was a plaque our children had given us years ago. It simply said, *"The most important thing a Father can do for his children is to love their mother."* Jerry would always occupy the chief place of honor in our family.

By God's grace, I was able to keep my china cabinet, dining room table and matching chairs and put them in my new living quarters. Some of the houses that we had looked at were not big enough to accommodate my dining room furniture plus Viki and Doug's. God was so good in providing us with the perfect home that He had picked out for us.

We replaced the badly cracked single driveway with a double wide one to accommodate three vehicles. We still had boxes to unpack that were stored in the garage. One day the garage door would not open so Doug used a crow bar to pry it open. We discussed having an electric garage door. Viki was so elated when the door was finally installed. Excitedly she drove the Oldsmobile into the garage only to be horrified when she found out that the car stuck outside five inches. She had measured the garage's inside width to make sure the Oldsmobile would fit, but never dreamed the length would not be long enough. For the first time she stood there absolutely speechless!

Several weeks later, Doug, Kirk, and two other men moved the wall separating the garage and utility room 16 inches. Finally, the Oldsmobile fit in the garage!

It was close to Christmas when all of the remodeling projects were completed. We even had the outside of the house painted white to cover up the ugly green and brown colors.

We decided to have an Open House the week before Christmas and invited relatives, friends and neighbors to come and see the transformation. Those who had seen the house before could not believe all of the changes.

On Christmas Eve my family gathered in my downstairs living area to exchange gifts. It was wonderful basking in the warmth, peace and coziness of the fireplace. No one wanted to leave.

The New Year was soon upon us and our tranquility was replaced with chaos and change. On January 3 we received the word that Dorothy Woodrum had gone home to her eternal glory. She and her family were some of the first members of the House of Prayer congregation. She and her husband, Paul, had lost their first spouses and together raised eleven children. Kirk helped with the funeral.

Six days later we learned that another church member, Dolores Marini, was having emergency surgery. God miraculously transformed her into a new creature after she accepted Christ as her Savior. She lived above a tavern named Changes and finally moved to a senior citizen hi-rise apartment where we helped her set up housekeeping. Her son Mark had been involved in our church youth group years earlier.

Kirk went directly to the hospital where Dolores was having surgery and visited with Mark and his fiancee, Bernice. Two days later I received a phone call from Chris who said there was a fire in the trailer where Mark lived with his fiancee and her four children. She did not know for sure, but thought someone might have died in the fire. Not only was Bernice killed, but so was her three-year-old daughter.

Mark had been at work and was beside himself when he found out. The other three children were in school. Apparently the fire had started in the living room and spread quickly. The mother tried to open a window to get the girl out, but a back draft came upon them and they died in seconds. Kirk spoke at the funeral for both victims.

The next morning Chris called again with bad news. The church had just been robbed! Someone waited to break in until after Teresa left for work at 5:30 a.m. A ladder was propped outside the second story window of Kirk's office. Three desks were rifled through as though someone was looking for cash. A pair of scissors was used to pry open the locked file cabinet. Checks were strewn everywhere. Amazingly, an envelope with the tithe money was overlooked.

Chris was upstairs asleep in the church apartment while the robbery occurred. I suddenly feared for her safety and wondered what would have happened if she had come downstairs and found someone robbing the church.

"Mom, if I saw that it was a teenager, I would have chased him until I caught him," she remarked.

We received word that Dolores Marini was dying. Mark was torn between spending time with her and trying to be a father to his fiancee's three remaining children.

Dolores' kidneys and heart were failing and her body was full of bacteria. Although she was only 65 years of age, she had lived a hard life. The doctors wanted someone with her at all times so several people from church took turns staying at her bedside. By the time Chris and I left to drive to Washington, D.C., for a Sunday School Convention, Dolores was on a ventilator. Mark made the difficult decision of having all life support systems removed. His mother had suffered enough and there was no chance for survival.

Several people from church plus Mark and Dolores' sisters gathered around Dolores for one last time. They sang her favorite chorus "Majesty." Around 7:15 p.m. Dolores went home to His Majesty, King Jesus.

I believe Jerry was on the welcoming committee in heaven, ready to receive another saint into eternal glory. Mark's aunts had Dolores' body flown to California for burial. She was back home at last. Later we had a wonderful memorial service for Dolores at Harvest Christian Center. Everyone loved her. She was such a spark of life during the few years we were associated with her.

Chris and I encountered terrible weather during our stay in Washington, D.C. Deep snow was piled everywhere. Adding to our misery was getting lost in the freezing cold while trying to catch a bus back to the metro station where our car was parked.

We had experienced bad weather at the Central Illinois Sunday School Convention in Peoria a couple of months earlier. Normally that convention is held in February, but it was changed to November with hopes that the weather would be much better. The inevitable happened! Rain turned to freezing rain and snow—one of the earliest winter storms to hit the area.

Chris and I weren't home very long from the Washington, D.C. convention, when we packed our bags and headed toward Atlanta, Georgia. We drove as far as Nashville, Tennessee, and spent the night with Jeanette's sister and family. By the time we woke up the next morning, the weathermen were forecasting ice. Chris was determined to get to Atlanta so we left quickly.

We arrived safely at the convention site and set up our exhibition booth. By 8 p.m. freezing rain coated everything outdoors so the convention officials ordered everyone to leave the building. We got up early the next morning and discovered about ½ inch thick ice covering our station wagon. It took forever to scrape and chip the ice. The roads were extremely treacherous, but Chris managed to drive to the big church where the convention was held. Lo and behold, only the "Yankees" showed up! None of the "Southerners" attempted to get out and drive. Even the conference coordinator did not show up. We stood around for a while and then came the announcement. "The conference is called off. Everyone go home."

Chris and I tore down our booth and headed back to our hotel to get the rest of our belongings. We canceled our reservation for that night and decided to drive to Chattanooga, Tennessee, to stay with some friends a day earlier than originally planned.

But first, Chris wanted to see some friends in the Atlanta area who lived about 30 minutes away. Two hours later we pulled up in their driveway. Along the way, we saw cars that had skidded off the roads and were abandoned. We were nearly creamed by a car that could not stop. Over and over again, we thanked God for His protection.

Soon we headed to Chattanooga. The road conditions were terrible. It started sleeting on top of the snow and ice. Visibility was extremely poor and only two lanes were opened for travel. If you tried to pass a vehicle, you would end up in the ditch. We stopped counting after seeing over 100 cars and semi trucks in the ditches. At one location there was an 11-car pile up. Only by prayer did we make it to Chattanooga, but our battle was not over.

The Schumann family we were going to stay with lived on top of a mountain. As Chris drove higher and higher, I was never so petrified in all of my life. Try as hard as she could, Chris could not get the wagon to go up the steep icy incline.

"Hang on and pray," she shouted and then put the car in reverse. We coasted down the mountain on a sheet of ice over several inches of snow. Chris then put the car in first gear and made it to the top of the mountain. I believe some strong angels helped push us to the top.

On Valentine's Day I received a phone call from Kim who casually asked if I would like a "Valentine" number 10. I couldn't believe it was possible to have another grandchild, but had always wanted 10. Kim said Libby had a doctor's appointment next Thursday.

Of course, we all concluded that it was to confirm Libby's pregnancy and to determine how far along she was. Just eight days later on February 22, which also happened to be Kirk's 36th birthday, a jubilant Kim called to announce that another girl, Kiana Donné, had joined the Henneberry family. She weighed 5 pounds and 13 ½ ounces. Her sisters had watched the birth and Kim once again cut the umbilical cord for a newborn daughter.

It would be busy in Kim's household–a newborn baby plus two other girls, Kim finishing up his bachelor's degree and studying for finals, and Libby finishing her master's degree in June. In addition, Kim was scheduled to do a marathon session of tuning pianos for 24 hours straight for a school district.

"He's a workaholic just like his father," I mused.

On the evening of April 18 Northwest Christian Campus had its annual Academic Fair. It started to rain and then stormed violently. It even hailed. Viki was on the clean-up committee so we were the last ones to leave the school.

When we pulled into our driveway, we could see two lamps in the livingroom were turned on. They were "touch lamps" that would go on when someone touched the metal parts or if there was a surge in electricity. Shortly after we got in our house, the power went off and we were plunged into darkness.

Viki turned on her transistor radio and began shouting that a tornado had just hit the southeast section of Decatur along Lake Shore Drive. In a 16-block area, a major grocery store was demolished and many other businesses and homes were heavily damaged or destroyed. Miraculously, no one was killed. The Dairy Queen on Cantrell St. had its windows blown out. Ironically, a big tree limb blew into the mouth of a large fish that was mounted on top of Mike's Tackle World. It would serve as a reminder of the tornado.

Throughout the next day, storm warnings were announced by the news media. Michael was invited to Nick Bushong's birthday party and Sarah was scheduled to have a friend spend the night. Michael was dropped off at Nick's house and Sarah waited patiently for Taylor Van Natta's arrival.

Shortly after supper, the sky began to turn an eery yellow-green color. The air seemed thick and heavy. Doug and I stood outside as it began hailing marble to golf-ball size hail. I picked up several stones and put them in our freezer. The phone rang and it was Taylor's parents canceling her overnight stay.

Back inside the house, the television weather forecaster reported a tornado had been spotted in Jacksonville, Illinois, and was heading north. Doug said the excitement was over because the storm was out of our path. Viki decided to turn on her transistor radio and suddenly the tornado sirens were warning everyone to take cover.

We looked at each other, wondering what to do because we had never planned where we should go in the event there was a tornado. As we headed down to the utility room, Doug shouted, "There

186

it is! I can see the tornado!"

Viki and I stared outside the utility room window. There it was, behind our house, swirling debris everywhere. We lifted Sarah on top of the freezer so she could see her first tornado. Suddenly, we came to our senses and dove under the big desk in Viki's office. We prayed and asked for God's safety and protection as our house shook from the fierce strength of the tornado. Rather than hit our house, we saw the tornado go through the woods behind our home. It wreaked havoc and destruction to homes on Gary Drive, Home Park Avenue, Ravina Park Road and many, many other side streets. Over 200 homes were damaged or destroyed.

At one house a Volkswagen was lifted up and planted on the doorstep of a house across the street. Big trees were uprooted and electrical lines dangled everywhere. The tornado skipped along and heavily damaged a lumber yard, a used car lot, more homes and a nursing home. St. Teresa's Convent suffered extensive damage.

When we felt it was finally safe to emerge from our hiding place, we went outside to find our house covered with a fine layer of debris and dust. Corn stalks from fields a mile and more away plastered the outside of our house and were strewn throughout our yard and the neighbors yards. We met several neighbors walking around outside with flashlights. Viki turned on her portable transistor radio to WSOY Radio Station which did a marvelous job of keeping the Decatur community informed of the latest developments.

My first concern was our church and whether it sustained any damage. We called a church member who lived near the church and she said everything looked all right. What a relief! Not too far from the church, an automobile body repair shop was hit by the tornado.

As nightfall came, we heard police and fire sirens coming from all different directions. About two miles west of us the Sharon United Methodist Church was completely destroyed. Other homes in the Wilcox Addition were heavily damaged. The home on the corner of Kirk's street was completely gone.

Kirk, his family and his next-door neighbors, the Bivens, raced down Kirk's basement to take refuge when the tornado sirens went off. Kirk's phone would not work so he had to use Bivens' phone to call and tell us everyone was all right. Kirk's house was pelted with all kinds of debris from the tornado's tail end. There wasn't one inch of his lawn or driveway that was not covered with glass. His house alone sustained $14,000 damage.

Everyone at the birthday party Michael attended was pretty scared when the tornado hit. Viki kept in touch with Michael by phone. However, she could not drive to pick him up because the power was out over a large part of the city and traffic lights were not working. It was not safe to drive.

The next morning most of the Home Park housing addition was sealed off so that looters and "gawkers" could not get in. Even though houses on our street were not hit by the tornado, we were told by the police there was no guarantee we could get back home if we left our area. As a result, Viki made arrangements for some friends to drop off Michael at Grand and Home Park Avenues. She drove her car as close as she could get and then got out and walked to meet Michael. He was never so happy to get home!

On Sunday morning Kirk capitalized on the tornado's destruction and preached to a full house his sermon entitled "Getting Your House in Order." Everyone praised God for His divine mercy that no one was killed. No one had ever heard of two tornadoes hitting a town on two successive nights.

Later that afternoon Doug, Michael, Sarah and I walked a little over a mile to Kirk's house on Dennis Ave. We were aghast at all of the destruction along the way. It looked like a military war zone where bombs had gone off. People's belongings were scattered everywhere. Insulation, siding, ripped boards and sheet metal hung from houses and even trees. It was an awesome site! Even First Lady Hillary Rodham Clinton came to view the damage. It took over a year before many of the homes were repaired or rebuilt.

On May 5 we learned that Tina Scribner, a member of our church, was dying of cancer. She was five months away from being cancer free for five years when cancer was discovered again. She was in terrible pain and would often cry out, "Lord, why can't You take me home now?" I tried to console her with a poem I had written several years earlier entitled "Drama of Life."

Drama of Life

The world is the center stage
*   And the drama is life itself.*
We are the members of the audience
*   Till we turn to Christ for help.*

Then we become the characters
*   In the play that's been well-run.*
We seek to be over comers
*   As we rely on God's dear Son.*

The Writer is our heavenly Father
*   Who knew all from the beginning.*
He knows which actors will endure
*   To see the final ending.*

The Spirit is the Producer
*   And the Spiritual Director too.*
The script is all God's Holy Word
*   Which gives us all our cues.*

Jesus is the leading Actor.
*   We're an understudy to Him.*
We follow in His footsteps
*   Which lead us away from sin.*

Our attire is the armor of God–
*   We apply it every day.*
We wear it to fight the battle scene
*   And be victorious in every way.*

The final act is being staged.
*   Christ stands behind the curtain.*
His entrance to this world is readied
*   And a climax is for certain.*

You alone have the right to decide
Which ending you will choose.
You can be the good guy or the bad one
And either win or lose!

"Drama of Life," *School of Learning* © 1979 Dottie Henneberry

I gently reminded Tina that all of us are actors and actresses on the stage of life. Our parts keep changing and sometimes we are assigned scripts that are distasteful. Our scenery can change also, but we are required to do the best acting job possible and pass the test in the final act.

Tina was only 39 years old, but had suffered much. Before she surrendered her life to Jesus, she didn't think God could possibly love her. When she finally came to the realization of how much Jesus loved her, she yielded her life to His Lordship. Her loving and caring ways helped bring people to our church.

She always had a terrific sense of humor and exemplified it during our church's Hallelujah Night which was an alternative to Halloween. Our theme was Noah's Ark and she came dressed as a cow–udder and all!

As Tina's health began to fail more and more, I tried to make it a priority to visit her in the hospital. Oftentimes I sang to her my new song "I'm Going Home" and she would open her eyes and look upward.

On May 17, which was also Kim's 41st birthday, I arrived at the hospital just in time to see Tina's mother, "Skip," come running out of her room, down to the nurse's station. She then ran back to the room and I raced in after her, just in time to see Tina take her last breath. I ran out of the room and told the nurses, "This is it. Tina's gone!"

The nurses came in and tenderly straightened Tina while I held Skip in my arms. I told her the gates of heaven had just opened wide. Jesus and all of the saints were waiting there to welcome Tina as she entered in. A royal crown was being presented to her for a life lived to the fullness of His love.

"She is now His beautiful bride," I continued.

Earlier I had told Tina she had my permission to give Jerry a great big hug from me.

"I never met your husband, but I believe I'll know him when I get up there," she replied.

Now Tina was a butterfly, set free from the body that had tied her down. I thanked God He allowed me to be at the hospital for Tina's appointed time into eternity. Kirk had her funeral and read my poem "Courage" which described Tina perfectly.

Viki decided it would be a good idea for Chris and me to attend the Christians in Theater Arts Conference in Chicago. I sat in one of the workshop classes for writers and was shocked from what I heard. In all of my years of writing drama, I always strived to present a powerful gospel message, but at this workshop the instructor boldly stated that the skits should not be preachy. He represented one of the fastest growing churches in the country which used "Christian" drama in its services. He stressed that no gospel words were to be used. Conflict should be established, but the message should be kept light and vague. Let the preacher have the answer.

The workshop leader explained that at his church the pastor would give the actors a title of the presentation two weeks in advance. It was their assignment to write a sketch, rehearse it for five hours, bring in full orchestration for one song and then perform the skit before the Seekers Service (unbelievers) on Sunday morning. If a person attended services for seven weeks, then he could become a believer and come to the worship service on Wednesday nights.

I couldn't believe it! I always believed it was the Word of God that divided the soul and the spirit and convicted people of their sins. I wondered how Jesus felt about using entertainment to get people to come to church.

I expressed my concern to a regional representative of CITA, but it was to no avail. I was standing pretty much alone on my convictions.

On the last day of the conference, one man finally had the boldness to stand up and say, "Give me some honest, unpolished, God-fearing little people that will boldly proclaim the Gospel and souls will be saved." Then he added, "The little churches need them."

"Yes!" I shouted emphatically.

Chris shared with some aspiring actresses about her acting experiences including being Coach Chris on the local Christian television station. She told them she left the station and all its "fame" when occultic cartoons that were contrary to God's Word became part of the daily programming.

"Do you think Christians should not be in the theater then?" they asked.

"I didn't say that," Chris replied. "All I can tell you is if you're only in the arts for the fame and glory, it will only burn up on the day your works are tested by God. Only what is purely done to glorify Him and His kingdom will be left standing."

II Corinthians 5:10 "For we must all appear before the judgment seat of Christ, that each one may receive what is due him for the things done while in the body, whether good or bad."

As we left the conference, people came up to Chris and asked her where she got her drama training and where she learned her facial expressions. They had watched her act out the part of a gorilla on Noah's Ark during the conference's opening night meeting. She had raced up to the stage when a last minute volunteer was needed. She did such a good job that she almost stole the show!

"I had one semester of drama in high school 20 some years ago. The rest is all God-given ability," she told her admirers.

Doug, Viki, Michael and Sarah left the middle of June for a vacation on the east coast. I stayed home to "guard" our new home and to take care of our two cats. A yellow tabby that Sarah befriended and named Nibbles had officially been adopted into the Scherer family. At first Midnight greatly disliked this rival, but eventually he enjoyed Nibble's company and would even cuddle up to him.

I decided to prove to Doug and Viki that I was "a big girl now" and could take care of myself. I meticulously checked every door and window to make sure they were locked before I took an early shower, having been soaked and covered with mud while trying to water the flowers.

At 10:30 p.m. the doorbell rang. I froze. I was dressed in my mumu and had rollers in my hair. The doorbell rang again so I carefully tiptoed downstairs to see who was there. A voice on the outside was yelling. "Dottie, it's Linda! It's Linda!" I opened the door and there stood my neighbor from across the street. She was in her pajamas too! She knew Doug and Viki were gone and since her phone was not working, she just had to tell me that my garage door was wide opened. I praised God for such a caring neighbor and for His divine protection.

One morning I went outside and found my keys still in the front door. I had forgotten to remove them when I came home the day before. Again, God had watched over me when disaster could have been lurking. My "senior moments" were increasing!

Kirk received word that Greg Nash, his close Christian friend from high school gymnastics days, had just passed away from an enlarged heart. At the tender age of 37, Greg had been ushered into the presence of the Lord.

I reminisced about the first time Greg spent the night at the big England mansion shortly after we moved into it. He and Kirk were about 14 years old and had stayed up late. Around midnight they turned off the lights when all of a sudden the front door to the house opened and a flashlight beamed their way. These "courageous" boys froze for a few seconds and then dove under the covers. It turned out that a drunken man who still had a key to the house came inside and then left muttering to himself.

Like Tina, Greg was taken from this world at an early life. At his funeral, Kirk read from Charles Spurgeon's *Morning and Evening Daily Readings* that had ministered to me the night after Jerry's funeral. The message dealt with the young and the best being taken because Jesus was praying to His Father that they could be with him. By faith, we let them go.

Nibbles, the adorable yellow cat that Sarah found, became very ill with asthma. We had no idea cats could get asthma. He got better after some expensive treatments, but then became ill again. Viki let him outside one morning and he never returned home. All indications are he found a secluded spot where he could die in peace. We searched and searched the woods for him, but never found him.

I couldn't endure the heartache of his loss so I set out to find a replacement. At the local animal shelter I asked the attendant to let me hold the scraggly gray kitten with the loud voice. Immediately he started purring and climbed all the way to the top of my head and nested down like he belonged there.

"That's the one!" I exclaimed to the worker.

We named him Friskie and he lived up to his name. Now Midnight had a "brother" to keep him company.

The year of 1996 was definitely a year of change. The great Author and Finisher of our life was directing the scenery changes. Many people we knew and loved were taken out of the picture for a better heavenly role. In God's infinite wisdom He builds up and He tears down. If we could catch a glimpse of what goes on behind the scenes, we would applaud and throw bouquets of admiration to our Heavenly Father as He unfolds events in His Book of Life.

23

He Is the Potter, I Am the Clay

The phone rang late at night on February 22, which also happened to be Kirk's 37th birthday. I did not recognize Kim's voice. He was crying so hard. He had been tuning pianos all day and stopped at a store on his way home to buy a present for baby Kiana's first birthday. Upon arriving at the trailer, he found to his horror that it was empty. Libby had taken the girls and some of his belongings were missing. In between sobs, he told me that he had come home earlier in the week to find Libby's wedding ring and a note stating that their marriage of 12 years was over and she wanted a divorce. Kim was devastated!

Libby had received her master's degree in May while Kim had obtained his bachelor's degree in January. He made straight A's, tuned pianos over the eastern half of Montana (sometimes pulling all-night marathons at schools and fairs) and for the most part raised the three girls. Now the marriage was suddenly over. Kim would give her a divorce, but he wanted custody of the children.

I was in shock! No one in our family had ever been divorced. We all prayed and believed Libby would change her mind. Kim now had the full responsibilities of raising Chantelle, who would be 11 in July; Katlin, who was five; and Kiana, who just turned one. The emotional stress caused Kim to lose 10 pounds in 10 days. His back gave out and he slept on the floor to ease the discomfort.

In the meantime, Chris and I left for Akron, Ohio, to participate in another Sunday School convention. It was snowing and the wind blew fiercely when we arrived so we quickly set up our booth and left the convention site at 8:30 p.m. When we came back the next morning, we discovered someone had taken 10 of our skit books, probably thinking they were free. God would have to make up the financial deficit and He did! Chris did such an outstanding job presenting her drama and prayer workshops that we had people standing in line at our exhibit booth wanting to buy our drama material.

From Ohio we drove to Charlotte, North Carolina, where everything was budding and blooming early. It was 27 degrees with a wind chill of 10 degrees when we left Akron, but it was a gorgeous 77 degrees when we hit Charlotte. Needless to say, the weather change played havoc with my allergies.

The next day as Chris drove on a multiple lane highway, a lady driver in front of us stopped abruptly, nearly causing a four car pile-up. I thanked God for watching over us and for His protective angels that surrounded us at all times.

Chris had never been to the Biltmore Estates in Asheville and decided to take a tour of it while I shopped at the nearby Biltmore Shopping Center. When we met up later, she told me she never made it inside the building. Instead, she had been getting estimates on getting the brakes fixed on the station wagon. She knew from the near accident the day before that the brakes were going bad. One repair man told her we could make it home all right even with all the mountain driving, but we would have to get them repaired as soon as possible once we arrived home.

We drove to Otto, North Carolina, and stayed with the Jorgensens for a couple of days before driving back to Charlotte where we were scheduled to participate in the Mid-Atlantic Christian Education Association's Convention. I did not feel well so Chris went alone to the convention on the first day. I was queasy, nauseous and had a headache caused from sinus pressure.

I was determined to go the last day of the convention. In the booth across from us was Joni Eareckson Tada, a paraplegic who founded JAF Ministries. She is an internationally known mouth artist who has authored 20 books. When the crowd cleared out after she signed autographs, I went over and introduced myself to Joni. I read her my poem "Assorted Roses." She was delighted and asked for a copy of my poem book which I signed for her.

Kim called from Montana and said he had just finished tuning 100 pianos in a marathon session, working day and night. I told him that at the age of 41 he was getting a little old to be working that hard.

Kim said he had some good news–he and the girls were planning to come visit in July and would stay for a couple of weeks. I was elated! It would be the first time all of my children would be together since Jerry died four years earlier. Chantelle, Katlin and Kiana would get to spend time with their cousins.

Viki told Kim that his muscle would be needed to help put a new roof on our house. He had experience working on roofs and we needed as many people as possible to help with this huge project.

For the 1997-1998 school year, Kim was hired to teach in a one-room school house that was located 37 ½ miles south of Miles City. He and the girls would live in the lower basement area.

Members of Kim's church embraced Kim and his daughters with love, giving them caring help and support during the divorce proceedings. Some fixed meals while others babysat when Kim had to go away to tune pianos. The mother of one of his students said she would babysit Kiana during the day while Kim taught school. I was so grateful God answered our prayers and provided for Kim's needs.

I wanted everything beautiful in the yard for Kim's homecoming. Trees and flowers were planted everywhere. Chris helped me plant a small rose garden in the back yard near the patio. Doug helped with various outdoor projects. We were thrilled when the Decatur Public Transit System named him Bus Driver of the Year for the fifth time.

I began to experience tremendous abdominal pain and was finally tested for a hiatial hernia. The doctor said I had the beginning of one. I was also diagnosed with esophagus reflux which was a terrible disease to live with. Several times a week I ate lunch at a fast food restaurant or would meet Eileen for breakfast. God began to deal with me about my weight and eating habits. Little did I know I was going to lose weight the hard way.

Chris decided to buy an old dilapidated house located a few doors down from our church. The price was right, but the entire interior had to be gutted. There was much work to do! For three days I raked grass that was three feet tall, pulled weeds and shrubbery from around the house, carried bricks, and last but not least, pulled out carpet staples from three rooms. Using a screw driver and a pair of pliers, I jerked and twisted to get them out.

"Isn't it great a woman my age can work like this?" I asked myself.

My glory was short-lived. When my granddaughter Natalie's fifth birthday party came around, I could hardly sit. All of the family members went outside to play softball, so I decided to get in on the action. I took my turn at bat, hit the ball and slid into first base. I was in excruciating pain!

The next day I knew I should rest, but instead I baked four cakes and got food ready for a funeral dinner at the church. Viki and I also got ready for another rummage sale. It rained off and on during the sale, so we had to run out of the garage several times to cover up the rummage on the tables. Even though the sun was not shining, I got a terrible sunburn. I was on an antibiotic and later read that I was supposed to avoid all exposure to the sun while taking that medication.

On my 63rd birthday Decatur was hit with a terrible storm. Water poured through a crack in our back patio, gushed through the crawl space and came into the closet under my stairway. In just seconds mud and water came pouring out onto my living room's white berber carpet. Viki screamed for help and started grabbing my silk flower arrangements, crafts, photo albums, wrapping paper and cassette tapes that I stored in the closet. It took hours to clean up the mess. Some of the flowers were ruined immediately while others eventually had mold appear over them.

Every time I stayed down in my living room area for any length of time, I always got a headache. I eventually discovered mold on my refrigerator door. In addition the carpet was still wet in some places. Since Kim was going to stay in my living room and sleep on my sleeper couch, I decided to purchase a dehumidifier so that extra moisture in the air could be taken out.

Kim and the girls finally pulled in around 4 p.m. on July 10. It was an exciting moment! Little Kiana had cute ringlets all over head. Soon she began calling Viki, "mommy" and would not let go of her.

That night we gathered in the Scherers' living room for an impromptu music practice. Kim played the piano, Michael played the keyboard, Kirk played the guitar and I sang. Our neighbor, Tim Littrell, who was a friend of Kim's in high school, came over and listened to the "concert." Kim played two songs he had just composed. It was the first music he had written in 12 years. There were no words, but you could feel the emotion.

When Tim started to leave, Kim asked him to stay and listen to the song he composed and sang to Libby on their wedding day. We were all touched and tried to hold back the tears. I just stood there and bawled. How much heartache he must have endured since Libby's announcement that she wanted a divorce!

On Monday, July 14, I took Chantelle and Katlin on a three-hour shopping spree and purchased seven pairs of shoes. When we got home, the storm clouds burst wide open. Bolts of lightning flashed everywhere and loud claps of thunder pierced the atmosphere. To divert the girls' attention from the storm, I told them about the surprise graduation party we were going to give their dad that night. We felt it was a big accomplishment for him to graduate from college and we wanted to honor him for it. The girls thought that was a great idea and helped decorate my downstairs living area with crepe paper. We invited some relatives and several of Kim's friends from the past. It was a great evening and let Kim know how much he was loved and appreciated.

Two days later the Scherers and Kim and his two oldest daughters left for St. Louis to do some sightseeing. I was assigned the duty of watching one-year-old Kiana. I was not feeling well so I called Chris. She came and spent the night. I went to the doctor and was given an antibiotic, plus was told not to lift the baby.

On Friday the "vacationers" returned and I was elated to see them. I was in terrible pain so I called Dr. Eloy. He told me to go to the hospital emergency room and admit myself. I delayed going, hoping I would feel better. Plus, this was the weekend several church members were helping put a new roof on our house. Doug, Kim and Larry Hughes had already started tearing off the old shingles.

Finally, I could not stand the pain any longer. I had Viki drive me to the hospital emergency room at 10:30 p.m. I was given something for my nausea, but was not admitted into a room until 4 a.m. I was exhausted! Viki finally went home and got two hours sleep. The workers were coming at 7 a.m. to put on a new roof.

After two days of IV's and pain medicine every four hours, Dr. McGhee released me from the hospital and said no further tests were needed. But when I got home, I started limping on my right leg.

I still was not feeling well a week later and happened to meet up with Dr. Kelly's wife in a grocery store parking lot. She noticed I was limping and suggested that her husband could maybe help me since he was a neurologist.

They came over to my house that evening. After a short examination, Wayne stated that I did not have any nerve damage, but rather a classic case of myofascitis. It concerned the fibrous tissue that connected the muscle to the bone. I had greatly aggravated the lower abdomen with over-exertion when working at Chris's house. He suggested complete bed rest and ibuprofen.

The few days of bed rest turned into three weeks and my stomach pains worsened. Dr. Kelly had to go to New York for two weeks to see his ailing father. Since I knew Dr. McGhee was retiring soon, I knew I needed to find a new doctor. I did not know what to do and called my friend, Pat Storm, who was my insurance representative. She recommended I see Dr. Richard Fritz who was her doctor. A miracle occurred and I got to see him the next day.

After a thorough examination, he ordered blood work and x-rays that night at the hospital. Early the next morning I had to go back to the hospital for a CAT scan. I had the chills so bad that I had Viki put a blanket around me. By the time we got home, I was in terrible agony and had Viki call Dr. Fritz's home. He prescribed a muscle relaxer and to drink plenty of gatorade.

Hours later I could not bear the pain so Dr. Fritz admitted me to the hospital. He ordered a lot of tests and noted that my white blood count was up and that I was dehydrated. I was put on IV's and given pain medicine every four hours. He noticed that I had a goiter that would require medical attention later.

I was still in the hospital on Sunday so Viki brought Eileen up to see me. She had been very worried and concerned about me. She promised to treat me to a free dinner after I got out of the hospital.

"That's a great incentive to get better," I told myself.

Before I went to sleep that night in my quiet hospital room, I picked up Charles H. Spurgeon's book *Morning and Evening Daily Readings* for my evening devotion. I was stunned to read the caption for the night of August 17. *"This sickness is not unto death." John 11:4*

From our Lord's words we learn that there is a limit to sickness. Here is an 'unto' within which its ultimate end is restrained, and beyond which it cannot go. Lazarus might pass through death, but death was not to be the ultimatum of his sickness. In all sickness, the Lord saith to the waves of pain, 'Hitherto shall ye go, but no further.' His fixed purpose is not the destruction, but the instruction of His people. Wisdom hangs up the thermometer at the furnace mouth, and regulates the heat.

1. *The limit is encouragingly comprehensive.* The God of providence has limited the time, manner, intensity, repetition, and effects of all our sicknesses; each throb is decreed, each sleepless hour predestinated, each relapse ordained, each depression of spirit foreknown, and each sanctifying result eternally purposed. Nothing great or small escapes the ordaining head of Him who numbers the hairs of our head.

2. *This limit is wisely adjusted* to our strength, to the end designed, and to the grace apportioned. Affliction comes not at haphazard—the weight of every stroke of the rod is accurately measured. He who made no mistakes in balancing the clouds and meting out the heavens, commits no errors in measuring out the ingredients which compose the medicine of souls. We cannot suffer too much nor be relieved too late.

3. *The limit is tenderly appointed.* The knife of the heavenly Surgeon never cuts deeper than is absolutely necessary. 'He doth not afflict willingly, nor grieve the children of men.' A mother's heart cries, 'Spare my child;' but

no mother is more compassionate than our gracious God. When we consider how hard-mouthed we are, it is a wonder that we are not driven with a sharper bit. The thought is full of consolation, that He who has fixed the bounds of our habitation, has also fixed the bounds of our tribulation.

I knew my heavenly Father was watching over me and would guide me during this dark time in my life.

The next day I received a hospital roommate. She was in her fifties, suffering with many of the same symptoms that Jerry had before he died including emphysema, asthma and heart disease. She wanted the room's air conditioner turned on cold with the fan blowing on her at all times. She also had the television on at all hours of the day and night.

At one point I did not think she would live through the night because of her breathing difficulties. I got out of my bed and went over to her to pray. She nodded that she knew Jesus as her Savior and Lord. It was comforting to know, but at the same time I felt uneasy because it made me relive Jerry's last days on earth.

Kim called me at the hospital on Tuesday and reminded me that I devoured a lot of mixed nuts at his graduation party plus drank a lot of the delicious punch which Viki had made. It was loaded with citric acid which probably bothered my stomach.

Viki came in early the next morning as my breakfast was being served. A nurse came in and said all my tests were negative, indicating there was nothing physically wrong with me. Viki buttered a slice of my toast and the nurse bluntly asked, "Why are you doing that? She should be buttering her own toast." Viki smiled and replied, "Because she's my mom and I love her." I felt humiliated with the nurse's remarks.

Dr. Fritz came in shortly thereafter and said he was bringing in a specialist to look at me. I hoped it would be Dr. Victor Eloy who had seen me before. I rejoiced when he walked in later that afternoon. After a quick examination, he told me on his way out of the room, "We will get to the bottom of this."

In the hectic hours that followed, I was prepped all night for a lower bowel scan. One nurse remarked that I was the calmest hospital patient she had ever seen considering how much pain I was in. I said I felt like I was trying to deliver a baby for the last two months, but no deliverance came.

Dale McKinney, a red-haired lab technician, came into my room to draw blood. He knew Kirk and Viki from Northwest Christian Campus. I told him I was their mother. He saw a copy of my book *Fortress on a Hill* on the cabinet. I told him he could have it, but he insisted on writing a check for it. "I can just feel the presence of the Lord in this room," he remarked as he left the room. I was blessed!

Dr. Fritz said my lower gastrointestinal series test revealed that I had diverticulitis again. It also showed that my colon kinked and curved instead of going straight across. This caused me to have pain. In addition I had a tremendous amount of esophagus reflux–sometimes clear down to my ribs.

Dr. Fritz became positive and cheerful when he said, "This is the first day that we know what's wrong with you and can start to treat you."

He wanted me to stop taking the pain shots and have the IV's removed. The pain medicine was preventing my healing and could cause blood clots to form. I had to quit it cold turkey and could only take Tylenol® every four hours. In addition, I needed to get out of the bed and start walking the hospital corridors.

I found out what drug addicts go through when they have withdrawal symptoms. I talked to Lura Etnier for hours on the telephone just to keep my mind off of the pain. My body temperature dropped down to 96 degrees so I had a nurse put a heating pad across my stomach for the chills and pain I was experiencing.

Grace Jorgensen called and told me, "Dottie, just think about good things as you fall asleep tonight." Everyone was praying for me and believing I would get healed.

In spite of all the stress I was under, my blood pressure went down and I no longer needed to take medication for it. I had lost 20 pounds and that was a contributing factor to my lower blood pressure.

Dr. Fritz came in to see me and said I could go home. Viki zoomed over to pick me up. When I stepped into our lovely white house that I now called home, I cried like a baby. It was so good to be home after this long siege of sickness. Doug, Michael, Sarah, and our two cats Friskie and Midnight were on the welcoming committee.

I had to be extremely careful of everything I did. Reflux would attack. I couldn't walk fast any more. My stomach muscles were healing and it would take time before they worked normally. I was growing older and not embracing it very easily.

24

Be Anxious for Nothing

In the days and weeks that followed, I noticed another disturbing factor in my body. I simply could not slow down. I was extremely nervous. My eyelids fluttered, my hands shook and I could not fall asleep in my recliner chair. My stomach and intestines churned constantly ever since I was injected with iodine and had a CAT scan in August. I suspected it had something to do with my thyroid.

I contacted Dr. Fritz's office and told his nurse Phyllis about my condition. She said it might possibly be a goiter, but I would have to wait until all of the iodine was out of my system before any more tests could be ordered. I was given medication for anxiety, muscle relaxers, bowel pain killers and sleeping pills. Even with all of this I still only got five to six hours of sleep at night and then the shaking would start all over again. An ice pack and heating pad became my constant companions.

To help my hiatal hernia which always worsened at night, Doug elevated my bed by putting blocks of wood under the legs so that it would be raised several inches. I could not eat anything after 7 p.m.

My two-month waiting period for the iodine to be out of my system was finally over so I called Dr. Fritz's office. The nurse and I had a three-way telephone conversation with Decatur Memorial Hospital to set up the tests for my thyroid. They were scheduled for the following Monday morning and afternoon and Tuesday morning.

When the radiologist said he wanted to feel my neck, I exclaimed, "Oh, how romantic!" He quickly responded, "Quick! Open the doors. I'm a married man." We laughed and it relieved the tension I was experiencing.

He said he felt a hard growth on the right side of my thyroid and commented it might be hyper-active. He emphasized I would definitely need to have it treated.

"Yes," I agreed. For the first time I had hope that my condition would be diagnosed and treated.

The next day Dr. Fritz's nurse called to set up an appointment. Finally, we were going to get to the bottom of my ailments. My weight was still dropping and I just did not feel well. While examining me, Dr. Fritz said there was definitely something on the right side of my thyroid. He ordered a sonogram for early the next morning.

Test results showed there was a definite growth so Dr. Fritz ordered a needle biopsy of the thyroid. He recommended I select a surgeon. Dr. Steve Sobol was my choice and I got an appointment with him the following week. It was a miracle to get one that quickly. I knew God was working out the details on my behalf.

At the same time, I was worried about the medical bills and how they would get paid. Even though my insurance company paid for most of my previous hospital bills, it would not cover tests or doctor bills unless I was admitted to the hospital or had surgery within 14 days. Throughout most of my life, God never let me have an easy short cut, but I usually had to go the long, hard route in accomplishing anything.

I decided to call my brother and explained to him the medical bills I would soon be facing. He said not to worry, but to continue to get well. A check would be in the mail soon.

Just to let me know that God had everything under control, He sent a robin my way. I came out of Hickory Point Mall and happened to look up, straight into the eyes of a big, fat robin perched on the roof. He looked down at me as though giving me a nod of approval and then flew away. It was the end of October and usually the robins have all migrated south by then. God knew robins have special meaning in my life and He sent that one on a special assignment.

God allowed me to have several "divine" appointments with people who also had thyroid problems and eventually had surgery. Some even had cancer in that area. They encouraged me greatly and gave me hope that everything would turn out all right.

Dr. Sobol examined me and set up a biopsy the next morning. I was amazed at how fast things were moving. While reading my Bible that night, my eyes again fell on the Scripture verse John 11:4. *"This sickness will not end in death. No, it is for God's glory so that God's Son may be glorified through it."* What a wonderful God we serve! That was the second time the Lord gave me that verse.

My biopsy was scheduled for October 31, Halloween Day. As Viki and I walked down the corridors of St. Mary's Hospital, we saw the biggest, ugliest "woman" we had ever seen. "She" was actually a male doctor dressed in costume, trying to kiss the younger men. One man was so startled he just sputtered, "Uh, uh, who are you?" Everyone standing around was laughing and it helped relieve the tension I was feeling concerning my upcoming ordeal.

Dr. Sobol pierced the right side of my thyroid and then said he better do the left side also. My results would be in Monday. Monday came and went and it wasn't until Tuesday that my results were faxed to Dr. Sobol's office. Dr. Sobol said there was still a big question about the cells on the right side and he decided to order a CAT scan for that region. I finally asked him if the growth was benign and he said he still did not know. He instructed me to get the CAT scan on Thursday and carry the film over to his office at 1:30 p.m. so he could determine immediately if the growth was malignant or benign.

I was elated to hear the words "no cancer," but was shocked to hear there would be no surgery yet because the thyroid was still swollen from the biopsy.

I had an appointment to see Dr. Fritz and he expressed concern about the radiologist's report on the lymph nodes below the thyroid. He wanted to recheck the CAT scan on that area. To help me stay calm over the weekend, he ordered some tranquilizers.

Ten days went by and I still had not heard anything so I decided to call Phyllis at Dr. Fritz's office. She said there was still a big question about the lymph nodes so Dr. Fritz ordered a second CAT scan for Thursday. It turned out okay, but Dr. Fritz said the right side of my thyroid was now twice the size of the left side. In addition, I continued losing weight and my stomach bothered me. A panendoscopy procedure was ordered and revealed that I had a red sore and some bleeding in the stomach lining, probably from my acid reflux. In addition, all of the ibuprofen I took earlier did not help my system.

On top of all this, I was in agony with back pain and went to a chiropractor. He took x-rays and said I needed a lot of work from my neck to the middle of my back and down to my lower back. I started going to him three times a week in order to get some relief.

I was scheduled to see Dr. Sobol on December 18. I prayed for favor that I would have a good rapport with him and that he would agree to do surgery soon on my thyroid. I gave him a box of home-made candy and cookies plus a copy of my book *Fortress on a Hill*. When he walked into the examining room and saw the gifts, he exclaimed, "Why can't there be more people like you in this world?" He then asked why I did that. I replied that when I was a little girl we had very little money and I always believed in giving and making others happy.

He hugged me and gave me a list of reasons why he should not do surgery on my thyroid. He commented, however, that he also valued the opinion of his patients. Finally, I heard the blessed words, "But I will do it for you."

I asked if the surgery could be done before January 1 so that my insurance company could pay for it since I had already met my deductible. If the surgery was after January 1 then I would have to pay the deductible for that year. In addition, it was getting more and more painful to swallow. I wanted that growth out as soon as possible.

Dr. Sobol said he was planning a skiing vacation at the end of December, but something might be able to be worked out. At that point I asked him if it was okay to hug him again. He replied, "Sure, I can take all the hugs I can get today."

I called Dr. Sobol's office the next day to see when surgery was scheduled and was told the doctor would be on vacation from December 25 thru 31. There would be no surgery for me or anyone else during that time. "How about January 11?" I was asked.

I was devastated! I asked to talk to Imogene the nurse to explain my situation to her. She said to give her 10 minutes to see what she could do and then call back. It seemed like an eternity waiting those 10 minutes. When I finally called, Imogene elatedly announced, "Dr. Sobol will do your surgery on December 22 at 1 p.m. You will be home for Christmas. Your preliminary tests will be done two hours before the surgery."

I was ecstatic! God was working behind the scenes.

God gave me just enough energy to attend Sunday's church services at Harvest Christian Center. The children presented a beautiful Christmas pageant during the morning service and at night we had a candle light communion service.

When it was over, someone remarked she could not believe how calm I was considering what I was facing the next day. I responded that I was totally in God's hands and shared with her the promise Scripture verse I received during the service. *"Come and see what God has done, how awesome His works in man's behalf." Psalm 66:5*

Viki and I arrived at Decatur Memorial Hospital at 11 a.m. to have the preliminary blood work and tests completed before surgery. We soon found out that everything was running behind schedule. I was anxious to have the surgery done and each delay did not help my stomach. I was in a lot of pain so a nurse gave me some medication to stop the acid reflux from going into the esophagus.

I was finally "worked into" the surgery schedule at 4:30 p.m. The last thing I remembered was being told to take some deep breaths as two people strapped my arms straight out. I thought of Jesus being in the same position on the cross.

When I woke up, the first question I asked was, "Did they take all or just the right side of the gland?" I was greatly relieved to learn that only the gland on the right side was removed. The nurse did not think it was cancerous. A big tube was inserted in my neck and a very big red scar was present. But I could talk!

My three daughters came in to see me. Chris did not care to look at the scar, but Cheri came right up to me and estimated its length. She would have made a great nurse!

Originally my surgery was supposed to be same-day surgery, but because I did not actually have it until late in the day, I was allowed to spend the night. My stomach was in excruciating pain and it seemed to bore right through my back. I was given Demerol® every three hours, but relief only lasted an hour at a time.

Two nurses came into my room and helped me feel a lot better. They said they had two women patients who had thyroid surgery. One was 43 years old and one was 63 years old. They thought I was the younger one and I didn't even have on my make-up!

The next day the other patient visited me from across the hall. She believed her growth was cancerous. Dr. Sobol had removed her entire thyroid gland. I was blessed that mine was only partially removed.

Dr. Sobol came in my room and thanked me again for the candy and cookies I had given him previously. He then got serious and said the growth had been badly inflamed. It had to come out. I told him that I had shared with Viki on the way to the hospital that I believed the growth was inflamed or infected. Dr. Sobol said I had made the right decision to have the surgery.

I was discharged from the hospital and told I would have to take Synthroid® medication the rest of my life. The next day I returned to Dr. Sobol's office to have the tube removed. I nearly fainted when I found out it was embedded five to six inches down in my flesh.

I was home in time to celebrate Christmas with my family. All of my children and grandchildren except Kim and the girls gathered in my living room on Christmas Eve. I was extremely grateful that my "gory" drain tube had been removed so the grandchildren did not have to see it. Even still I was affectionately called "zipper throat" and "Frankenstein."

It was wonderful to be home, surrounded by my loved ones. I was still in a lot of stomach pain and my throat hurt greatly. Kirk surprised me with another precious porcelain robin.

Five days later I was back in Dr. Fritz's office. He prescribed some strong medicine for the reflux. Nothing seemed to stop the flow of acid. Pain was my constant companion. My vision became blurry at times and I had difficulty concentrating. There was no way I could drive a car, so Viki became my chauffeur. I was sure my condition was caused by hypothyroidism, but test results from the blood work never revealed that to be the case.

Dr. Fritz gave me permission to go back to my chiropractor, but he was not allowed to do any work on my neck which was still healing from the surgery.

I stayed home from the Sunday night service on January 4 because I was in terrible pain. I fell on my knees in my bedroom and sought the Lord for an answer. The pain was excruciating in my stomach and nothing seemed to help. I had spent over $1,100 on prescription medicines in just six months. I couldn't go on like this forever.

Lura recommended I go to the Country Nutrition Store in Spring Creek Plaza and talk to Audra. She proved to be extremely helpful and spent over an hour suggesting several health foods and products that would be beneficial to my system. To help gain back some of the 40 pounds I had lost, she recommended a protein drink to supplement my food intake. I agreed to eat flax on my oatmeal for breakfast and eliminate all sugar. Aloe vera and barley green were added to my daily food regime.

I was told green tea might help my stomach so I grabbed the first box I saw at the grocery store. Much to my alarm, I discovered after drinking a cup of it that it had enough caffeine to equal one chocolate bar. I went straight into orbit! I shook all over and never slept a wink that night, even with a sleeping pill! From then on I knew I could only have caffeine free drinks.

I had a check-up appointment with Dr. Sobol and he told me the gravity of the growth on the thyroid that he delicately removed. Not only was it inflamed, but it was embedded and wrapped around my windpipe. For the first time I realized my air supply would have been cut off, slowly suffocating me. Not only would I have lost my voice, but my breathing ability would have been affected. How marvelous of God to let the growth be found in time and removed!

A few days later I called Dr. Sobol's office and told Imogene about my shaking and inability to sleep. She said I could go off all thyroid pills for four days and then start taking the lowest dose of 0.05 milligrams of Synthroid®. I needed to go back two weeks later to have blood work done to make sure I was taking the right amount.

My sister-in-law Diane called with the devastating news that her brother Roger was diagnosed with cancer. A big man, Roger was 6 feet 4 inches and weighed about 300 pounds. In the last few months, though, he had lost 80 pounds. A fun loving guy who was a great eater, Roger now could only drink liquids and barely whisper. I worried about my mother-in-law and how she would handle the possible death of Roger, her second child. Jerry was the oldest child and his death was hard to accept.

Around the same time, Chris was experiencing a lot of pain. At first her doctor thought it was an appendicitis attack, but an ultrasound revealed she had a cyst on her right ovary that needed to be watched.

"Will it ever stop, Lord?" I cried out.

Dr. Sobol's nurse, Imogene, called me the day after my blood test to see if I was taking the right dose of Synthroid®. She said my Serum Thyroid-Stimulating Hormone (TSH) level had dropped so low that my thyroid kicked into full gear. I was going full throttle for months! We reasoned my stomach was also going full force too and that caused me to burn the fat right off and consequently lose weight.

I told Imogene that I was finally able to drive my car again after the Synthroid® dosage was lowered. Even my blurred vision had cleared up. My system was slowing down and I could fall asleep in my living room recliner.

For the first time I realized how God had directed my path. If I never had the CAT scan on my stomach in August, the iodine would not have allowed my thyroid to protrude. If Dr. Fritz had not been persistent in following up with all those tests and if Dr. Sobol had not agreed to do the surgery, my life would have really hung in the balance.

My heavenly Father had watched over me every step of the way and He would continue to do so until He calls me home to be with Him forever.

25

Once More "Round the Mountain"

"I Lift Up My Eyes to the Hills, from Which Cometh My Help." Psalm 121:1

My time of testing was far from over as my health continued to deteriorate rapidly. I had intense stomach pain and finally decided to see Dr. Fritz. He prescribed Zantac®–the same reflux medication I had taken nearly a year earlier.

Although I took the medicine faithfully, I got no relief. Dr. Fritz's nurse called Dr. Eloy to make an appointment for me. There were no openings until April 22. I was in total shock and cried out to the Lord.

"If this is a hiatal hernia, I cannot live with it!"

For nearly a year I had missed attending social functions and many of my grandchildren's activities. I couldn't sit in a chair or on a bleacher to see Michael's band performances or Sarah's gymnastic competitions. For some reason the pain always increased as the day wore on.

Out of the blue I started reading Scripture verses about healing that leaped out at me. King Nebuchadnezzar of Babylon had his health restored after seven years. King Hezekiah was given 15 more years of life from the Lord after experiencing a terrible disease. In addition I remembered the verse given me while I was in the hospital. *"This sickness is not unto death but for the glory of God, that the Son of God might be glorified thereby." John 11:4*

I noticed something different happening to my voice. While vacuuming the house, I started singing and to my amazement my voice

213

sounded strong and clear. I could even reach the high notes! My secret desire all along was to get back to Harvest Christian Center to help sing during worship, giving God all the glory.

That night while reading Charles Spurgeon's *Morning and Evening Daily Readings*, I read about King David seeking deliverance in Psalm 51:14. It ended with David saying he would sing aloud when the Lord delivered him. Was that just a coincidence? Again I thanked God for watching over me and encouraging me.

I kept busy by concentrating on helping Chris remodel her new house. A very slow process, it was literally inch-by-inch that the work got done. Although I could not help with the physical labor, I decided to help with furnishing and decorating it.

On April 7 I had an appointment at Dr. Sobol's office for a routine blood test regarding my thyroid gland. There was a 15-minute delay so I decided to go to Dr. Eloy's office which was in the same building. I asked if I could possibly see Dr. Eloy before my April 22 appointment and was blessed to be given the date of April 14.

The next day Diane called and said Roger passed away at 2:20 a.m. I was not well enough to travel to Arkansas for the visitation and funeral which were scheduled for Easter weekend. Chris and Cheri represented my family and drove to Arkansas. My sister Colleen also went to the funeral and stayed with Babe.

A week later Dr. Eloy thoroughly examined my stomach and colon. He could do another panendoscopy procedure, but did not think he would find anything. Would I consider going elsewhere, perhaps the Mayo Clinic? If the source of the problem could not be found there, would I consider seeing a psychiatrist? At any rate, another approach was needed.

My heart sank. I asked myself, "Do I really love attention so much that I'm making all of this up?"

Dr. Eloy ordered a special blood test and urinalysis. We talked about the possibility of my admittance to the Mayo Clinic. It was located in the hills of Rochester, Minnesota, about 40 miles from my hometown of Winona.

My dear friend, Pat Kelm, urged me to go to the Mayo Clinic. "They will find the problem and it will be a simple one," she remarked.

Other people also encouraged me to go, but I found out it would take three months before I could get an appointment. I didn't have that long to wait. I was living hour-by-hour, holding my stomach constantly because of the pain. I was losing a pound of weight a week and did not have strength to do anything.

Finally, I received a confirmation from God about going to the clinic. Spurgeon's *Morning and Evening Daily Readings* came alive again as I re-read what I had underlined on April 7. *"Go to the strong for strength, then wait humbly upon God and the mighty God of Jacob will surely come to the rescue and you shall sing of victory through His grace."* I prayed that Viki would be the one to drive me to Rochester.

Seven days passed with Dr. Eloy's office earnestly trying to get me an appointment at Mayo. There were absolutely no openings. The clinic was open Monday thru Friday. Walk-ins could try to get an appointment if one opened up. I decided to go for it. What did I have to lose?

The next day I picked up medical papers about my condition from Dr. Eloy and Dr. Fritz's offices. My brother suggested we get on the Internet to find places for lodging near the clinic.

That evening my nine-year-old granddaughter, Sarah, came up to me and said, "Grandma, I think I know why you have to suffer so much and go to the Mayo Clinic. It's so you can add another chapter in your book that will help others."

In order for Viki to drive me to Rochester, she had to make several arrangements regarding Michael and Sarah because Doug was oftentimes working 12 hour days. Everything was finally in place and we left Decatur at 7 a.m. on April 23. I laid down on the back seat of my station wagon. I could not endure the pain of sitting in the front seat with a seat belt over my stomach. Also, I was having problems with my equilibrium so the prescription medicine I took helped me sleep during the entire eight-hour drive.

Shortly after 3 p.m. we entered the doors of the mammoth Mayo Clinic. Viki got me a wheelchair and took me over to admissions. I kept praying and believing that I would get admitted to the hospital so that my insurance company would pay the medical bills.

After filling out numerous papers, we were directed to go to the 19th floor where the specialty of gastroenterology was located. God gave me great favor with Julie who worked in public relations on that floor. She took one look at me and suggested I go to the emergency room at St. Mary's Hospital, which is the hospital portion of the Mayo Clinic. She was sure a doctor there would admit me as a patient.

Blood work and urinalysis were done and then we waited for hours in a cold room for the results. Finally, a doctor came in and said everything was okay and there were no grounds to admit me. I was extremely disappointed, but kept believing God had everything under control. The last thing the doctor told me before going out the door was to "fast" in case particular tests would be ordered for me the next morning.

Viki and I checked into a motel and I finally got some rest. We got up bright and early the next morning and headed to the Mayo Clinic. At 7 a.m. we were back on the 19th floor, waiting for an appointment. I was in great pain and oftentimes went into the ladies restroom where I cried out to God to reveal His mercy and power during this ordeal.

Julie said that because I had my blood work done at the hospital the night before, maybe I would get to see a doctor of internal medicine. My sister-in-law Diane told me before I left home that if I could not get an appointment with a gastroenterologist, then someone trained in internal medicine could get the ball rolling and begin ordering tests. Sure enough around 11 a.m. Julie announced my name and told me Dr. Ketterling, a doctor of internal medicine, had an unexpected cancellation and would see me at 11 a.m.

I told Dr. Ketterling that either I was very ill or I was the biggest hypochondriac in the world. He peered at me over his glasses and remarked, "No, I don't believe either. First of all, they haven't found the answer yet; and second, the pain is not all in your mind."

What a relief to hear those words of comfort!

He said he thought I had irritable bowel syndrome. We discussed the bile duct being possibly obstructed after my gallbladder and a gallstone were removed in 1993. Dr. Ketterling ordered full x-rays of my stomach and more blood work. Because I had been fasting all morning, I could have the blood work done that afternoon.

I told him about my thyroid surgery and he commented, "I don't think you need medication for it anymore." He set up an appointment for me with a specialist.

While waiting to have my x-rays, I noticed a young man sitting across from me. He had a paper towel attached across his shoulders and looked in terrible shock. I told him, "God has everything under control. Give it all to Him. I am a pastor's wife and I know what it means to suffer. I will be praying for you." He cried and thanked me for those precious words of encouragement.

Dr. Ketterling was on the 17th floor so Viki wheeled me back up there to await the x-ray results. Some of the people had been waiting for days and even weeks for an appointment. By 5 o'clock the room was clearing out. Viki started sharing our family's testimony with two of the office workers who managed "grand central station." It was extremely hectic, but they wanted to listen to what God had done in our lives. They both wanted a copy of our testimony *Fortress on a Hill*, which we brought with us. One of the girls cried when she read my poem "Assorted Roses" while the other one said she had the goose bumps all over her.

As they started to read the book, it suddenly dawned on me that the opening chapter began with me visiting the Mayo Clinic. A psychic woman had sent me there, saying I had a brain tumor. It was incredible to think I was here for a second time.

The clock rapidly approached 6 p.m. and everyone was leaving the building. "Even at the Mayo Clinic we are the last ones to leave," I commented to Viki.

Because I had x-rays taken late in the day, there was not a radiologist on duty to read them. We were told the Mayo Clinic was closed on weekends and therefore we needed to come back Monday morning at 8:30 a.m. to see if there were any openings for appointments. Dr. Ketterling was setting up some tests for Tuesday and Wednesday. That meant we would have to stay in Rochester for several more days. We had an immediate fast decision to make–spend the weekend in a motel room in Rochester, or see if our friend Jackie Auld, who lived 75 miles away in Burnsville, could house us.

When Viki called her, she had her car keys in hand, ready to

217

walk out the door. God's timing was perfect! She would gladly open the "Aulds Motel" for us. It was a wonderful "home away from home!" Jackie and Charles' nine-year-old daughter, Rebecca, graciously gave up her bedroom for me for the next three nights. We enjoyed a great time of fellowship with each other.

We left early Monday morning to drive back to Rochester. Upon our arrival, I was promptly sent to the fourth floor for a stomach sonogram. We then waited for several hours to get an appointment for an ultrasound on my thyroid and to see a gastroenterologist, but there were no openings. At 1:15 p.m. Julie called me to the front desk. She said she could hardly believe it, but Dr. Levine, a thyroid specialist, had a last minute cancellation. A man who was scheduled to see him needed to switch his appointment time to Wednesday. Twice God gave me favor in allowing me to see a doctor without having an appointment scheduled months in advance.

Dr. Levine was from England and everything was "simply smashing." He also did not think I needed Synthroid® medication for my thyroid. Just to be sure, he was going to ask Dr. Michael Brennan, a world renown endocrinologist who happened to be in the building, to come in and talk with me.

"But I have no insurance to cover all of this," I lamented.

"That's okay. This won't cost you a cent. He owes me a favor," replied Dr. Levine.

After looking me over and discussing my case with Dr. Levine, Dr. Brennan agreed and said I did not need to take any more thyroid medicine. He recommended I go off the Synthroid® for eight weeks and then be re-tested. To verify his recommendation, he also recommended an ultrasound of my thyroid. The problem was there were no openings for an ultrasound.

We went back to the 19th floor where Julie was located at the gastrointestinal department's desk. Once again she was amazed when an opening occurred and I got a 10 a.m. appointment the next day for an ultrasound on my thyroid and a 12:45 p.m. ultrasound on my stomach.

The next day was April 28 and Viki and I were back at the Mayo Clinic at 7 a.m., hoping I could get an appointment to see a gastroenterologist. At 10:30 a.m. I had an ultrasound on my thyroid. As I was getting dressed, the technician came back in and said, "We don't normally do this, but we're going to go ahead and do the ultrasound on your stomach now instead of at 12:45 p.m."

When we came back and reported to Julie what had happened, she was utterly amazed. She could see God working things out on my behalf. Viki and I were able to minister to many patients while they waited for appointments. Jesus was the only hope for their problems.

We were back at the Mayo Clinic at 8 a.m. the next day to attend an Irritable Bowel Syndrome Clinic. I asked several questions and the dietician said I had more problems than irritable bowel syndrome.

I saw Dr. Levine again after he had a chance to look at the results of my ultrasound. He said there were little nodules on my thyroid but they should not present any problems and therefore I could go off the Synthroid®.

We went back up to the 19th floor where I soon learned there was a 1:30 p.m. cancellation with Dr. G. Richard Locke III, a gastroenterologist. Viki had noticed Dr. Locke's name on the roster of doctors on the 19th floor and wondered if he was related to the Dr. G. Richard Locke from Decatur who was a cancer doctor that she had interviewed for the *Decatur Tribune*. While Julie booked the appointment for me, Viki asked her about Dr. Locke. She did not know anything about him, so Viki asked the nurse who did the preliminary interview with me before I saw him. "Yes, he has blonde hair," she replied to Viki's inquiry. Sure enough, when he walked in the examination room, Viki knew he was the son of the doctor she had interviewed. We had a great time sharing about Decatur and the schools he attended. He had been at the Mayo Clinic for eight years.

Dr. Locke asked Viki if I ever smiled or had fun. Before she could respond I remarked, "I love to make silk flower arrangements, pull weeds, work 1,000 piece puzzles and go fishing, but I'm hurting so badly that I can't do anything."

Dr. Locke said he suspected my "gut" was super sensitive and probably had irritable bowel syndrome. Because of the intensity of the pain, he suggested I get a pain shot in the muscle and possibly attend a pain management clinic at a later time. I thought to myself, "My God is greater than any pain clinic," and promptly nixed that idea.

He ordered some tests which made me wonder how I would pay for them. I told him my insurance company would not pay my medical bills unless I was admitted to a hospital or had surgery within 14 days of tests.

Viki and I thanked him and went back out into the waiting room. Suddenly, Julie called my name and said I was to go immediately to St. Mary's Hospital for an endoscopy and biopsy of the small intestine. Viki quickly drove me over there. As I was being prepped for the test, a nurse at the desk asked Viki why I was there. She said the test should have been done at the clinic. "The doctor bent the rule to have her come here," she remarked.

The test did not go well with me. I had three panendoscopies previously and never felt a thing. This time I gagged and wretched the entire time. I had huge red sores in my throat and could hardly swallow. A nurse suggested I take Tylenol® and throat lozenges. I told her I could not have anything after midnight because I was scheduled for a gastric emptying test at 7 a.m. and I had to fast for it.

My brother Bob came to our motel room that night. We shared a lot about our childhood. He noted that he and Stefannie lived within a few blocks of the motel several years earlier. He shared his experience about having varicose vein surgery on one of his legs at the Mayo Clinic. The next day the surgeon came in his room with an assistant who very carefully unwrapped the bandages to examine his "fine work." The assistant then picked up the bandages and very carefully started wrapping Bob's other leg! Everyone held his breath until the surgeon blurted out, "Here at the Mayo Clinic we usually bandage the leg we operated on." Bob wished me luck and headed out the door to drive back home to Winona.

Viki and I were back at St. Mary's Hospital at 7 a.m. for the gastric emptying, small bowel transit and colon transit. The test would take place over 24 hours. The technician commented that the procedure was only 10 years old and therefore I had to sign my name on a form, giving the hospital permission to perform it.

I swallowed a radioactive pill and was checked an hour later in front of an imaging machine. I could see a picture of my stomach with the capsule exploding as if it was out in cyberspace. And yet the capsule was still in my stomach. Another man who was also doing the test was long gone because his capsule had apparently gotten into the rest of his system.

At 9:30 a.m. I was given another capsule, only this time it was crushed into scrambled eggs on wheat toast. I had to report back every couple of hours and stand before an imaging machine so both capsules' progress could be monitored.

I suddenly found myself having two appointments at the same time. The hospital wanted to check me at 2 p.m. and Dr. Ketterling also wanted to see me then. Since we knew I probably wouldn't get in to see Dr. Ketterling right at two, I did the hospital first and then Viki rushed me to the clinic.

Dr. Ketterling said all my tests looked pretty good, but pointed out that my stomach was "J" shaped. I also had a kinked stomach which altered the way my stomach emptied. It also pressed up against my rib cage. Dr. Ketterling suggested I eat smaller meals several times a day, which I was already doing on the advice of my nutritionist. I could not believe I had a kinked stomach since I already had a kinked colon. No wonder my insides fought constantly.

The next morning I completed the gastric emptying and then headed to the Mayo Clinic for more blood work, only to find out I should not have eaten breakfast. Everything worked out okay and I was able to have blood work done at 11 a.m. It took four phlebotomists several tries to get blood because my veins are so tiny.

With the afternoon quickly approaching, we realized the clinic would be closing at 6 p.m. for the weekend. We wanted to drive back home to Decatur and did not want to stay around until Monday when the clinic re-opened. We prayed I could get in to see Dr. Locke. Finally, I received a 3:10 p.m. appointment.

Now was the moment of truth. The answer to my stomach pain was in the doctor's hands. There was no turning back. Either my pain was real or God would not get any glory if I made all of this up in my mind. I had to face reality.

Dr. Locke said the transit study showed I had a very slow

221

moving stomach. After four hours of eating a meal, only 28 percent of the food had left my stomach. "Wow!" I cried. No wonder my pain was not so bad in the morning when I woke up, but by evening I was in excruciating pain. I had to take pain pills and a sleeping pill just so I could make it through the night.

Medication would make my stomach pump better. I was to take Propulsid® three times a day. It might take up to three weeks before I saw any positive effects from the medicine. By making the stomach empty better, I would get better. The colon and small bowel worked okay but not perfectly. To help my digestive system work better, Dr. Locke recommended I eat six small meals per day instead of three large ones.

The hiatal hernia that I blamed for my health problems really was not a problem at all. I actually only had the start of one. Dr. Locke said I could eat anything I liked, but in moderate proportions.

I literally floated out of his office! We found Julie and gave her a big good-by hug. She had been a tremendous blessing, teaching us the "ropes" about how to get around the Mayo Clinic and helping us with appointment scheduling.

Viki decided to drive straight home rather than spend the night with someone. She was anxious to see Doug and the kids who had "survived" nine days without mom.

I could hardly believe we had traveled all the way to the Mayo Clinic to receive the help and advice of a doctor who grew up in Decatur. If someone had told me ahead of time that I would be at the clinic for nine days and in a wheelchair, I might have had second thoughts about going.

Somehow while driving home, Viki missed a turn and we ended up at a rest stop. I stepped out of the car and looked up to see a beautiful rainbow. For me it was a sign that God was watching over me. I had almost purchased a plaque with Noah's Ark at the Christian bookstore located in the lower level of the clinic. Instead, my eye caught a smaller plaque with butterflies on it. The scripture verse was Jeremiah 29:11. *"'For I know the plans I have for you,' declares the Lord, 'plans to prosper you and not to harm you, plans to give you hope and a future.'"*

26

Metamorphosis

To occupy my time during these long months of pain and anxiety, I watched a lot of television. News commentators announced the deaths of several famous movie stars plus other well known personalities. I watched in horror the coverage of the tragic death of Princess Diana and then the passing of Mother Teresa.

When I heard that Mother Teresa was being considered a candidate for sainthood by the Roman Catholic Church, I reflected on Psalm 116:15. *"Precious in the sight of the Lord is the death of His saints."* In Ephesians 1:1 the apostle Paul addressed his letter to the saints in Ephesus. They were the faithful in Christ Jesus--alive, not dead, and were already called saints.

In II Corinthians 5:8 Paul wrote, *"to be absent from the body is to be present with the Lord."* According to I Corinthians 3:12-15, the true believer in Jesus will have his works tested by fire after his death to see if what he did was merely good deeds for himself or for the glory of God.

With the pain I was suffering, God quickened to me the agony of those who die without accepting Jesus into their hearts and lives. Their final judgment will take place after Jesus has ruled and reigned in Jerusalem for 1,000 years. In Revelation 20:11-15 each person will be judged according to what he has done and if anyone's name is not found in the book of life, he will be thrown into the lake of fire.

At this judgment seat, everyone will have to bow his knee before God and confess that Jesus Christ is Lord. (Romans 14:11) Even those being sent to hell will have to make this confession. According to Jesus in Luke 16:26 there is no intermediate place after death to help a person get good enough to go to heaven. *"...between us and you a great chasm has been fixed, so that those who want to go from here to you cannot, nor can anyone cross over from there to us."*

I have wondered many times what would have happened if Jesus had sinned just one time during His 33 years of testing on earth. I concluded there would not have been any hope for us. We would have all been doomed to spend eternity in hell. Nothing evil can enter into heaven–it is a holy place where entrance is only allowed by the righteousness of Jesus Christ.

I Timothy 2:5 states, *"For there is one God and one mediator between God and men, the man Christ Jesus."* Jesus said in John 14:6, *"I am the way and the truth and the life. No one comes to the Father except through me."* It is a lie from Satan himself that all religions lead to heaven.

Jesus emphasized that it is actually a narrow road that leads to life. *"Enter through the narrow gate. For wide is the gate and broad is the road that leads to destruction, and many enter through it. But small is the gate and narrow the road that leads to life, and only a few find it."* Matthew 7:13-14

Thirty years have passed since I accepted Jesus Christ as my Savior and became born again. I made a promise then that I would read my Bible through every year, and so far I have been able to keep that promise. One of my favorite verses is Colossians 1:16. *"For by Him were all things created, that are in heaven, and that are in earth, visible and invisible, whether they be thrones, or dominions, or principalities, or powers: all things were created by Him and for Him: And He is before all things, and by Him all things consist."*

Jesus, the Creator of all things, gave up His heavenly dwelling place to come to earth and die a hideous death on the cross. But through His death and resurrection, He fulfilled His Father's perfect will, allowing precious souls to enter into His Kingdom forever.

My church, Harvest Christian Center, showed several of the end time videos that were made in the 1970's. Each movie showed a different aspect of the rapture and seven years of tribulation soon to come upon the earth. There will be a one-world government and a one-world church. The Antichrist will first appear peaceful when he makes a treaty with Israel, but his true colors will show. He will be bent on the destruction of Israel and the Jewish people. No one in the world will be able to buy, sell or trade unless he takes the mark of the beast. *"He also forced everyone, small and great, rich and poor, free and slave, to receive a mark on his right hand or on his forehead, so that no one could buy or sell unless he had the mark, which is the name of the beast or the number of his name...His number is 666."* Revelation 13:16-18

Anyone who takes the mark of the beast will have a huge penalty to pay the rest of eternity. *"A third angel followed them and said in a loud voice: 'If anyone worships the beast and his image and receives his mark on the forehead or on the hand, he, too, will drink of the wine of God's fury, which has been poured full strength into the cup of his wrath. He will be tormented with burning sulfur in the presence of the holy angels and of the Lamb. And the smoke of their torment rises for ever and ever. There is no rest day or night for those who worship the beast and his image, or for anyone who receives the mark of his name."* Revelation 14:9-11

I truly believe our time is running out. I remember when I was a little girl and heard a priest read some scripture verses about the end days. I prayed that it would not be during my lifetime, but I'm afraid there are signs all around, fulfilling Jesus' discourse on the end days in Matthew 24, Mark 13 and Luke 21. Just the weather patterns alone indicate an increasing number of tornadoes, earthquakes, floods, drought and famine. Pestilence is everywhere. Moral decay is rampant. Few know good from evil. Occultic practices are flourishing as Satan knows that his time is running out. Deception abounds.

The prophet Daniel warned in Daniel 12:4 that *"Many will go here and there to increase knowledge."* Computers and the internet have become a way of life. It became apparent that the House of Prayer Ministries needed a web site to advertise its Christian drama books. Viki tried to take a class at Richland Community College on how to design a web site, but twice it was canceled because not enough people registered.

While surfing the internet one day, she found several Christian drama sites. She particularly liked the site titled DramaShare and decided to contact John Alexander in Canada and ask him some questions on how he designed it. During the course of their conversation, Viki found out that John was familiar with the House of Prayer's drama material and said it was some of the best out there. A "kindred spirit" developed between John and Viki and he said he would develop an internet site for the House of Prayer and hook it onto his site–the most visited Christian drama site on the internet. Over 100,000 people a year view it.

Viki knew it would be a great way to advertise my musical *Voyage*. Bob and Brenda Wilcott with Catchpenny Productions had the huge task of producing the soundtracks for 14 songs. Several times they said they felt the anointing all over the project. I felt an urgency to get it completed and did not want to stand before God on Judgment Day without it being finished.

Voyage is a captivating two-hour musical portraying a literal sea voyage as well as a spiritual voyage. An allegory for the church today, *Voyage* harnesses the present reality of every day life with the imminent return of Christ in the last days.

I believe according to scripture that the born again believer has the blessed hope of the rapture of the saints before the dreadful tribulation days of the unbeliever. I Corinthians 15:51-52 states, *"Behold, I shew you a mystery; We shall not all sleep, but we shall all be changed. In a moment, in the twinkling of an eye, at the last trump: for the trumpet shall sound, and the dead shall be raised incorruptible, and we shall be changed. (KJV)*

The Apostle Paul continues with these beautiful words of hope in I Thessalonians 4:13-18. *"But I would not have you to be ignorant, brethren, concerning them which are asleep, that ye sorrow not, even as others which have no hope. For if we believe that Jesus died and rose again, even so them also which sleep in Jesus will God bring with him. For this we say unto you by the word of the Lord, that we which are alive and remain unto the coming of the Lord shall not prevent them which are asleep. For the Lord himself shall descend from heaven with a shout, with the voice of the archangel, and with the trump of God: and the dead in Christ shall rise first: Then we which are alive and remain shall be caught up together with them in the clouds to meet the Lord in the air: and shall we ever be with the Lord. Wherefore comfort one another with these words." (KJV)*

Jerry always envisioned himself going to heaven in the rapture of the church. Instead, he and Charles Volle are already up in gloryland. I told Eileen that I have a hard time imagining Jerry and Charles in white robes, singing in one accord and in perfect harmony.

I looked forward to the day when I could sing again after my thyroid surgery. One day while in Wal Mart I talked to a clerk about my operation. She showed me her scar where Dr. Sobol had operated on her thyroid gland five years earlier. "How long was it before you could sing again?" I asked her. She shot back, "I couldn't sing before Dr. Sobol operated on me and I still can't sing after he operated on me!" I laughed and laughed.

I know that my testing time on this earth is not over yet. I am still learning to trust God and to thank Him for the little miracles that occur daily on our behalf.

On the trip home from the Mayo Clinic, I didn't sleep a wink. I was "hyperactive" for three weeks. I discovered I was extremely sensitive to the iodine capsule I was given and it affected my thyroid. I thanked God it did not take any longer than three weeks to get the iodine out of my system.

Although I had to take Propulsid® medication at $188.00 a month, I was grateful the terrible pain was gone and I could live again. Dr. Sobol emphasized my thyroid condition did not cause my stomach problems.

"No connection," he said emphatically over and over again.

For some reason God had allowed two major health problems to hit me at the same time, causing months of suffering.

On June 26, 1998, we lost a wonderful "saint" from our body of believers at Harvest Christian Center. Brother Don Etnier, the elderly pastor who had given his church, Bethel Tabernacle, to Jerry in 1986, went home to be with the Lord just nine days before his eighty-seventh birthday. Two days after his body was laid to rest, his wife, Lura, was admitted to the intensive care unit at the hospital with two blood clots on her lungs. I prayed and "argued" with my heavenly Father that I needed her here on this earth a little longer. She was a good friend and we talked a lot on the phone. God honored my request

227

and she pulled through okay.

My heart's desire was to go see the Jorgensens in their beautiful Smokey Mountain home in North Carolina. Chris surprised me just before my 64th birthday and said she had some vacation days. She thought about driving to North Carolina to see the Jorgensens. "Would you like to come along?" she asked.

I had long ago abandoned any such thought of traveling again, but suddenly I believed I could make it. We went and had a fabulous time. Chris even went white water rafting.

When we got home from our trip, I needed to have my blood tested for my thyroid. Much to my dismay, the doctor said I had to go back on Synthroid® medication because my remaining gland was being overtaxed. My TSH level had gone from 2.9 at the Mayo Clinic to 7.36. Dr. Sobol reassured me that the small amount of medication was no big deal and would regulate me. I was now "hypo" instead of "hyper" with a slow acting gland. I think that helped me to pick up a few pounds that I had lost.

I took pain medication to help me sleep, but now it was time to be weaned off of it. I can honestly say it was a terrible experience and helped to give me compassion for others who go through withdrawal.

God granted me the ability to be able to walk around the three-day Decatur Celebration—one of the largest outdoor festivals in the Midwest. I could even eat some of my favorite foods! I shared with many people about the dark tunnel the Lord had just seen me through.

Although I enjoyed being active once again, I had to learn the balancing act of when to rest and not overdo. One of my favorite scripture verses is Isaiah 30:15. *"In returning and rest shall ye be saved; in quietness and in confidence shall be your strength." (KJV)*

As summer stretched into early fall, the Jorgensens arrived in Decatur and blessed us with a short visit. After seeing our beautiful home, they took me out for dinner. We noticed that our waiter named Mark was bubbling over with joy. He insisted on taking back my "bloody" steak and returned with another whole dinner. I commented that I had not eaten steak for a year and had spent several days at the Mayo Clinic in May. I told him how my health problems were being

228

taken care of and he shouted. "Well, praise the Lord!"

Grace looked him square in the eye and asked, "Young man, are you a Christian?"

"Yes, ma'am," came the instant reply. "Born again on the Fourth of July one year ago. I should have been locked up then. My friends thought I was crazy. You see, I was a drug addict. I even jumped out of a second story window. I hurt my head real bad and scraped and punctured my side. Well, Jesus told me He wore a crown of thorns on His head for me and had his side torn open for me."

Someone eventually took him to an evangelistic meeting where he witnessed a young girl's feet get totally straightened. He said he had to know more about that God Who healed people.

Mark came up closer to us and whispered, "You see, I was a homosexual, but when I got baptized and came up out of the water, I knew I was free!"

As quickly as I could, I shared my testimony with him about becoming born again on my 39th birthday. In one year's time all five of my children came to know the Lord as their personal Savior. I mentioned how my husband, Jerry, had been a district manager for Prudential Insurance Company which was the number one financial institution in the world. At the age of 45 he gave up his job and everything we possessed to start a ministry in the big England mansion and called it the House of Prayer.

Mark's eyes grew bigger and bigger and he started murmuring, "Oh no, oh no. I was your next door neighbor, living in the Staley mansion. We used to make fun of you. We called our place "the House of Sin."

Suddenly his face lit up. He remembered me talking to him in our back yard. "You gave me a copy of your book, *Fortress on a Hill.*

By this time the Jorgensens and I had tears in our eyes. I remembered my conversation with the young man. How gracious God was in letting me know that my words were not in vain. We will reap a harvest if we faint not. Isaiah 55:11 says, *"So shall my word be that goeth forth out of my mouth; it shall not return unto me void, but it shall accomplish that which I please, and it shall prosper in the thing whereto I sent it."*

As we parted to go our separate ways, I turned to Mark and commented, "Mark, Jesus has truly set you free, free as a butterfly. We will meet again in the rapture one day soon."

I marveled at God's precious timing, allowing us the opportunity to share with Mark. What an awesome, caring Creator! Only He can make something beautiful out of an ugly past during these closing days of time.

27

What Do You Mean, Lord, Another Chapter?

Months went by and I rejoiced with my new health. Not only was I feeling like a new creature, but our church was undergoing a major restoration project. Under Kirk's direction, the sanctuary was being transformed from the orange and brown colors of the fifties to soft white walls accented with burgundy and blue decor. New carpet, drapes and a center aisle completed the picture. I used my talents to make flower arrangements and swags.

Just before Christmas in 1998, I made a lovely big planter of silk flowers and sent it to my brother and his wife. Much to my delight, Bob called and said Stefannie wanted to put it in the Minnesota Conservatory for the Performing Arts where she taught ballet.

On December 23 members of our church met at Harvest to go Christmas caroling. Chris met me at the door and excitedly told me that a big box had arrived from my brother. It might be perishable and therefore I needed to open it right away. I went into the nursery and started to unwrap a huge package. Chris interjected, "No, lift it straight up!" I did so and out popped my six-year-old granddaughter Katlin from Montana. I was speechless and wondered where the rest of Kim's tribe was. Suddenly the nursery's bathroom door opened and there stood Kim holding 2-year-old Kiana and beside them was 12-year-old Chantelle. I cried buckets of tears! It was our first Christmas family reunion since Jerry died nearly six years earlier.

Chris had called Bob and asked if he had my Christmas gift yet. When he said no, she told him the greatest gift he could send was the airfare for Kim and the girls. Chris picked them up at the

Bloomington Airport and smuggled them to her home until it was time to go caroling. I never sang so loudly and jubilantly as I did that night. The words for many of the Christmas carols had greater meaning than ever before.

My "to do" list for Christmas Eve day was jam packed. Kim's favorite pie is black raspberry so I thawed several packages from the freezer and made four pies. I got my hair done at the beauty shop and bought more gifts for Kim and the girls. After getting the presents wrapped, I had a huge turkey to prepare for Christmas Day's dinner. At 7 p.m. all of my family gathered for the traditional Henneberry Christmas Eve gift exchange. I was exhausted by the time the evening's activities were over, but I was so grateful that my heavenly Father allowed us the opportunity to be united for the holidays.

After a luscious turkey dinner on Christmas Day, I asked Kim if he wanted to go over to Kirk and Jeannette's house. "No, mom. I'm home and this is where I want to be," he simply replied.

Two days later I read in the newspaper about the death of Vera Davis. She was an elderly lady who worked at New Art Beauty Salon where I got my hair done. I was the last customer to leave the shop on Christmas Eve and turned to wish everyone a Merry Christmas. The only ones left were Betty, my hairdresser; Ruth, the owner; and Vera. Someone suggested we give each other a hug. Little did we know that would be the last time we would see Vera. She died in her sleep on Christmas Day. Her Bible was opened to the book of Exodus. I made a sign and placed it over her booth at the beauty shop. It simply stated, "Gone home for the holidays."

Kim and I listened to the sound tracks for our musical *Voyage*. We met with Bob Wilcott and suggested some changes that we wanted made. Viki had already received some inquiries from people on the internet who were interested in doing the musical at their church.

The new year of 1999 was upon us and I thanked God for seeing me through another life threatening and emotional year. It was time to look forward to the new millennium.

On January 21 I received a telephone call from Colleen at 6:45 a.m. I wasn't fully awake yet and couldn't believe what she was telling me.

"Stefannie passed away last night at the Mayo Clinic."

Colleen explained that Bob had taken her there on December 30 for what was diagnosed as a small cancer on her lung. It was successfully removed, but she developed a blood clot that claimed her short life.

Her death was a great loss to the art world as she had danced and taught ballet in the United States and abroad. She was truly a "Grand Dame" of the arts. Her two beautiful daughters, Lara and Monique, would miss their mother tremendously. Chris drove me to Minnesota in a blinding snowstorm. Over a thousand people attended Stefannie's funeral mass.

On March 8 I received a phone call from Bob. He said if the Republican Party would have him, he would run for the vacant state senator seat in Minnesota. Two other candidates ran for the position. On April 13 a very happy Bob called to tell me he had won the election by a landslide with 53 percent of the vote. I was thrilled and congratulated him on his great accomplishment.

It was a beautiful spring and I thanked God for all the things He had brought me through. I had gone a whole year without any major health problems. Little did I know my greatest challenge was just ahead.

Although my 65th birthday was not until June 25, I was eligible to start Medicare the first of June. I also started a large supplemental health insurance policy at that time so that any medical problems not covered by Medicare would be covered by my insurance company.

On June 6 Viki and Doug gave Michael an eighth grade graduation party. He was finally starting his growth spurt and was ½ inch taller than his mom. He was looking forward to high school and auditioning on both the trombone and piano for the MacArthur High School Jazz Band. His grandpa Scherer's prediction of being a piano player had exceeded all expectations.

Later that night I started having severe chest pains near my heart. They continued off and on during the night. The next morning I called Dr. Fritz's office and was given an 11:15 a.m. appointment. My blood pressure was up a bit and my ankles were definitely swollen.

233

A diuretic would solve that problem. Dr. Fritz listened to my heart and it was fine. He always faithfully did a breast exam. Suddenly he stopped and said he felt something on the very tip of the left breast. "That wasn't here before," he commented. It was a hard lump about 1 and ½ centimeters around the nipple area.

"Does that mean surgery?" I asked hesitantly.

"No, probably aspiration will take care of it," was his reply.

He ordered a mammogram for two days later. I left the office in shock. When I got into my car, I found another car had parked behind mine. "Well," I thought to myself, "I'll just go forward."

Suddenly I heard an agonizing crunch. I locked the front end of the station wagon onto a concrete parking lot block. I envisioned needing two doctors to help lift my car off, but with great determination, I gunned the car and it came loose.

By this time I was anxious to get to Lura's house. We had made plans to go out for lunch and I wanted to share with her about my latest medical condition. While backing out of her driveway, I did not see a car that had just driven up and was parked illegally in the driveway across the street. I hit the driver's door! Lura called the police immediately. I said I wanted Kirk there too. He quickly arrived and remarked that the man was parked illegally. The owner of the car said he did not want any problems and he would have his mechanic fix the door at a cost of under $400.

Kirk noticed my front fender was sprung. He looked it over and popped it back into place. No damage done. I thanked my heavenly Father for looking after me.

The next evening I called Babe in Arkansas to tell her the news about the lump. Colleen was with her. I mentioned I had been looking at a deluxe electric bed. I explained that my head had to be raised because of the hiatal hernia and my feet also had to be raised because of my varicose veins. If my legs were not raised at night, then my ankles would swell because of water retention. Both Babe and Colleen said to go for it. Buying the bed would help take my mind off my health situation and make a nice birthday gift to myself. I chose a double bed with a deluxe mattress. My grandchildren loved going up and down in the bed and also the massage it provided. The house had

234

a new "toy" and I was fortunate if I had it to myself at night!

The night after Dr. Fritz discovered the lump, I read Numbers 11:23 in Charles Spurgeon's book *Morning and Evening Daily Readings. "Thou shalt see now whether My Word shall come to pass unto thee or not."* I knew according to Jeremiah 29:11 that God had promised to prosper me and not to harm me; He planned to give me hope and a future. I decided to hold my Lord to it. He had spared my life so many times already, could He possibly do it again?

I had the mammogram the next day. The nurse came back in and asked if I could stay for an ultrasound. I saw a big black area in the center of the image and knew something was not right.

Sure enough, Karen from Dr. Fritz's office called the next day and said there was an abnormality. I needed to see a surgeon as soon as possible. We were on a three-way phone conversation with different doctor's offices, but most surgeons could not see me for several weeks. I was in pain all the time now and knew I could not wait a long time. I was getting scared.

Viki was nearby and suggested Dr. Scott Sherwood who did my gallbladder surgery in 1993. An appointment was set up for the following Wednesday. Over the weekend the pain increased in intensity and by Monday I was feeling miserable. Viki suggested I call Dr. Sherwood's office to see if there had been any cancellations.

We were also racing against the clock because Viki's family, ` Kirk's family and Cheri's family were all leaving early Friday morning on June 18 to drive to Maryland for my nephew's wedding on June 19. The following day everyone was gathering at his parents' house to celebrate the 90th birthday of my mother-in-law, Clara Henneberry. Many family members had extended vacations on the east coast they had been planning for months.

Chris volunteered to stay behind and take care of me plus be in charge of all the church services. She was now a licensed minister and also a volunteer chaplain at Decatur Memorial Hospital.

The Sunday newspaper had a special section devoted to the Race for the Cure...Breast Cancer, but I did not want to read it. I couldn't begin to think about chemotherapy because of my reflux and stomach condition. To be honest, I just did not want to think about it at all. I was in the denial stage.

I called Dr. Sherwood's office and the staff worked me in for a 1:30 p.m. appointment. Dr. Sherwood immediately stated he did not like the feel of the tumor or the way it laid underneath the skin. He gave me the choice of either having a biopsy the next morning or going directly to the hospital for an aspiration. I asked if that would hurt and he replied smiling, "It won't hurt me a bit."

Viki and I raced over to the hospital. It was already after 3 p.m. and usually aspirations are not done after that time. However, God gave me favor and I was able to have the procedure. A doctor inserted a needle into the left breast, without numbing it. I must have gotten tougher in my old age because the pain really was not that bad.

Dr. Sherwood remarked that if the lump was benign, then he would do a lumpectomy the next day. However, if I had cancer, then I would have to wait and have the surgery done after my family came back from vacation.

At 4:30 p.m. a nurse called and triumphantly stated the report was benign. Hallelujah! Surgery would be at St. Mary's Hospital at 10 a.m. the next morning. I called everyone and shared with them the good news. I was going to be okay! There was no cancer!

Early the next morning I received a telephone call from my dear friend Pat Kelm. I had talked to her the night before about my benign growth. Her husband, Dick, was on some new medication for his ongoing health problems. He was basically confined to a wheelchair and on oxygen most of the time. Pat and Dick were one of the first couples to come to services at the House of Prayer many years earlier. They even repeated their wedding vows during a special ceremony we held at the mansion.

I was surprised to have Pat call so soon after our conversation last night. Pat then proceeded to tell me that Dick did not awaken that morning. Their son went into the bedroom to check on him and discovered he had slipped away into eternity. Pat wanted Kirk to do the funeral, but since he was leaving Friday for Maryland, I suggested Chris help with the funeral. I rejoiced that Dick did not have to suffer any more and that he was now in heaven with Jerry.

Viki drove me to St. Mary's Hospital for my 10 a.m. scheduled lumpectomy which Dr. Sherwood said would take about 20 minutes. Viki and Kirk waited in the waiting room, but the procedure took a lot longer than expected. Both Viki and Kirk knew something was wrong. Dr. Sherwood finally came and told them that he removed a tumor the size of three centimeters or a small marble. It was definitely cancerous and there were some feelers that would require more extensive surgery. Either my children could break the news to me or else he could when I went into his office the next day.

Viki and Kirk quickly discussed their options and knew if they waited to tell me, then I would be calling everyone and telling them everything was okay. They agreed to tell me once I came out of the recovery room.

I was sitting up, trying to eat some soup and a sandwich when they found me. I was freezing cold after the surgery so the nurses wrapped me in blankets. I could tell by the looks on Viki and Kirk's faces that something was wrong. Kirk tried to smile, but finally said I had cancer after all. The aspiration report was wrong. They told me the size of the growth and that I would have to have surgery again to remove the feelers. I was in total shock and denial. I couldn't believe it! But it was true and it was reality. Kirk drove me home while I contemplated what the future held for me.

The next morning Viki took me to see Dr. Sherwood. He said the biopsy tested positive for cancer and therefore I had to pick one of three options. I could either have a moderate radical mastectomy, a mastectomy and radiation, or undergo another lumpectomy plus have radiation. Even at my age I could have reconstructive surgery. Dr. Sherwood talked about radiation and chemotherapy, but those procedures frightened me. He commented how amazed he was that I had pain with my breast cancer. Usually pain means the growth is benign.

Grace said God allowed me to have pain so that I would go see a doctor pronto. As a result, my problem was quickly diagnosed and I could receive treatment much sooner. Dr. Sherwood said I had six weeks to decide which way I wanted to go.

I went to the old mansion to share the bad news with Dr. Kelly and asked for his advice. He advised me to take charge of my life and recommended I opt for a moderate radical mastectomy. His mother had recently had breast cancer which ran in their family and had both breasts removed. Kelly said the sooner I had the cancer removed the better.

On June 17, Viki's 45th birthday, I was back at Decatur Memorial Hospital for a bone scan, blood work and chest x-rays. Viki's family, Kirk's family and Cheri's family were all departing early the next morning for the wedding and birthday celebration on the east coast, leaving me to ponder my fate by myself.

I put aside my decision making and attended Dick Kelm's funeral. Chris did part of the service and read my poem "Beyond God's Veil" that Jerry and Kirk often read at funerals.

Afterwards, Pat's daughter, Patty, came up to me and said, "Dottie, get all of that (cancer) out of you and go on living."

"Yes!" I shouted back.

I was instructed to call Dr. Sherwood's office at 2:30 p.m. on Friday for my test results. I asked my next-door neighbor, Mabel, to be with me then or else I would be "climbing the walls" if I was alone.

"Thumbs up, Dottie," said Kathy from Dr. Sherwood's office. "There is no cancer in the bones, but some arthritis in the knees and ankles. The chest x-ray was okay and the cancer showing in the blood work was only in the very early stage. The cancer appears to be self-contained."

I felt like 100 pounds of weight came off of me! I turned around and hugged Mabel with joy! Kathy said I needed to protect my left arm from cuts and scratches. All blood pressure and blood work would have to be taken on the right arm from now on.

Monday morning I awoke with a terrible pain on my lower left side. A quick visit to Dr. Fritz's office revealed a bad bladder infection. "Is there ever a 'good' one?" I jokingly asked.

I told Dr. Fritz how he had saved my life three times. He was the only one who took me in as a patient when I had stomach problems. He found the thyroid growth and now the cancer in the breast. How could I ever thank him?

"Just be cancer free when this is all over," he replied.

Shelly Miller took me to Decatur Memorial Hospital for more

blood work and a potassium test. Because my veins are so tiny, the nurse had a hard time getting my blood. As oftentimes happens, she had to get another nurse to help.

Shelly took me back to the hospital the next day for an ultrasound test on my stomach. Over and over again I thanked God for His perfect timing allowing me to be eligible for Medicare and having a supplemental insurance; otherwise, I would be in the poor house.

The next day Kirk took me to see Dr. Jordan Youngerman, a cosmetic surgeon. When the doctor mentioned taking skin from my stomach to make a breast, I quickly interjected, "Stop! I don't want to hear it." I was, however, interested in having him do saline injections on my legs' ugly varicose veins. That would be after I healed from my mastectomy. By the time we left his office, I was pretty sure I wanted Dr. Sherwood to do a modified radical mastectomy and not have reconstructive surgery. I would just go for a prosthesis.

My chest pains came back that night. I called Dr. Fritz's office in the morning and the nurse told me to be there in 20 minutes. They did an immediate EKG and learned that my heart was okay. Dr. Fritz said my shooting pains were from the surgery and nerve endings that had been affected. He agreed the sooner I had my mastectomy, the better off I would be.

Kirk took me to K-Mart for breakfast. Two weeks earlier I had breakfast there with Eileen. Two of the waitresses discussed if I was 55 years old and qualified for the senior citizen's discount. I was flattered! Now one of the gals asked Kirk if I was over 50. That made my day! I think God planted them there just for me!

June 25 was my 65th birthday. I awoke that morning thinking that the greatest gift I could give myself was added years of life. I knew I had to take charge of my life just as Dr. Kelly had said.

I opened my stack of birthday cards and found among them a get well card from Viki. The outside of the card had a picture of butterflies. The inside verse read, *"The tiniest and most delicate of God's creations shout the most clearly His beautiful message of Love. He brings New Life to those who trust."*

I decided then and there not to wait any longer to schedule my surgery. Even though Doug and Viki were supposed to get home that

239

night from their vacation, I knew if they were around I would have to work my surgery around baseball games and band concerts.

I called Dr. Sherwood's office and asked Kathy if there were any openings the first of the week. She called back and said surgery would be Tuesday morning at 8:30 a.m. A peace flooded my soul and I knew that I had made the right decision.

That afternoon I had an appointment with oncologist Dr. Benjamin Esparaz. I couldn't believe I was seeing a cancer specialist on my 65th birthday. He gave me some good news and said the actual tumor size that Dr. Sherwood removed was only 1.2 centimeters according to the pathologist. When he checked my left arm pit, he felt something and I winced. I was sure cancer was in my lymph nodes. Kirk commented that my body just might just be reacting to all the other surgeries I had been through. Time would tell.

Viki and Doug made it back that evening. I remarked that it was my first birthday without a cake. Two hours later when Viki returned from grocery shopping, she sneaked in with a Dairy Queen® ice cream cake. I had a great birthday celebration with many gifts.

Viki took me to Decatur Memorial Hospital on Monday, June 28, for pre-admission registration and some preliminary tests. Everything looked good and was in my favor. I was ready for the big day Tuesday. I had to think positive! I told Dr. Sherwood's nurse to give him a message for me. "Take your time and be sure to wear your granny glasses!"

The next day we arrived at the hospital at 7 a.m. I saw Dr. Eloy as I was waiting for my name to be called. I walked over and told him I was having breast cancer surgery at 8:30 a.m. He was shocked!

"Yes, another chapter in my book!" I exclaimed.

A breathing tube was inserted to ward off any problems from reflux and would be removed before I woke up from surgery. The anesthesiologist came in to prepare me and asked if I was ever able to sing again after my thyroid surgery. That was the last thing I said before that surgery and it had been recorded on my medical records.

"Yes," I replied. "It took me six months to recuperate, but I can sing for the Lord's glory!"

I came out of surgery with two drains. I was very nauseous and

240

in a lot of pain. I was given morphine and told my lymph nodes on the left side had been removed as a precaution. I was fuzzy, but could not sleep. I could hear everything.

That evening when my daughter Cheri came up to see me, she emphatically said, "Mom, get off the morphine. That's what is making you so sick." She was speaking from personal experience when she had surgery for cervical cancer. The pain medicine Toradol® was ordered, but after I took it my stomach and colon reacted immediately. I had to be very careful with medications.

Coincidently, my hospital roommate and her parents knew Jerry's side of the family. They were from Lovington where Jerry and several of his siblings went to school. Patty, my roommate's mother, had a modified radical mastectomy on her left breast 25 years earlier. She greatly encouraged me, giving me hope for what was ahead. I firmly believed that God had orchestrated and arranged everything.

I shared part of my testimony with a nurse that night and she emphatically remarked that I should write a book

"I did and I am," I commented. "I'm just completing another chapter."

I did not feel very well the next morning so a decision was made for me to stay another day in the hospital. Mary Greve from church came in to see me and shared how she had endured chemotherapy.

"Dottie, it saved my life," she emphasized.

I knew if I had to face chemotherapy the Lord would see me through it, but I still wanted to see God's promise for me come to pass where I had hope and a future.

That evening while lying on the hospital bed, I decided to read Spurgeon's *Morning and Evening Daily Readings*. A card fell out of the book. Viki had given it to me on April 23, 1995, when I was sick with diverticulitis. Romans 4:20-21 was on it. *"Yet he did not waver through unbelief regarding the promise of God, but was strengthened in his faith and gave glory to God being fully persuaded that God had power to do what He had promised."* Once again I marveled at how Almighty God communicates with His earthly creatures at just the right time. I would continue to trust Him, but would also be prepared for

241

whatever He had in store for me.

Dr. Fritz arrived early Friday morning and sat down in a chair near my hospital bed. I anxiously awaited the pathologist's report. If it wasn't in today, then I would have to wait over the long Fourth of July weekend.

Dr. Fritz took a deep breath and said, "The pathologist report is in. There were no cancer cells in any of the lymph nodes. You said all the right prayers and you did the right thing by having a modified radical. When Dr. Sherwood did the second surgery, there was still a piece of that tumor in there."

He pointed out that 24 lymph nodes were removed. If I had chosen a second lumpectomy, then it may have proven fatal later because the cancer could spread without having the piece of the tumor removed.

I just stood there and cried. I was so relieved! No radiation and no chemotherapy were needed. I had beaten the odds and was cancer free! I did opt to take the pill tamoxifen to prevent cancer later on, as long as I could outlive the medicine's side effects.

"God is so good!" I exclaimed over and over again. He had kept His promise to give me a hope and a future.

I called Viki and we had a "glory fit." She would call Chris and Cheri, but I wanted to call Kirk who had been preparing me for the worst. My grandson, Michael, told me later that during the next Sunday morning's church service, Kirk asked the congregation if they had ever seen me laugh and cry at the same time. I had the victory!

Dr. Fritz said he would see me in a month and would be checking my right breast every three months. I was released to go home from the hospital. Praise the Lord! A nurse came in to remove a drain tube and instructed Viki how to change my dressing.

I held off taking a shower for one more day. That's when reality finally set in. Seeing a part of me missing, but knowing its removal was the only option of saving my life, made it more bearable. Even Sarah came in my bedroom to watch Viki change the dressing. It didn't seem to bother her at all.

"She'd make a good nurse or doctor some day," I thought to myself.

I knew I needed to use my left arm as much as possible. I decided to cut my hair, wash and set it. I also "walked" my left fingers up the wall, an exercise I was told to do often so that my left arm had movement.

Finally, eight days after my surgery, I saw Dr. Sherwood who removed the staples and the second drain. Boy, was I ready! I did not know, however, that the tubing was embedded seven to eight inches inside my body. The surgery had been a success according Dr. Sherwood. Even Dr. Esparaz said I was extremely blessed.

I shared with Dr. Sherwood that I thought God could only get glory if the growth was benign, but He showed me that even if we have to go through the fiery furnace, He is still there waiting for us. Dr. Sherwood had now saved my life twice—once with the gallbladder surgery and now with this cancer ordeal. He agreed God uses doctors for His purpose. He said I could do anything and urged me to "get on with life."

While getting ready to leave the examining room, I reminded Dr. Sherwood that my cancer ordeal was going in my book.

"Keep it decent," he remarked.

I laughed and said, "This book has got to come to an end soon. I'm running out of body parts!"

The day after my last drain came out, the mall's annual sidewalk sale was going on. Secretly I wanted to go, and Viki said she would take me. I had to rest often, but I did it!

"Good therapy," Viki commented.

Two Wal Mart "padded specials" were tucked into a medical sports bra until I could be fitted for a prosthesis. I already had a pretty lacy bra picked out!

As I looked back on all my ailments, it was staggering at what my heavenly Father had seen me through. Tonsils and adenoids removed twice as a child, had five babies in eight years, varicose veins on my legs stripped and ligated, numerous allergies and sinus infections, a deteriorated disk in the lower back, two D&C's surgeries (one in which my heart stopped beating), a hysterectomy in which my bladder was punctured, three broken toes, gallbladder surgery where a diseased gallbladder and a gallstone the size of a large marble were removed, diverticulitis, hiatal hernia, right thyroid gland removed with a growth embedded and wrapped around the windpipe, a trip to Mayo Clinic where the diagnosis was a slow moving stomach and curable by taking an expensive pill before each meal, and lastly this death defying cancer episode.

I reflected on those 22 days of darkness before my cancer surgery and realized that if I had been diagnosed eight days earlier, I would not have been insurable by Medicare. If I had not had the chest pain, I would not have gone to Dr. Fritz who detected a lump in my breast. If the aspiration report had shown a malignancy, Dr. Sherwood would not have performed the lumpectomy the next day. I would have had to endure the pain during the whole time my family was on vacation on the east coast. If I had not elected to have a modified radical mastectomy, I could have been harboring a "silent killer" in me. God had orchestrated everything. I was an over comer, designed to tell everyone about the great God I serve. He had indeed guided all my steps and I would have all of eternity to praise and thank Him.

Chapter 28

The Grand Finale

Following my cancer surgery, I had three doctors encourage me to have varicose vein injections on my right lower leg. I had a massive network of veins in about a four-inch circle that throbbed intensely whenever I stood for any length of time. The doctors said it was a simple procedure that I could have at my convenience. There shouldn't be any complications.

I mustered up all the courage I could find and made an appointment with Dr. Youngerman who I had seen earlier for possible breast reconstruction.

On September 22, 1999, Viki took me to my 10:30 a.m. appointment. Dr. Youngerman checked my leg and said he would try to do the lower mass and possibly an upper thigh area that had come back after being stripped and ligated over 30 years earlier.

I grimaced as I had to lie on my "battered" left side when the injections went in. After about 20 injections, Dr. Youngerman announced he was finished. A nurse quickly covered the area with cotton balls and lots of tape.

"But what about the higher mass?" I asked.

"I'm sorry," he replied. "I've already used 20 cc's and that's the limit. It could affect your heart if I did more," he added.

After big brown bandages were wrapped around the entire leg, I was released to go home. I was in a lot of pain and went straight to bed where I put my feet up.

Two days later, Viki slowly and carefully unwrapped the bandages and took off the tape and cotton balls. I held up pretty good until she said, "Oh, oh, mom, you're not going to like this." There was a deep open sore about an inch in diameter that was bleeding badly.

We quickly found my discharge paper which said if there was an open sore that resembled a cigarette burn to call the office immediately. I made an appointment to see Dr. Youngerman and thus began a ritual every two weeks of seeing him. It took months before my leg healed.

October came and it was time for the annual fall bazaar at the mall. I stood for hours making swags and flower arrangements. My problem was I never knew when to quit. I remember twisting ever so slightly to reach for something on the floor when suddenly something popped in my right knee. Swelling set in along with pain. When I tried to walk, the leg often gave out.

Dr. Fritz said I had a Baker's cyst and arthritis in the knee. I also had some arthritis in my left wrist and thumb. How observant he was! He pointed out that the occasional swelling in my left arm was attributed to the fact that I had 24 lymph nodes removed when I had the mastectomy. His observation confirmed the results of my bone scan for cancer in June. I did not have cancer in my bones, but the scan did show that I had arthritis in both knees and ankles.

Dr. Fritz ordered x-rays for my knee and would not let me travel to North Carolina to the Jorgensens unless I stopped every hour on the hour and walked around. He explained that I was a prime candidate for blood clots. I was terribly disappointed! Nearly every October I had taken a trip to North Carolina. Both Grace and Chris said the risk was too dangerous and not worth it if something happened.

Praise God, the x-rays did not show any broken bones or tumors. However, I had to see an orthopedic doctor so something could be done about my bad knee. I immediately asked for Dr. M. Stephen Huss who had put a cast on the three toes I broke in California years earlier.

His schedule was full and I could not get in for another month. I could not endure the pain for a month and asked if an appointment could be set up with Dr. Robert Kraus who formerly had his medical office near the old House of Prayer mansion. He was Michael's orthopedic doctor when he was a baby and had to wear corrective shoes with a bar to straighten out his feet. Dr. Kraus was also Sarah's doctor when she broke her left arm.

Amazingly, I was given an appointment three days later. Dr. Kraus suspected arthritis and torn cartilage. He ordered an MRI and said I could have it done at the South Shores Medical facility which had an open imaging machine.

After looking at my ugly ulcerated sore, the kind doctor said he would like to inject my knee with cortisone to help deaden the pain, but could not until the sore healed. It was far too risky. He did order, however, 12 weeks of physical therapy and an ultrasound of my knee.

The day after the MRI, Dr. Kraus called and confirmed that there were three things wrong with my right knee–arthritis, a Baker's cyst and much torn cartilage. Arthroscopic surgery was the only answer, but it could not be scheduled until the sore on my leg healed.

A few days later on November tenth, I was limping across the back yard, enjoying the warm sun on my back. The temperature was in the 60's and it was beautiful outdoors. I pondered what the future held for my knee and if I would ever be healed.

I began praying and then did a strange thing. I asked my heavenly Father for one violet flower to be blooming. If I found one, I would know that He had everything under control. Many years earlier I had written a poem entitled "Violets in November." It concerned finding violets growing behind the carriage house at the old mansion. I compared them to born again Christians who blossom the second time around. They were few in number, but they were the strong ones who endured.

I glanced down at my feet and suddenly cried for joy. There was a tiny purple tuft, blooming in all its glory, just for me! I scooped up this lonely violet and held it close to me. Immediately I started looking for more, only to be chided when these words came from deep inside of me.

"Hey, you only asked for one!"

God used the violet to reassure me that He was leading me. I need not be afraid.

Besides my knee hurting, I noticed my heart was racing all the time. At first I thought it might be my thyroid, but a trip to Dr. Sobol's office confirmed the thyroid was right on target. Something else was happening to me.

Kirk accompanied me to Dr. Youngerman's office on November 17. It was time for the doctor to remove the ugly black scab from the ulcer. Kirk sat and watched as the doctor cut around the scab and then lifted it off. Because it was an open wound, I had to protect it with ointment and large bandages.

I saw Dr. Fritz two days later and he did an EKG on me. There was some heart palpitation, but my primary illness was a bad sinus infection.

Within a few days of placing bandages over the sterile gauze on my ulcerated leg sore, I discovered that my skin had turned bright red. Soon I lost all of the skin. It looked like raw meat! I was allergic to the bandages and had to invest in non-allergic tape.

Adding insult to injury was the fact that my left leg was now in great pain. Not only did the knee hurt, but the pain radiated all the way up the back of my leg, through the thigh and back down the inner leg to my ankle. Would it never end?

I felt horrible and woke up one morning with my head spinning. I still had the sinus infection and drainage, but now both ears were infected. I never made it Christmas caroling with the church group that night.

I told Dr. Fritz I could not take the heart pounding so he put me on a small dosage of Propranolol. I could take it three to four times a day as needed.

Christmas was an exciting time. Kim flew home for three days. Chris made arrangements for him to fly on Christmas Day. He came without the girls this time because Libby had them for the holiday. None of us wanted him to be alone for Christmas. Instead of the traditional family gathering on Christmas Eve, everyone decided to wait until the evening of December 26 so Kim would be able to participate in the gift exchange. Everyone brought in food and I "feasted" on chocolate, cheese, nacho chips, cookies, candy etc. I completely forgot about the blood work I would have the next morning at Dr. Esparaz's office. It had been six months since my cancer surgery.

My triglyceride level was 240 and my sugar was sky high. I learned my lesson and knew I had to stay away from sweets and fattening items at least prior to my cancer check-up.

Dr. Esparaz took one look at the knee high stockings I was wearing and remarked, "I'm no expert, but those stockings are cutting off your circulation and doing you more harm than good." He recommended I wear full length support hose. I heeded his advice and got fitted for a pair, but because the pain in my knees was so severe, in days to come I could not get the hose on.

I was determined to hit all of the "after Christmas sales." My legs ached and before long I was sick in bed. I had inner ear problems which caused dizziness and nausea. My doctor ordered me to stay in bed for a couple of weeks because of the swelling in my legs. I had to keep them elevated at all times. I thanked God for my gift to myself—my electric bed!

Chris took me to see my orthopedic specialist Dr. Kraus. He checked the ulcerated sore on my leg and my upper respiratory problem.

"No way will I inject anything in your knees or do surgery while you have these two problems," he remarked.

The sore actually looked worse. I was not to return to Dr. Kraus until I was healthy and then we would talk. I was to go back to bed and do nothing.

Three days later Babe called from Arkansas. She was suffering with arthritis in both hands and wrists, causing difficulty when she drove her car. She was alone now since Roger died two years earlier.

Babe then told me to take a deep breath because Bob was getting married on May 27 in Winona, Minnesota. He had known Mary, an employee of the city, for some time. They had served on committees together. It would be a small wedding with only the immediate family present. On the following Saturday there would be a big reception for other family members, friends and business associates. I could only bring one guest and I knew it would be Chris.

Suddenly I had something to look forward to. My last trip to Winona was to attend the funeral for Stefannie, Bob's first wife. My two sisters and I were so happy for Bob! Colleen said she wanted to sing at the wedding even though she couldn't sing a note! I declared that Babe and I would dance at the wedding, provided we could get out of our wheelchairs!

On January 25th, Viki burst through my bedroom door with the newspaper in her hand.

"I think we just found the source of your heart problems," she said.

Propulsid®, the drug I had been taking for 18 months for my stomach after my visit to the Mayo Clinic, was basically recalled by the Food and Drug Administration. There had been 70 deaths and over 200 people ended up with heart conditions from taking this "wonder drug." All patients on this medication were to see their doctor immediately and have an EKG. It was recommended that patients switch to an alternate drug.

I got in to see Dr. Fritz that day and he did an EKG. It was normal, thanks to the heart pills I was on. Dr. Fritz then looked me in the eye and said, "I want you to quit cold turkey Propulsid®."

Inwardly I wondered if I had the faith to follow his directive. Those pills were my life-line. Without them I could easily drift back to the condition I had before I went to the Mayo Clinic. For two years I had endured terrible stomach pain, nearly dying until the proper diagnosis was made.

Dr. Fritz ordered me to go back to bed and rest my legs if I was ever to be ready for knee surgery. I looked into the alternate drug for a slow moving stomach, but found it to be so harsh that very few people stayed on it very long. Another complication was the possibility of the medication causing motor disability. I wanted nothing to do with those complications. I decided I would have to trust the Lord, my great Physician, one more time.

Finally, on February 1, 2000, Dr. Youngerman pronounced my leg ulcer healed. I could call Dr. Kraus to set up an appointment for arthroscopic knee surgery. Perhaps he could also drain the Baker's cyst. It was a long time coming, but I could finally see daylight at the end of the tunnel.

I decided to cut back on my heart medicine to only two pills a day. My heart was beating strongly on the second beat which frightened me. Praise God, I made the right decision because I could finally relax and go to sleep.

I called Dr. Kraus' office on February 9 and told the office nurse that I was finally healthy and ready for knee surgery. There was a long pause and the nurse quietly informed me that Dr. Kraus was seriously ill and would not be seeing any more patients. I needed to select another doctor. My records and files would be forwarded to him.

I was devastated! I had waited a long time for this moment and now it was back to the drawing board. I called Dr. Fritz's nurse and told her the news about Dr. Kraus. I asked if she could get me an appointment with Dr. Huss who was also an orthopedic physician. Amazingly, I got one with him on Friday at 7:30 a.m.–just two days away. I could hardly believe I got one that quick! God was still in the miracle working business!

I found out that Dr. Kraus had an inoperable brain tumor and resigned from his medical practice immediately. It was a terrible blow to the medical profession and to his patients. He sent letters to all of us and wished us the very best of health and happiness. I reflected on his last words to me, "You just concentrate on getting well, then call me and we'll talk."

Kirk took me to see Dr. Huss and in my haste, I forgot my purse which contained all of my insurance cards and my reading glasses. Kirk went to retrieve my purse while I started to fill out papers.

A lady sitting next to me offered to be my "eyes" and read the questions. Suddenly she asked me who my husband was. When I replied it was Jerry Henneberry, she incredulously asked, "And you're Dottie?" She explained that she came to the services at the House of Prayer in our early days and had attended Jerry's funeral visitation. It was the longest line she had ever seen!

I shared a little bit of my family's testimony with Diane the nurse. I mentioned I had written the book *Fortress on a Hill* about 15 years earlier and had given Dr. Huss a copy. Diane left the examining rom and within a few minutes returned with Dr. Huss, who was carrying my book.

"Look what we found in the ancient archives," Dr. Huss

251

proudly stated.

He asked me if I remembered how I signed it and tossed it to me to read. I commented he would definitely be in my next book.

Dr. Huss ordered more x-rays for my right leg and told me I was a candidate for knee replacement surgery. I told him my left leg was in worse pain than the right one. He asked if I would consider a MRI on it. Instantly I agreed. He said if the Baker's cyst was big enough, he would drain it. He also suggested that a cortisone injection might alleviate some of the pain.

Before Diane left the room, she turned and remarked, "You know, Dottie, many people today believe God quit performing miracles some time ago. But you are a living miracle!"

While getting ready to leave for my MRI, I heard a funny sound in my bedroom. It seemed to be coming from under my electric bed which I had lowered 15 minutes earlier. It took all of my strength to get down on my knees and look. To my horror, there was our big fat cat Friskie wedged in the bottom of it. He couldn't move one way or the other. I feared the electric bed had injured him. Somehow I managed to manipulate the controls so the bed came up and I was able to grab him. I was grateful I had not left the house yet because I may have returned to find a squished cat! Lo and behold, the silly cat did the same stunt again several weeks later! I saw one of my bedroom slippers shoot out from under the bed. I guess it was his way of trying to get my attention.

As each week passed, I counted my blessings that my stomach was working again. I was saving a bundle of money not having to buy Propulsid® every month. I started taking alfalfa pills on a daily basis and believed they helped my "plumbing" work properly. I could finally eat fried chicken and salads again, foods I hadn't touched in three years. I still had to be careful, though, because my hiatal hernia was always present. I carried Zantac® in my purse whenever I went out to eat in a restaurant. The "honeymoon" was great, but I knew in my heart that I had to get back to eating healthier foods. The only bothersome problem confronting me now was getting food stuck in my esophagus.

On February 17 while gathering all of my prescription papers for Kirk so he could do my income tax filing form, I found a blue paper lying on the bottom of my desk drawer. It was for the medication dicyclomine, something I had taken years earlier for my diverticulitis and irritable bowel syndrome.

In big bold print it stated, "Slows the stomach down!" I couldn't believe my eyes! God was revealing the source of my slow moving stomach after all those years of pain. It had helped a lot of people I knew who had stomach and colon problems. But as for me, I was the exception to the rule. It worked on me "overtime," slowing my stomach to the breaking point.

Viki got on the internet to see what was happening with Propulsid®. She discovered it would no longer be marketed after July 14, 2000. There were now over 80 deaths and 341 reports of heart abnormalities.

"There but for the grace of God go I," remarked my neighbor, Mabel, about me when I shared with her the news. I could very easily have been included in those statistics.

Looking back, I knew I had to take the Propulsid® medication when I did or else I would have slowly died from starvation. As it says in Ecclesiastes chapter three, there is a time for everything under God's heaven. Now I was off the drug and surviving. A miracle!

I was free again like a butterfly, ready to fly home. I told the congregation at church on Sunday that my goals were short term. I didn't have to live to a ripe old age, just survive until the rapture.

A week later I called Dr. Huss for my MRI results, only to be told they had not come in yet. I called back on Friday and Dr. Huss informed me that I had a lot of degenerative arthritis and many tears in my knee. The torn cartilage would require arthroscopic surgery as soon as possible. Injections of cortisone or draining the Baker's cyst would not help at all.

A real inspiration to me at this time was my 90-year-old mother-in-law who underwent hip surgery and came through it beautifully. With therapy she learned how to walk with a walker, enabling her to leave the nursing home and move into an assisted living residence. If she could accomplish that at her age, then I could overcome the obstacles in my way.

I was determined to go to Millikin University on February 19 and hear Michael play trombone and piano in the MacArthur High School Jazz Band. I hobbled to different places on campus despite the cold wind and sleet. It was all worth it when the jazz band was named the top band.

When leaving the school's auditorium, I met Dr. Fritz and his wife. Their daughter, Becky, played saxophone in the jazz band and had the "honor" of getting blasted with Michael's trombone since she sat directly in front of him.

Finally, I received a telephone call from Dr. Huss's nurse. I was scheduled for preliminary lab tests on March 14, would see Dr. Huss on the 17th and have arthroscopic surgery on March 22. I was grateful for those dates, but wondered how I could wait that long. At times both legs gave out on me.

During the late afternoon of March 8, I received a telephone call from Kirk. He was in the emergency room at Decatur Memorial Hospital with Chris. She had been cleaning a machine at Wood Printing Company and somehow the rag she was using got caught in it and so did her right index finger. The finger was crushed, but no bones were broken. It would take a long time to heal, but she was determined to go back to work as soon as possible. One tough lady, she went back two days later, even though the finger remained numb for a long time.

On Saturdays I looked forward to watching Sarah play indoor soccer at the old Bethel Education Academy gymnasium. She loved playing goalie and helped her team win many games. She was aggressive and had such power in her skinny legs. She always gave her all.

My other outings included watching Michael play his trombone and the piano at band concerts. We rejoiced and praised God when Michael won two scholarships to attend jazz band camp. The Juvae Jazz Society awarded him a scholarship for his piano audition and the Symphony Guild of Decatur gave him a scholarship for his trombone audition. He used the scholarships to attend the University of Wisconsin-Whitewater Jazz Band Camp in July. In August he won second place at the Illinois State Fair in the instrumental/keyboard talent contest for playing on the piano from memory "Bumble Boogie" adapted from "Flight of the Bumble Bee."

My grandson Joel auditioned on his clarinet and won a scholarship from the Symphony Guild for a year of free music lessons at Millikin University. A talented soccer and baseball player, he was a born leader and president of his 4-H Club.

Kirk taught a tumbling class after school at Northwest Christian Campus. His daughters Kayla and Natalie plus Sarah did a show for the school's fund raiser. For the grand finale, Kirk and Sarah did a series of back flips. "Not bad for an 11-year-old girl with spindly legs and a 40-year-old man," I quietly thought to myself.

I am so proud of all ten of my grandchildren who are growing up quickly. Each one is blessed with his or her own unique talents and abilities. At the age of twelve Brianna won first place at her church for a paper she wrote entitled *What I Believe and Why*. The most crucial element in each of my family members is his spiritual foundation. It was comforting to know that even though Jerry was gone, his legacy would continue and live on through his children and grandchildren.

I was reminded of a poem I had written entitled "Children."

Children

God took the warmth of a sunny day
And caught a tiny moonbeam at play.
He gathered all the laughter that He could find
And added a bit of His love divine.

He asked a rose for its beauty
And sweet honey from a bee.
He sought for tiny drops of dew
And coaxed the rainbow for different hues.

God took the strength of the northern wind
And found the most infectious grin.
He laughed and almost gave a shout
For He greatly enjoyed what He was about!

The purity of the whitest snow,
*   A curious mind that wants to know,*
The swiftness of a running deer,
*   God put together in loving cheer.*

His labor of love was all too soon over
*   So He called for His angels to guard and to hover*
Over this His great masterpiece of art
*   For "children" are truly the work of His heart.*

The day for my arthroscopic surgery finally arrived. I was at the hospital by 11:30 a.m. Things moved slowly until 1 p.m. when I heard over the loud speaker, "We're ready for Henneberry." I was quickly hooked up to an IV and then whisked away.

When I came to in the recovery room, my leg was bandaged so much that I thought my knee was swollen twice its size. The nurse laughed and said it was just a lot of padding and gauze. Dr. Huss informed Viki that the torn cartilage was the primary source of my pain. Arthritis had settled into more than one-half of the inner knee.

I was given Tylenol® with codeine for pain, but it had an adverse affect on me–it kept me awake all night and I stared at the walls. I changed the medication and by Saturday I was off all pain pills. I managed to attend my granddaughter Kayla's ninth birthday party and was introduced to her family's latest addition–a blonde Labrador puppy named Princess Jasmine Pure Joy. She was a 40th birthday present to Kirk from his family.

With all of the illnesses I had endured, I thought about Job in the Old Testament and pondered his ordeal. Satan could not do anything to him unless God gave him permission. At the same time, Satan could not take away Job's life. In a way, the same was true for me. I was preserved to write my story for others so that it would encourage them. As much as I longed to be in heaven with Jesus and Jerry, God still had a purpose for me on earth.

Ironically, my arthroscopic knee surgery was performed on the seventh anniversary of Jerry's funeral. Time had gone by quickly in those seven years, still only the beginning of eternity for my husband.

As much as I would like to conclude this story with a testimony of a glorious healing, I have to write that God had other plans for me. My newly operated left knee seemed to get worse instead of better. At times the pain was almost unbearable.

My biggest disappointment was not being able to attend Bob and Mary's wedding on Memorial Day Weekend. I just could not have endured the pain and circulation problems on a trip to Winona, Minnesota. Viki accompanied Chris instead of me and they had a great time visiting their cousins and other relatives.

I went back to Dr. Huss's office and had x-rays taken of my left knee. The reason for my pain was made clear–the surgery had stirred up the arthritis, making my left knee worse than before. I was given a cortisone injection for pain, but it did nothing. Pain pills were ordered and I was to take them every four hours, but I tried holding off until evening to take any.

I used a four-prong walking cane and was issued a temporary handicap card to park my station wagon in handicapped designated parking spots. I was grateful that Dr. Huss only ordered it for 6 months because it gave me hope that he believed I would eventually be walking normally.

Before he would do knee replacement surgery, Dr. Huss wanted me to have the procedure of injecting synovial fluid called Synvisc® in both knees. For three weeks he injected the fluid into each knee. My insurance company covered the $1,000 needed for each knee.

My swallowing problems continued to get worse. One Sunday morning while getting ready for church, I choked on a pill that got lodged in my esophagus. It was a frightening 20 minutes before it finally went down. I shared this incident with Helen Johnson, the grandmother of Michael's friend, Nick Woodcock. She came to Harvest Christian Center that day to hear Nick and other youth group members testify about their mission trip to Wisconsin to work with Teen Serve Ministry. It was the first time she visited our church and she calmly told me, "Go see Dr. Eloy. He stretched the esophagus of a friend of mine and now he can swallow again."

Two choking incidents at a restaurant convinced me it was time to see Dr. Eloy. He performed surgery quite successfully. I thanked God for guiding me and helping me once again. How often we take the simple things for granted, even swallowing!

On September 7 I received a much awaited phone call from Dr. Huss's office. A complete knee joint replacement surgery would be scheduled for November 7 at 9:30 a.m.

I needed to donate two pints of blood beforehand plus attend a clinic for several hours on October 25. Papers explaining the seriousness of the operation were sent for my consent. I was, however, grateful to know that relief was coming. There would be weeks of pain and therapy, but I would be near normal once again. The right knee would be replaced later.

I was so elated that I was finally going to have the surgery that I called Babe and shared with her my good news. Colleen had been staying with her for several weeks.

Babe finally said she hated to burst my bubble, but she needed to tell me her news. She had breast cancer. She found out in January, just six months after my discovery, but opted against all surgery and treatment. It was her desire to choose to die with dignity. Colleen helped change her dressings and planned to bring her to her home in Winona, Minnesota, to live during her final days. She wanted to be buried next to Roger. Babe remarked that the arthrititic pain in her hands was too terrible to live through another winter alone.

I cried for days, knowing I would never see her again. Although I didn't agree with her decision, I knew I had to honor it.

Viki and I discussed the topic of healing. I mentioned that many people believe the greatest faith is having an instant healing, but I learned from my "archives" of experience that the greatest test of faith is going through the battle with the Lord by your side.

Once again I envisioned the Israelites going through the Red Sea with the Egyptian army right behind them. I recalled my poem "Going Through" where the Israelites had to take one step at a time, knowing the enemy was right behind them. They had to keep looking forward, believing the two walls of water would not close in on them as they made their way to the other side.

There were times in my own life when I couldn't even walk, but had to crawl, one inch at a time. God was always with me and is

258

leading me to the promised land. I've often said I could never have endured Jerry's suffering, but God had a special course designed specifically for me. I just thank God He doesn't reveal all of our "race" down that course ahead of time.

During one of my frustrating moments with my knees, I decided to call my author friend Frances Roberts in Ojai, California. We talked for a long time and she shared how her daughter had to endure chemotherapy for her stomach cancer. It had been a time of great suffering for her.

I was reminded of a passage that Frances wrote in *Come Away My Beloved* that God used to speak to me so clearly. I was to live what He had ordained and then I was to write about it for His glory.

Frances said she had never met anyone who went through as much physical testing as me. In her closing remarks she commented, "Dottie, keep smelling the roses and looking for robins out of season. And keep searching for violets in November."

"And I'll still believe in butterflies for the wonderful way God has been re-arranging my life," I replied.

After we hung up, I knew I had to live one day at time, enjoying God's beauty around me. Never again would I take anything for granted.

I praise God for His mercy and grace without which I would not be here today. If I had been born and lived at any other time in history, I would not have survived because the medical procedures would not have been around then. I thank God for the medical professionals we have today. I was given a report of cancer free on my first anniversary since my breast surgery.

Two days later another blessing came my way. While getting my hair done at New Art 2000, I received a telephone call from Sarah. She was so excited! An employee from Family Drug Store had called to say that I had won a 19" color television set as the result of a drawing from the Senior Rama held at the Decatur Civic Center. God let me know that He was still on the throne and in the blessing business. I concluded there were some advantages to growing older.

My days of suffering and trials were not over. When I donated my first pint of my blood prior to knee surgery, it took three nurses to "nurse" my only vein. I became anemic so iron pills were ordered. I just barely met the requirements for my blood count to be high enough to donate the second pint of blood. I was greatly concerned if my blood count would be high enough for Dr. Huss to even perform the surgery.

In desperation I cried out to my heavenly Father and asked for a sign like a flower blooming out of season and then I would know everything was going to be okay. Every day for two weeks I walked around my house, looking for an iris or a gladiolus in bloom.

Early in November I drove around the old mansion on College square to see the brilliant colorful leaves adorning the streets. My former neighbors, Alvie and Elmira Sparr, were just pulling up in their car. They lived behind the mansion and had been a great support to my family.

We visited for a while, sharing about the will to live despite life's difficulties. That very morning I had given up hope of ever seeing a flower out of season bloom. As Elmira walked me out of her house, I suddenly gasped as my eyes beheld a magnificent purple blooming iris on the east side of their house, underneath a big evergreen tree.

"It's the strangest thing, Dottie. Look all along the fence. There are dead gladioluses and irises everywhere, but this one is different. It comes up again every fall!" Elmira remarked.

She bent over and picked the double-bloomed flower. I told her it was a symbol of both my knees and compared them to an overcoming people who are willing and able to bloom gracefully in spite of all the obstacles surrounding them. The iris was not just a flower, but God's assurance that He would see me through my surgery.

I took comfort in His assurance when my blood count dropped down to nine following the surgery and I had to be given back both pints of blood that I had previously donated.

Much to my delight and prayers, God was doing a work in Babe, who was slowly dying from breast cancer. She was down to 84 pounds. I telephoned her every Sunday night and always ended our conversation with prayer. Even Colleen said to "keep it up" because Babe enjoyed it so much. Oftentimes I quoted God's Word, shared about our lovely Jesus, His salvation plan for us and how beautiful heaven will be for the believer.

One night I asked her if she truly believed Jesus was her Savior and Lord. I emphasized that she needed to take the time that night to invite Him into her heart so that He could reveal Himself to her in the days ahead.

"I will and I love you," she quickly replied.

I greatly rejoiced in my spirit and felt a burden was lifted, knowing she would wake up in paradise some day. I could finally turn her loose. She was in God's hands.

I told her she was beautiful and would some day turn into a lovely butterfly that would simply fly away. Amazingly, God Himself reinforced that belief when I drew out a scripture verse for Babe at my church's Christmas Eve candle light communion service. *"He has made everything beautiful in His time"* found in Ecclesiastes 3:11 said it succinctly.

By early February it was apparent that Babe's days were numbered. On February 5 I sought for answers in Spurgeon's book *Morning and Evening Daily Readings*. Over and over again God used that book to comfort and guide me throughout the chapters of my life.

My hands skipped over to February 7 which had the title, *"Arise ye and depart"* found in Micah 2:10. The reading continued. *"The hour is approaching when the message will come to us, as it comes to all–'Arise, and go forth from the home in which thou hast dwelt, from the city in which thou hast done thy business, from thy family, from thy friends. Arise, and take thy last journey."*

Across the page for the evening devotion was the scripture verse found in Revelation 11:12. *"And they heard a great voice from heaven saying unto them, Come up hither."* I shared with several people that I believed Babe would pass away on Wednesday, February 7, and it would be before midnight.

The darkness of the night passed without any word from Minnesota. At 6:30 a.m. as daylight approached, I received the call that Babe had quietly passed away just before 11 p.m. I cried with joy, knowing that Babe had emerged as a beautiful butterfly. She was free from all pain and safe in the ever loving arms of Jesus. What a great God we serve!

It is glorious to live on the mountaintop where you can be closer to heaven and survey the entire picture, but it is in the valleys where the fruit is produced. Pruning and cultivating cut deeply, trying one's patience over and over again.

Times are even tougher in the desert where the soul cries for living water. It's barren and lonely there. The sand swirls all around you and any direction seems utterly impossible. How can anything possibly grow? Yet it is precisely at this level that one is closer to a caring God Who never leaves us nor forsakes us. He is the Author and Finisher of our faith. He truly works all things together for our good when we simply let go and trust Him. One day He will transform us into beautiful butterflies and our redemption will be complete.

My thoughts drifted back to the first fall in our new home on Florian Court. Doug decided to pull out the old ivy that was growing rapidly and taking over a corner of the flower garden in our front yard. He uncovered an ugly toad and several big wooly worms. Michael quickly took the toad to the nearby creek and Sarah scooped up a jar full of the crawling critters–big ones and small ones with a variety of colors.

Days later I was trying to dose off in my big recliner, when I noticed something moving slowly by my new sofa. Sarah came in and immediately picked up a giant wooly worm.

"Sarah wouldn't put a proper lid on the jar, but merely placed a paper towel will holes over the jar. They have escaped and are everywhere!" exclaimed Viki.

She found some crawling over her kitchen counter, on the walls and elsewhere.

"How symbolic of the souls of men," I thought to myself.

These little creatures come in different colors and sizes, looking for a place to spin their cocoons. With the help of their lovely Creator, they will emerge one day as gorgeous butterflies.

I long for the day when I can leave this old worn out body with all of its imperfections and scars and by God's process of metamorphoses change into a lovely butterfly and fly away to the paradise above. In the meantime I'm slowly becoming the first "bionic" grandma. When I finally get my "wings" and fly away, all of my body parts will be perfect again! The only scars in heaven will be the nail-scarred hands of Jesus–a magnificent reminder of His awesome grace, mercy and love. Those hands will be a perpetual reminder of the sacrificial cost He paid for our admission into heaven.

It will be wonderful and beyond description when I finally enter eternity and spend it with my loving Father and His precious Son Jesus. He is the Bridegroom calling His precious bride to come away with Him to His Father's mansion that He has prepared for us, His church. The bride must be without spot or wrinkle and longing for His appearance. How anxiously I await the call, "Come up hither!"

One day I realized that I have two bridegrooms waiting for me in heaven–Jesus and Jerry. I've often told people that I don't know which one I will hug first. "Why, Jesus should be your first one," they often chide me. "But He's the One with the long line," I facetiously countered. Even so, come Lord Jesus!

> *Yes, I still believe in butterflies*
> *For what they were–*
> *Once so was I.*
> *And like the tiny butterfly*
> *Emerging from the past,*
> *My life through Christ is changing*
> *Till I fly away at last!*
> *Fly away....*